Corinne Adams

English Speech Rhythm and the Foreign Learner

Mouton

Adams, English Speech Rhythm and the Foreign Learner

JANUA
LINGUARUM Series Practica 69

Studia Memoriae
Nicolai van Wijk Dedicata

edenda curat

C. H. van Schooneveld
Indiana University

Corinne Adams

English Speech Rhythm and the Foreign Learner

Mouton Publishers
The Hague • Paris • New York

Corinne Adams,
Lecturer in Phonology,
Teaching English as a Foreign Language Programme,
The University of Sydney.

ISBN 90 279 7716 X

Preface

This study of native and non-native utterance was based on the theory that the impression of rhythm in spoken English is produced by the serial recurrence of more or less isochronous intervals marked off by stressed syllables and that the periodic movement associated with the rhythmic impulse is produced by the respiratory muscles. Thus a major part of the experimental work was concerned with stress which, in a stress-timed language such as English, is fundamental to the phenomenon of speech rhythm, since it is the feature by which the temporal units are marked. The relationship of the acoustic parameters of fundamental frequency, amplitude, and duration to stress was examined, and electromyographic (EMG) investigation of the internal intercostal muscles in connected speech was undertaken as a means of determining whether increased activity of these (expiratory) muscles could be associated with the utterance of stressed syllables.

Although it has long been recognized that disjuncture is an essential constituent of English speech rhythm, both as a means of delimiting groups of words in close grammatical relationship and as a means of defining the structure of the rhythmic unit, little is actually known about the organization of this feature. On this account, an investigation of the position and duration of pauses in connected speech was also undertaken.

Since the object of the research was to establish the nature of the differences between the speech rhythm of native and non-native speakers of English, all the experiments involved comparative investigation of the utterance of individual speakers and groups representing both categories of subjects. On the basis of the findings, learning activities were devised which, it was hoped, would assist the foreign learner in his acquisition of English speech rhythm. The results obtained with an experimental class of graduate Asian students suggest that at least some of the strategies used by young native learners of English in their acquisition of normal speech rhythm could be adapted successfully for this type of foreign learner.

The study was four years in preparation, and during that time I was greatly assisted in the several phases of the investigation by a number of my colleagues and students in the University of Sydney who acted as subjects. To them I am extremely grateful.

I am most appreciative of the guidance and encouragement given to me by Emeritus Professor W. F. Connell, Dr. H. Bluhme, Mr. G. A. Pittman, and Dr. C. V. Taylor, all of whom listened patiently while I talked about theories, described experiments, and reported results. Discussions with them were always fruitful for they invariably asked the right questions, and throughout the study provided me with a continual supply of helpful criticism.

I wish to express my sincere thanks to Mr. E. A. Atkinson of the Phonetics Laboratory, who constructed the electronic speech/silence indicator used in a number of the experiments, and with exceptional good humour repeatedly made necessary adjustments to the intensity meter, the pitchmeter and the oscillograph; to Messrs. G. Williams and B. Bowden of the Department of Anatomy for their much valued technical assistance in the course of the EMG experiments; to Mr. P. Mills of the same Department for his graphic representations of some of the data; to Messrs. H. T. Brown and R. W. Tully of the Department of Photography, for their preparation of the prints used in this text; and to Mrs. J. M. Cook for her excellent typing services.

I am especially indebted to my husband, Associate Professor Robert R. Munro of the Department of Anatomy, without whom a considerable part of the research associated with this study could not have been accomplished. I am grateful for his constant criticism and unfailing support at every stage of the project, for his generosity in giving freely of his time and equipment in the conduct of the EMG investigations, and for his actual painstaking statistical analysis of much of the data.

Finally, my thanks are due to my parents, the first to foster my interest in spoken English, for their endurance in tolerating my excursions into the prosodic features of our language—firstly intonation and more recently stress and rhythm—over such a prolonged period of time.

Contents

List of Tables

List of Figures

Abstract

Although stress has been variously associated with a number of physiological and acoustic parameters there is still considerable disagreement among phoneticians regarding the actual nature of this feature.

In the investigations of the nature of stress reported in this work account was taken of both production and perception aspects of the phenomenon. This approach was considered necessary in view of the wider objectives of the study—examination of stress in relation to speech rhythm and the development of learning activities designed to assist speakers of syllable-timed languages to acquire the stress-timed rhythm of English. Thus the search for the correlates of stress included investigation of the physiological mechanism believed to be involved in its production, and examination of the acoustic parameters generally regarded as cues to its perception.

Determination of the stress placement of two groups of speakers, one native English-speaking and the other, foreign, was made independently by 10 adjudicators, themselves native speakers of English, who listened to 12 test items recorded by the two groups and indicated the words in each utterance which seemed to them to be stressed.

The two groups were found to differ quite considerably both in the number of words which were stressed and in the placement of stress—a difference found by Chi-square to be significant at both word and sentence level.

The next stage of the study consisted of a pause interval investigation by means of which the position and duration of pauses in the utterance of the two groups were determined. Analysis of the data revealed certain characteristic features in the utterance of the non-native subjects which pointed towards first language interference, foremost among these being the large number of pauses made by this group and its relatively high ratio of pause interval time to total duration of utterance.

As a result of an electromyographic investigation of the activity of the expiratory muscles believed to be associated with stress, it was found that increased internal intercostal muscular activity could not be correlated with this feature in the connected utterance of either native or non-native speakers.

Examination of the relationship of fundamental frequency, amplitude, and duration to stress revealed that although all three parameters were associated with the phenomenon, duration was by far the most frequently used cue (being used by 81% of the speakers), and that amplitude was the least used. No evidence was found to suggest that native and non-native speakers consistently employ different acoustic parameters to signal stress at the sentence level.

The final stage of the study was the devising and testing of a programme by means of which it was hoped that the foreign learner could be assisted to acquire an acceptable English rhythm. All 30 students who participated in this experimental programme showed improved performance in the post-test as compared with their performance in the pre-test but the improvement of the experimental group was significantly greater than that of the control group. It was concluded that the highly successful results obtained by the experimental group could be attributed to learning activities based upon the timing and organization of the rhythm unit, this being the essential feature of the programme.

Introduction

Division of spoken language into equal or proportionate intervals is a phenomenon as normal as is the division of walking into steps and circulation into pulses. However, while it is not at all difficult for most people to recognize steps and pulses as markers of spatial and temporal intervals, it appears that recognition of the rhythmic impulse in language is beyond the faculty of the vast majority of those who daily communicate by means of the spoken word. For most of us, this does not matter. As native speakers of a given language we early in life acquire the skill to produce the impression of proportion between the rhythm units of our utterance and the ability to recognize temporal ordering in the speech of others, and thus, usually, it is only when a speaker fails to demarcate the intervals as anticipated that we become aware of the phenomenon at all.

The non-native speaker, on the other hand, is almost always painfully conscious of his failure to realize the rhythmic impulse of the foreign language but, as often as not, has no idea of the nature of the elusive system he is trying to cope with; for while all languages are characterized by rhythmicality there is considerable diversity among languages both in the arrangement of the rhythm units and the means by which they are marked. The whole question of speech rhythm in English is complicated by the fact that the features which in this language are concerned with transmission of the rhythmic impulse are also concerned with the marking of attitudinal contrasts, with the transference of emotional overtones, and, following the rules of grammatical integration, with the sequential organization of meaningful units; thus phonological transgressions can have far-reaching implications at the semantic level.

However, if—as I believe—the rhythmic impulse is the primary phonological fact of language, it follows that command of rhythm is the key to mastery of the spoken language, and inadequate control of this feature, the ultimate barrier to fluency and comprehensibility at all levels of usage. Unfortunately, there are always likely to be problems of facilitation and interference when an individual who has learned the systems of one language to a high degree of competence attempts to learn another in which as John Carroll, the American educator, puts it, ''his competence is, initially at least, virtually nil."[1] In language learning, although the aim is to supplement rather than to replace original skills, the speaker's first language habits can be remarkably tenacious, and in certain systems—particularly the early acquired prosodic systems—L_1 interference can be a major obstacle to proficiency.

One of the main reasons for my concern with the problems of English speech rhythm in relation to the foreign learner is connected with my work in phonology with overseas students taking the course leading to the Diploma in the Teaching of English as a Foreign Language in the University of Sydney. These men and women—graduate teachers of English from a number of Asian and South-East Asian countries—come to Australia, not to learn English themselves, but rather to upgrade their professional skills and to develop a general theory of language teaching. However, they invariably bring to their pronunciation of English, errors in sound production, stress, and rhythm, while many, who are native speakers of tone languages, in addition allow discrete phonemic tones to interfere with their control of intonation. Frequently, the degree of their foreign accent is such that their efficiency as teachers is impaired.

It was in order to determine the nature and cause of the speech rhythm anomalies of successive classes of these students that the study described in this work was undertaken. It seemed that if L_1 interference were found to be responsible, approaches to the teaching of this feature of English might profitably be re-examined. This led inevitably to consideration of the whole issue of phonology in language learning and of the question raised by Corder[2] in a slightly different context; namely, whether any parallels exist between the processes of learning the mother tongue and foreign language learning. Current theories of first language acquisition were then reviewed, (not included here) and some characteristics of child speech considered with a view to determining whether, if parallels did exist, the creative principles employed intuitively in the one could be applied advisedly to the other.

However, it was first necessary to ascertain in precisely what ways the rhythm used by my foreign students when speaking English differed from that of native English speakers. Since stress patterning and pause placement play a major role in the production of English speech rhythm, it was decided that these issues should be investigated in a comparative study of native and non-native utterance. Thus stress and temporal ordering became the focal points of the research.

Analysis of recorded readings by a group each of native and non-native speakers revealed significant differences between the two groups of subjects in the number and position of stressed syllables spoken in the test items and in the number, placement, and duration of pauses made in the same utterances. No significant difference was found between the native and non-native subjects with regard to the parameters used to signal stress.

As a result of these investigations, I concluded that the foreign speakers' faulty organization and timing of rhythm units could be attributed to several factors:

1. the syllable-timed nature of their first language
2. their method of learning English
3. their lack of experience in speaking English

Part I of this book consists of an historical survey of stress and rhythm studies; Part II deals with the several experiments involved in the investigation of stress and pausing in relation to speech rhythm; and Part III, with an experimental programme designed to test strategies employed in the teaching of English speech rhythm to a group of non-native (Asian) speakers.

1. John B. Carroll, "Contrastive Analysis and Interference Theory", *Report of the Nineteenth Annual Round Table Meeting on Linguistics and Language Studies*, Washington D.C.: Georgetown University Press, 1968, p. 114.
2. S. Pit Corder, "Significance of Learners' Errors", *International Review of Applied Linguistics in Language Teaching*, Vol. V, 1967, 161 169.

PART I

Historical Survey

CHAPTER ONE

The Nature of Rhythm

From ancient times, man, fascinated by the very idea of rhythm, has sought to define its nature. However, despite its all-pervading presence in the universe, it has eluded exact definition and agreement among observers regarding its essential characteristics has been rare largely, I believe, because the numerous manifestations of the phenomenon which cause it to be apprehended in different ways according to the researcher's sensory perception and experience are described as a rule, instead of the phenomenon itself.

Thus, for one, rhythm may be the simple ticking of the hall clock or the swing of its pendulum; for another, it may be the successive flashes of the beams from the lighthouse; for another, the alternating rise and fall of the onward movement of waves; yet another may apprehend it in the human heart beat or in the regular breathing of a sleeping animal. None would deny the existence of rhythm manifested in the polka, the waltz, the tarantella, but there are also those who would point to physical phenomena: light, heat, sound, cosmic periodicity; even life itself, as illustrative of the rhythmic principle. Bolton[1] points out that Herbert Spencer, for instance, who treated the subject of rhythm in considerable detail in his philosophical masterpiece, seems to hold that rhythm is the only possible form of activity, that continuous motion is an impossibility. Some 50 years after the publication of *Principles of Psychology*, we find Warner Brown in his discussion of the time factor in rhythm implicitly supporting this view in his assertion that there is "hardly an act performed by us, either mentally or physically, into which rhythm does not enter as one of the obvious factors."[2]

For the Greeks, who regarded rhythm as the application of order to movement, a correspondence existed between ordered movement and the movements of the soul—thus rhythm was seen to have an ethical function.[3] Harmony, they maintained, cannot exist without rhythm, harmony of the soul, when perfected, being virtue. Thus, as well as denoting harmony or symmetry in its more general sense of the right relation of the parts to each other and to the whole, rhythm for them was fundamental to their theory of the good and the beautiful, and as such a distinctly human characteristic:

. . . whereas the animals have no perception of order or disorder in their movements, that is, of rhythm and harmony as they are called, to us the Gods who, as we say, have been appointed to be our partners in the dance, have given the pleasurable sense of harmony and rhythm, and so they stir us into life.[4]

Considering this view, we should be in no way surprised to note their insistence that rhythm must be nurtured by proper education. Both Plato and Aristotle assert a direct connection between music and character—hence their emphasis on music in the education process. But if we do not normally think of music as developing moral qualities it must be remembered that Greek music was mostly sung and that song itself derives from the attempts of the human personality to co-ordinate music and speech—that single possession of *Homo sapiens* which most clearly of all distinguishes us from the rest of the animal species and marks our specific type of mental organization.

Furthermore, as Lucas[5] points out, music normally accompanied the dance and this, too, would have contributed to the association since, for the Greeks, the dance could express character as well as emotion and action. He says that it was easy for them to explain the connection between the movement of dance and these qualities on the basis of a correspondence between internal (i.e. of the soul) and external movements, even though dances as meaningful as those referred to by Plato (Laws II) must have depended largely upon a conventional language of gesture.

For Aristotle,[6] according to Lucas, rhythm was essentially a pattern of recurrence imposed on speech or on other sounds and giving rise to expectations which are more or less fulfilled so that even in over-rhythmic prose, he says, one waits for the recurrence.

In recognizing the patterning aspect of rhythm Aristotle appears to have come closer to defining the actual characteristics of the phenomenon than any of his predecessors had done, although it was his pupil Aristoxenus—often referred to as the father of Greek music—who by his definition of rhythm as an "ordering of times" drew attention to its all-important temporal factor. According to Thomson[7] this definition contains an error of the most fundamental sort because it is not the time which is rhythmical but rather the beats.

> The most fundamental error made about rhythm is that
>   it is 'an ordering of times'.
> The most fundamental truth about rhythm is that
>   it is 'an ordering of blows'.[8]

This point is taken up by another modern critic, E. A. Sonnenschein, who points out[9] that Aristoxenus himself says in his *Rhythmica Stoicheia* Section 6: "Time does not divide itself: something else must be present to divide it"[10]—further, that not even a "defined ordering of times is necessarily rhythmical."[11] Sonnenschein himself defines rhythm as "that property of a sequence of events in time which produces on the mind of the observer the impression of proportion between the duration of the several events or groups of events of which the sequence is composed."[12]

In this definition of the genus *rhythm* which, he says, is not intended to account for particular manifestations of rhythm as perceived by the several senses, he makes no mention of repetition or recurrence. The function of repetition in rhythm, he explains, is "to secure that the rhythm shall be *recognized* as such by the mind of the observer; without repetition it might easily escape observation."[13] Thus for him a certain amount of repetition is "a condition without which rhythm would not be brought home to the ear."[14]

Not all observers would agree. Elsie Fogerty for instance, points out that recurrence can be of a series of single drum beats or of detached notes, of falling water drops, of the reiteration of echolalia, even the repetitive hesitation of a stammer—all examples of repetition, but every one of them "devoid of any natural or acquired rhythm."[15] While Stetson[16] maintains that a movement may be perfectly regular, uniform, and recurrent and yet not give the impression of rhythm. According to him:

If one moves the hand or arm in a circle, the hand may be made to pass a point in a circle much oftener per second than the tempo of the slower rhythm requires and yet there will be no feeling of rhythm *so long as the hand moves uniformly and in a circle.* In order to become rhythmic in the psychological sense, the following change in the movement is necessary: the path of the hand must be elongated to an ellipse; the velocity of the movement in a part of the orbit must be much faster than in the rest of the orbit; just as the hand comes to the end of the arc through which it passes with increased velocity, there is a feeling of tension, of muscular strain; at this point the movement is retarded, almost stopped; then the hand goes on more slowly until it reaches the arc of increased velocity. The rapid movement through the arc of velocity and the sudden feeling of strain and retarding at the end of this rapid movement constitute the beat. In consciousness they represent one event, and a series of such events connected in such a movement-cycle may be said provisionally to constitute a rhythm.[17]

On the question of beat he says:

Every rhythmic beat is a *blow.* The origin of rhythm as Bücher has suggested was in forms of concerted worth which required blow on blow. That is possibly the genetic reason why the beat, the blow, is the primary thing in the rhythm-consciousness. In all forms of activity where a rhythm is required, the stroke, the blow, the impact is the thing; all the rest is but connection and preparation.[18]

Thomson takes a similar view, emphatically asserting that time—and rhythm—without accent simply cannot exist. Time without accent, he says, does not exist, and that which does not exist cannot be emphasized.[19] However, he points out that in order to create the effect of rhythm and time the accent need not be strong—provided it is perceptible—since emphasis, or lack of it, in no way affects the nature of time. It indicates only that time is more or less strongly marked.

Brown,[20] on the other hand, while conceding that accentual features are necessary, says that they are not at the root of the phenomenon. He makes this assertion on the basis of his finding that accent was not the distinctive feature in the rhythms examined in his study. Discussing the so-called "time" and "accent" theories of rhythm he points out that all recurrence is a temporal matter. "A rhythm is temporal in so far as there is any regular return of similar features. But at the same time such a rhythm will also be accentual since there must always be points of emphasis whose return can be marked."[21] The idea of accent as the organizing principle of rhythm had also been recognized by Bolton, who, while supporting the view that "accent simply arranges the material already rhythmical through some temporal recurrence"[22] says that a rhythm which depends wholly upon either the time element or the accent is less forcible than one which combines both factors.[23]

Thus argue some of the protagonists in the *time* versus *accent* controversy which has been debated with varying degrees of intensity over the centuries—a sterile exercise, it seems to me, since clearly the rhythmic impulse must be marked in some way for perception of rhythm to occur at all. One thing is certain, however. There is no question that the impression of regularity occasioned is, as Brown insists, the only undisputed characteristic of rhythm:

"Some hold that this impression arises from the regular recurrence, in time, of certain features of the rhythmic series; others claim that the regularity resides in the structure of the elements composing the series."[24]

On the issue, which is fundamental to the rhythm—the uniform time of recurrence or the uniform character of the thing that recurs, he argues:

If the movements or sounds vary in intensity more than in duration or more than the interval separating them, I submit that the rhythm is primarily temporal. No very extended argument seems to be required in support of this view, for regularity is essential to rhythm, and if the regularity is predominantly in the time relations the rhythm may be presumed to have its seat there also.[25]

It is my belief that any repeated movement (and this includes sound) over a given period of time—tends to be subjectively organized into series of perceptually uniform intervals which constitute for the observer rhythmic experience, so that even if the intervals are not objectively equal the impression gained is one of periodicity. Obviously the durations of such intervals cannot be so long that the mind is unable to take cognizance of them. According to Bolton,[26] the conception of a rhythm demands a perfectly regular sequence of impressions within the limits of about 0.1 sec. and 1.0 sec. However Wallin[27] says that so strong is our inclination towards rhythm that the margin of irregularity may be quite considerable; while Miyake has shown that even irregular movements "have a constant tendency to become rhythmical notwithstanding the voluntary effort of the subject to execute the movement at irregular intervals."[28]

Wallin suggests that rhythm is more a matter of feeling or rhythm sense than of judgment. In order, therefore, "to occasion a genuine rhythmical reaction a movement in time must arouse those sensory processes and motor responses or physiological reactions which lie at the basis of the feeling of rhythm."[29] Without an active functioning of the physiological or neural substrata, he says, "the rhythmical consciousness would consist of only a certain awareness of a quasi-rhythmical movement in time."[30]

Stetson,[31] in supporting Wallin's earlier research findings, points out that the mere presence of movements which might be the basis of rhythmic experience does not necessarily imply *perception* of that rhythm. According to Stetson, although the muscular apparatus whereby the sensational basis of rhythm is produced is developed in the lower animals, and many of their actions are rhythmical, no one would credit them with a sense of rhythm. He argues:

The trotting of a horse produces a vigorous rhythm, but one has only to listen to a well-matched team veering slowly into perfect unison, and veering just as gradually out again, to realize that their trotting is rhythmical, but that they have no sense of rhythm.[32]

This notion is strongly reminiscent of the view presented by Aristotle which we have already noted. However, Stetson offers a more scientific explanation of this sense of rhythm than had the great psychologist of antiquity. He says that

. . . the simplest suggestion would be a 'centre which combines the motor sensations to a rhythmic perception or a rhythmic emotion. But the multiplication of 'centers' never simplified a problem; it is much more nearly in line with what we know of co-ordination to assume that rhythm is simply a special form of the ordinary co-ordination of movement experience.[33]

On the question of the distinction between rhythm produced and rhythm merely perceived, he maintains that although the movements involved in the production of a rhythm are always there as the basis for the experience of the produced rhythm, we have quite as vivid and satisfactory a sense of rhythm when we merely *perceive* the series. The movements at the basis of 'sensory' rhythmic experience, he says, are produced by muscles of the body capable of producing rapid and varied movements not visible to ordinary observation. Some of these muscles are in the arms and legs; some in the head and trunk; but the most important natural rhythm-producing apparatus is the vocal apparatus. He explains that the tongue is extremely mobile, and that slight movements of its muscles and those of the throat in conjunction with the expiratory muscles (which according to him mark the main accents of speech) play a significant part in rhythmization. Every rhythm is dynamic he says, consisting of *actual movements*. However, it is not necessary that joints be involved; it is the changes in muscular conditions which stand in consciousness as movements which are essential to any rhythm, whether "perceived" or "produced". Most researchers would agree.

Ruckmich,[34] reviewing two decades of studies on the perception of rhythm states unequivocally:

"Kinaesthesis of one sort or another, or motor expression consciously represented in the form of imagery or perceptual complex, is regarded by most investigators in this field as essential to rhythmic grouping and accentuation."[35] And, on the basis of his own investigations he concludes:

Under the conditions of these experiments . . . whatever was the material presented for rhythmisation (equal and equally spaced sounds for subjective rhythm; sounds of different intensities; tones objectively varying only in duration, in intensity, in pitch; flashes of light differing in intensity); kinaesthesis was essential for the establishment of a rhythmical perception. That perception once established, however, rhythm might be consciously carried, in the absence of any sort of kinaesthesis, by auditory or visual processes.[36]

Some years earlier, Bolton, in his seminal paper on *Rhythm*, had also commented on the phenomenon of motor rhythmization. So strong is this impulse, he says, that "no one is able to listen to music in which the rhythm is strong and clear without making some kind of muscular movements. With some people these movements tend to increase in force until the whole body becomes involved and moves with the rhythm."[37] This kind of response is especially marked in primitive peoples and in children, for both of whom, he points out, the accents in a given rhythm may have the effect of "summated stimuli" and thus produce various emotional states. He instances the chanted rhythms associated with religious and other rituals which occasion frenzied responses in some primitive peoples, and the rhymes repeated by children to the accompaniment of clapping and other physical movement which induce states ranging from sleep to wild excitement.

In his opinion a highly civilized people is not easily affected by mere rhythms; yet in our own times we have seen the phenomenon of mass hysteria induced by the impassioned repetition of catchwords and slogans at mass rallies where vast audiences of very cultivated and responsible people can be caught up in waves of rhythmic emotion. One thinks immediately of Hitler's audiences in pre-World War II Germany in this respect, and possibly of large contemporary assemblies of fans of the various pop arts. However, mass motor rhythmization is by no means a recent social trend. At the turn of the century it was recognized as a significant form of group behaviour by Triplett and Sanford[38] in their discussion of the phenomenon as displayed in the yells and cheers of collge students. These and other such utterances, they point out, have the same metrical patterns as those occurring in traditional English nursery rhymes and evoke similarly emotional responses.

As individuals, independent of group influences, we are less inclined to respond physically to rhythmic experience, although the gestures used by the native speakers of a language even in ordinary unemphatic utterance are an index of a very profound sense of rhythm. According to some linguists,[39] gesture is in fact the original form of language, and speech merely a system based upon natural instinctive movements. This is an interesting theory, but as Abercrombie argues,[40] languages differ gesturally in many ways—particularly in the extent to which gesture is used as an accompaniment to speech, and in the movements which constitute gestures of similar meaning. We should also note that languages differ quite markedly in the timing of the movements which accompany spontaneous utterance, depending upon the events in speech (syllables or stresses) which mark the rhythmic beat. Thus although gesture may be "the only speech that is natural to man" and therefore "the general language of human nature", as Bulmer asserts,[41] it is nevertheless a language-specific characteristic. This, I believe, could be a factor accounting for the difficulty experienced by some non-native speakers in maintaining the rhythmic flow of a foreign language, who when finding themselves unable to produce the appropriate word, abruptly break the speech continuum by indiscriminate placement of pauses[42] which are, for the most part, noticeably unfilled. In similar circumstances the native speaker's hesitation would be filled in by some sort of bodily movement and/or paralinguistic expression, intuitively made to preserve the rhythmic pattern while the required word were being recalled.

The native English speaker very early in life associates particular auditory patterns with kinaesthetic sensations through frequent repetition of holophrastic expressions and such auditory forms as nursery rhymes which, with their strongly metrical patterns, not only evoke a natural response in the child by effecting a synthesis of sound and movement but also provide him with a rhythmical framework into which his own spontaneous utterances can be fitted. Thus it is that the mature native speaker tends to produce sentences, the rhythms of which bear a strong correspndence to the rhythms of traditional rhymes, and to maintain the rhythmic impulse of these utterances by means of muscular tensions which, as often as not, have originally been stimulated in childhood by rhythmic motor activity. For example, such everyday expressions as:

Wait there!
Bring round the car.
Come in!
Where have you been?
Coffee or tea—
Which will you have?

are quite clearly echoes of

One, two
Buckle my shoe,
Three, four,
Knock at the door, etc.,

while the rhythm of the fabricated sentences:

If she's leaving, please let me know—sixteen students still want a place

When you get there, see all you can; I can't be there much before ten

can be traced to the old familiar

Humpty Dumpty sat on a wall,
Humpty Dumpty had a great fall.

Rhymes such as these, as Triplett and Sanford[43] point out, are very similar in structure to Old English poetry with their stanzas of alternating stressed and unstressed syllables arranged in 2- and 4-stress patterns and are a direct link with Early English. So ingrained are the rhythms of these verses, they say, that it is by no means uncommon for a speaker in attempting to recall a forgotten phrase or stanza to recapture the rhythm or lilt of it, while the actual words escape. As they point out,

> . . . we recall the form or plan of the phrase, but not the filling in. At other times, as in listening to a conversation indistinctly heard . . . we are able, from the familiar cadence of the sounds, few of which are distinct enough to be fully recognized, to reconstruct the phrases which we can hardly be said to hear.[44]

The non-native speaker is able to make no such reconstructions, being, as a rule, unfamiliar with native speech rhythms and certainly unaware of patterns of auditory-kinaesthetic sensations. However, according to Seymour Chatman,[45] kinaesthesis is not a *sine qua non* of rhythm. He says that while the early theorists drew attention to what they regarded as the significance of motor sympathy with manifested rhythms, authoritative modern observers "warn against overestimating the role of kinaesthesia, observing how frequent it is that the sense of rhythm is quite abstract, being conceived by sophisticates (for example, musicians and composers) as an idea rather than a percept."[46]

While it must be admitted that rhythmic grouping is very much a psychological event, the fact that rhythm may also be conceived as either a physiological or as a physical phenomenon cannot be questioned. Nowhere is this dual conception of rhythm more evident than in the case of English speech rhythm, which has at least some degree of correspondence with the rhythmical movements made by us in other ordinary life activities and is therefore basically kinaesthetic, yet is at the same time clearly psychological in so far as its units are based on an impressionistic isochrony of stressed syllables. Swindle[47] believes that although there is little danger of our confusing the psychological and physical conceptions of rhythm, confusion of the two organic rhythms—that is, the physiological and the psychological—is of common occurrence. He explains that this is because any systematic accentuation and subordination of the elements of a series is regarded as rhythm by the psychologist, so that even the walk of a lame man is rhythmical in this sense, whereas to the physiologist normal walking is a rhythmical act and the gait of a lame man, for instance, non-rhythmical.

He says that for some reason it is a characteristic of human beings to divide repeated movements into certain numerical groups or rhythm units so that

. . . a normal adult if asked to beat a long succession of like strokes or to listen to such a succession of sounds manifests a tendency to group the elements into periods, that is, into successive unit groups numerically the same. The grouping factor may be an exceptionally extended pause, an exceptionally heavy stroke, a change in pitch, or any other means, although we need not assert that any or all would serve the purpose equally well.[48]

If this grouping factor does not exist objectively, he says, then it must exist subjectively, as an illusion. The time factor is important in rhythmical grouping only in so far as the movements occur in time—the chief factor for him being the principle of subordination and accentuation. He explains the role of accent in rhythm as follows:

Our movements in rhythm must correspnd to the normal movements of our organs involved. The fact that our large members require more time than the smaller ones gives a basis for understanding the function of the accent, or why it is insisted upon in rhythm. There are other things which contribute a meaning to the accent, viz., the fact that in ordinary life we find it quite necessary to make lightly certain tentative or preparatory movements before the real purposive action is strongly executed. Further, there is the fact that we are bilaterally symmetrical. This affords us two means for executing like acts. One member of a pair usually becomes subordinated to the other. One makes the strong, but possibly unskilled, movements and leaves the production of the finer movements to the more skilful member. It is in this way that right or left handedness (and "footedness") exerts its influence. Our inherited structure is such that in performing purposive actions that require the use of the two hands serially we must often make weak and strong movements alternately, or one hand make two movements while the other hand makes only one.[49]

The great 18th century phonetician, Joshua Steele,[50] presented a similar explanation. Comparing the cadences of ordinary speech to the rhythm of breathing, of heart beats, and of walking, Steele says that there are always two alternate motions: the one coming down as it were with *weight* and the other being more *remiss*—these movements, which correspond to the Greek *thesis* or "setting down" and *arsis* or "raising", he called *heavy* and *light* respectively.

"When we lift our foot in order to walk, that motion is *arsis* or *light*; and when we put it on the ground, in order to proceed, that act of posing is *thesis* or *heavy*."[51] He goes on to point out that if we count on our fingers every step or cadence we make in walking we find that each one of them consists of these two motions, and is thus subdivided by them. If we count only on every second step, we then find that there are four motions—two heavy and two light—sub-dividing each pace. Steele says that "this division of the step by the even number 2, and of the pace by the even number 4, naturally arises from the walk of a sound or perfect man."[52] The halting of a lame man, on the other hand, makes a pace divisible into 6 instead of 4 because the thesis of one of his feet rests twice as long on the ground as that of his other foot. Consequently, says Steele,

> . . . in each pace of this lame walk, there will be one *thesis* of so much greater weight or emphasis than the other, that the second thesis appears, in comparison with it, to be light. Wherefore this whole pace is considered only as one cadence, divided unequally into heavy (Δ) lightest (. .), light (∴), and lightest (. .).

Here then are two general modes or MEASURES of time. The *first*, wherein each step makes a *cadence*, and is divided equally by the even number 2, and the pace, or *double cadence,* by 4; and is in music called *common time*, andante, or the MEASURE of a march. The second, where the whole pace, making only *one cadence,* may be equally divided by the number 6, as the double of 3; and is called *triple time*, or the MEASURE of the minuet and jigg. But the two steps composing the pace of triple time, are so far dissimilar, that one of them is composed by $\overset{\wedge}{3}$ + ï, and the other by ï + ï; as,  which

diversity, when slow makes the graceful variety of the minuet; and when faster, the merry hobble of the jigg.

Now all speech, as well as other music, is subject to the influence of CADENCE, by *arsis* and *thesis*, or the *light* and *heavy*, as well as of MEASURE, which determines those cadences to the *common* or the *triple*, and likewise to the affection of QUANTITY . . . by the *long* and the *short*. And as the length of syllables, as well as their particular affections to the *light* and the *heavy*, is various, according to the genius of the *language*; some words and sentences must be measured by *common time*, and some by *triple time*.[53]

The quantitative view of English speech rhythm which, according to Crystal,[54] was propagated by scholars well versed in the Classics who believed that they could interpret English metrical rhythm in terms of a Classical frame of reference, has been much criticized since the 18th century. However, as recently as 1960 Sheridan Baker[55] argued that English meter *is* quantitative explaining that in English stress makes quantity. He points out that whereas in Latin syllables are long by the intrinsics of nature or position and that they stay in place, "in English stress alone makes quantity; and what one minute you think is stressed may not be the next time you look."[56] Although Baker's discussion is concerned with English metre, precisely the same comment could be made of the rhythm of ordinary English conversational speech.

In his discussion of the close relationship which in early times existed between the primitive dance, music, and poetical recitation, Bolton also comments on the fact that in our English verse rhythms we still retain some vestige of the all-important time element which, he points out, was a distinctive feature of our early poetry and was not entirely superseded by stress features when English poetic rhythms became accentual.

He observes, however, that in English we have never assigned fixed time values to our syllables for rhythmic purposes, as was done in the Classical languages,[57] and suggests that English speech becomes rhythmical "not simply by sounds succeeded by pauses but also by the regular recurrence of strongly accented sounds in a series."[58] Since every word of more than one syllable in English consists of both strong and weak elements, the rhythm of our spoken language very early lent itself to metrical organization. However, the language of this early literature at first took the form of the simplest possible rhythm, consisting merely of an alternation of accented and unaccented syllables.

It is sometimes suggested that because this early poetry was sung to musical accompaniment, it was obliged to be kept in exact time and that the verses, which consisted of two sections separated by a medial pause, had to begin—as does the musical bar—and end with a strong beat. This, it is said, necessitated another pause between the verses in order to preserve the rhythm.[59] Bolton points out, however, that although some regard was paid to the timing of syllables, "no such exact time was maintained as modern musicians keep in their music."[60] Cassidy and Ringler support this view:

We metronome-minded moderns, influenced also by the regularity of machines, take for granted exactness of timing. Even if the *scop* used a harp to keep his rhythm regular there is no certainty that he did not use rhetorical pauses, prolongations for emphasis, and other devices which to a modern musician would seem quite irregular.[61]

They go on to point out that according to Pope[62] who assumes that the verse was isochronous "the harp was often struck at places calling for stress where no word was being said or sung".[63] Pope himself argues that "the only way to maintain an unbroken rhythm in *Beowulf* without doing violence to the meaning of the words or the alliterative pattern is to make use of initial rests before the majority of verses beginning with unimportant syllables''.[64] However, he says that *Beowulf* is not alone in this respect. "Most of the other Old English poems begin in the same way, and the long ones all contain initial rests at points where a reader might wish to resume after a pause.''[65] As our poetry developed, it was marked by the more wide-spread use of feet containing more than one unstressed syllable and by an increase in the number of accents in each verse. Although as many as eight accents might occur in a verse this number never really became popular and eventually it was the verse of five accents which proved to be most favoured of all English verse structures. The most popular rhythm in our literature has been the two-rhythm measure, consisting of the disyllabic foot which is the simplest possible rhythm, corresponding to the movement of normal walking. A rhythm of remarkable versatility, it has remained the basic measure of English verse from the simple patterns found in Early English poetry to the highly complicated arrangements of speech stresses and metrical values counterpointed to produce complex rhythms of great variety and expressive powers in the verse of our later poets.

According to McAuley,[66] the secret of the variety and power in English verse rhythms is to be found in the two-value system of the metre with its accented/unaccented syllable dichotomy and the stress-profile of spoken English which, while maintaining a regular pattern of stress prominences, yet uses a wide gamut of stress fluctuations. It is the very elusiveness of the stress profile which is largely responsible for the rhythm anomalies in the pronunciation of the non-native speaker who is confused as a rule both by the identification of stress and the precise location of stress placement. Nevertheless, given some basic rules for mastery of the stress-profile, it is my belief that the non-native speaker can learn to produce an acceptable speech rhythm. As we shall see in the survey of English speech rhythm studies in the next chapter, most of those who have sought to explain the phenomenon of speech rhythm have recognized the importance of speech stress. Thus it is that a number of these studies seem to be more closely related to investigations of stress than of rhythm, an obvious approach since without a marker of its pulsation rhythm cannot be perceived. That marker of the rhythmic impulse in English is stress.

CHAPTER TWO

A Survey of English Speech Rhythm Studies

According to Crystal[1] it is now generally agreed that before the phenomenon of rhythm can be explained, the phonetic nature of stress must be established. This is the *raison d'être* of the investigation presently reported. But the theory upon which this study was based; that is, that the impression of rhythm in spoken English is produced by the serial recurrence of more or less isochronous intervals marked off by stressed syllables, is only one of a number which have been proposed over the centuries, and so before we consider some noteworthy modern investigations of the nature of stress we shall review some selected investigations which, in my opinion, have added significantly both to our understanding of the elements which combine to produce the speech rhythm of English, and to our knowledge of the so-called "temporal tradition" in rhythm studies.

It would seem that the earliest extant discussion of any length on stress in English is that of John Hart[2] who in *The Opening of the Unreasonable Writing of Our English Toung* examines both lexical and syntactic stress in some detail. One of Hart's main concerns was the devising of an appropriate system of notation, for he believed that the writing system of a language should be "framed to the manner of speaking [it]",[3] and thus, in addition to an adequate representation of the actual sounds,

> to have an absolute writing we must use (163) therewith accidents to signifie the accidents of the voices; and use souche an ordre in pointing for the distinction of the wordes and sentences of our commune speech, as the reader may read perfectli and the hearer understand easili and readili. Whereof me thinks yt mete to be spoken in this treatise: for that with a convenience, they may be reasonabli signified by their figures, as the voice (in evri condicion) useth in pronunciation: and that almost as necessari as the veri and self letters spoken of before.[4]

His first recommendation is concerned with stress. He sets out a table[5] showing how accent may be indicated by the use of six diacritical marks; these being:

´	"sharp tune"	(strong stress)
`	"flat tune"	(weak stress)
^	"time"	(length)
'	"turner"	(omitted letters)
-	"joiner"	(linking)
"	"sundrer"	(separation of syllables)

Thus strong and weak stress would be indicated by means of acute and grave accents respectively, length by means of a circumflex accent, elided letters by an apostrophe, linked sounds by a hyphen, and separated vowels by a diaeresis.

Hart also devised a system of notation for sentence stress. He discusses in some detail the words in the phrase which usually take stress (the nouns, adjectives, demonstratives and interrogatives, pronouns, principal verbs and adverbs), and shows how the relative stress of such words in a phrasal group is determined by their general importance. In his emphasis on the significance of the phrasal group in English, Hart shows himself to have been a remarkably perceptive observer of both syntactic and phonological features. Not only was he the first of our English phoneticians to provide detailed information about the structure of the phrasal group and the organization of stress in the sentence, but by his recognition of the importance of linking immediate constituents in speech, he secured for himself a place in the vanguard of latter-day observers of connected English utterance. Of the "joiner" he says:

So this ioiner geveth knoledge which two syllables or (193) words (though naturalli devided in writing) the use of the toung doth pronunce and sound in one, as yt doth the other divers syllables of one word. As in theis wordes: *never-thelesse, not-withstanding, none-other*, and souch lyke: which sounds as though they were simple wordes.[6]

He goes on to point out that there are groups of words in English which also "ought to sound as though they were writen together";[7] for example, the preposition-article-noun sequence, the article-adjective-noun sequence, the subject-verb sequence, and he demonstrates how the idea of linking can be conveyed in the written language by having sub-linear marks connecting words in close grammatical relationship: of_an_apple, from_the_Citie a_noble_man,   may   moch   help   the_poor,   a_company   of_men, thow_didst_rune. Two centuries were to pass before the features of catenation were again discussed in length by any other British writer.

Although intermittent interest in the prosodic features generally was shown during the next two hundred years, it was not until 1775 that a major study appeared. This was *An Essay towards establishing the melody and*

measure of speech written by Joshua Steele at the request of the President
of the Royal Society in reply to the assertion made by Lord Monboddo in
The Origin and Progress of Language that "the music of our
language . . . [is] nothing better than the music of a drum, in which we perceive no difference except that of louder or softer."[8]

Steele's primary concern was the tonal variation of English but his study
of pitch led him to an investigation of several prosodic features including
length and stress when he realized that he could not discuss the melody of
speech without also considering its measure. Remarkably modern in his
empirical approach to his subject, Steele's ultimate appeal was to the
observable rather than to theories of language and the kind of authoritative
pronouncements which had to this time defined the framework of studies
on language.

Like Hart, he believed that the accidents or properties of language should
be distinguished and clearly marked, and thus we have from him an
elaborate system of notation representing the several prosodic features of
speech.

He says:

> The puzzling obscurity relative to the *melody and measure* of speech
> which has hitherto existed between modern critics and ancient
> grammarians has been chiefly owing to a want of terms and characters,
> sufficient to distinguish clearly the several properties or accidents
> belonging to language: such as, *accent, emphasis, quantity, pause,* and
> *force*; instead of which *five terms*, they have generally made use of *two*
> only, *accent* and *quantity*, with some loose hints concerning *pauses*, but
> without any clear and sufficient rules for their use and admeasurement;
> so that the definitions required for distinguishing between the expression
> of *force* (or loudness) and *emphasis*, with their several degrees were
> worse than lost; their difference being tacitly felt though not explained or
> reduced to rule, was the cause of confounding all the rest.[9]

Steele, who may be regarded as the first of the temporal theorists, was at
pains to emphasize the lost connection between poetry and music, and, at
the beginning of Part II of his *Essay*, notes the relationship between speech,
movement, and music:

> The art of music, whether applied to speaking, singing or dancing, is
> divided into two great branches, *sound* and *measure*, more familiarly
> called *tune* and *time*. Instead of which words, I use (for the most part)
> the Greek terms of *melody* and *rhythmus*, being more significant, as
> generals, than our vulgar terms.[10]

He argues that, because our "animal existence" is regulated by our pulse, we have an instinctive sense of rhythmus which is connected with and which governs "all sounds and motions".[11] It follows, he says, that all people feel the effects of *rhythmus*, and so it has been passed over as a self-evident truth. However,

> . . . we must pre-suppose an exact periodical pulsation, as regular as the swings of a pendulum, the length of which periodical pulsation we may vary according to our pleasure, as often as we would chuse to quicken or slacken the movement; and then all continuation of sounds or pauses are to be subserviently measured and regulated by this uniform and steady pulsation, as long as that proportion of pulsation (or pendulum) shall be continued.[12]

Obviously, as Steele recognizes, this pulsation, or "thesis" as he sometimes calls it, must be marked. However, he points out that since rhythmical pulsation implies no sound or noise at all, *heavy* and *light*—not *loud* and *soft*—are necessarily the governing principles of rhythmus, for they are as constantly alternate and periodical as the pulse itself, continuing even during rests or pauses. "The affections of *heavy* and *light* were always felt in music, though erroneously called by some moderns *accented* or *unaccented*; however, the *accented*, or *heavy note*, was never understood to be *necessarily loud*, and the other *necessarily soft*."[13] Likewise, loud and soft, although they may be "accidentally coincident" with rhythmical pulsation, are not—contrary to the view still sometimes asserted—governing principles of the rhythm of speech.

Steele explains[14] that the concepts of accented and unaccented cannot possibly be equated with thesis and arsis since the accented/unaccented dichotomy relates to tonal features whereas thesis/arsis, in relating solely to *pulsation* and *remission* are emphatic features by which the modes of time are pointed out and the measure governed.

In reply to Lord Monboddo's suggestion that rhythm must consist "in one or other, or all of the four following things: the quantity of the syllables; the variety of loud and soft; the pauses, and lastly . . . division into bars,"[15] he states emphatically:

> Now I say that the affections of *heavy* and *light* are the most essential governing powers of rhythmus, for since the accents, *acute*, *grave*, and *circumflex*, are common both to the *heavy* and to the *light*; And since quantity, or the *long* and *short*, are likewise common to each; And since the accidents of *loud* and *soft* are also common to each; And lastly, since the accidents of *accent*, *loudness*, and *quantity* occur not periodically, but occasionally, whilse *cadence* is strictly *periodical*, and divided into

heavy and *light* alternately; which affections are to be accounted for in the mind, whether *sounding* or *pausing*, continued or articulated,

It follows, that *heavy* and *light* (as the certain alternate division of cadence) are the most essential governing powers of rhythmus both in poetry and prose.[16]

Steele explains that whereas the Greeks used the term *rhythmus* to signify the number of metres in a line or sentence, he uses it both to signify the number of cadences in a line or sentence, and as a general term for the division of a cadence into the long and short quantities of its subsections. A difference between his *cadences* and the Greek *metres*, he points out, is that cadences "are exactly equal in duration of time to each other, and are commensurable by even steps, or by the pulses of a pendulum"[17] whereas the Greek metres "are not always of equal length; some being simple metres of one *foot*, and other compounded by *copula* of two feet, of various lengths."[18] Since this is so, he says, they are

> not always reducible within the compass of equal periodical pulsations like our cadences. For cadences always begin with *thesis* or △ the *heavy* syllable, and end with *arsis*, or ∴ the *light*; consequently, between step and step, or musically speaking, between *bar* and *bar*, the whole of each cadence is included.[19]

On the other hand, he points out, some Greek *feet* begin with *arsis* and thus, "the Greek metres cannot always be included, as our cadences may be, between the pulses of even time."[20]

As can be observed from his notation of the following utterance, the cadences represented *are* of uniform duration; this, as a result of the recurrence of emphatic impulses at regular intervals.

Steele[21] points out that in the first section of the sentence (Fig. 1) which he has written in common time (as marked by $\frac{2}{4}$) he has noted the *accents*, the *quantity* and *cadence*, whereas in the second, which is in triple measure, he has marked only *quantity* and cadence, together with the *rests* or *pauses* he has shown throughout the notation. He says, "where this mark

minu   in the
 ⌒ or ⌒   is used, it is to show, that as many syllables or rests as are
△   ∴

written over the line or embrace are all to pass as one in respect of the △, or the ∴."[22]

From Joshua Steele we have the earliest statements I know of the theory of isochronism in English. Not only did he initiate a new approach to prosody by pointing to the inapplicability of the Greek system to the analysis of English rhythm,

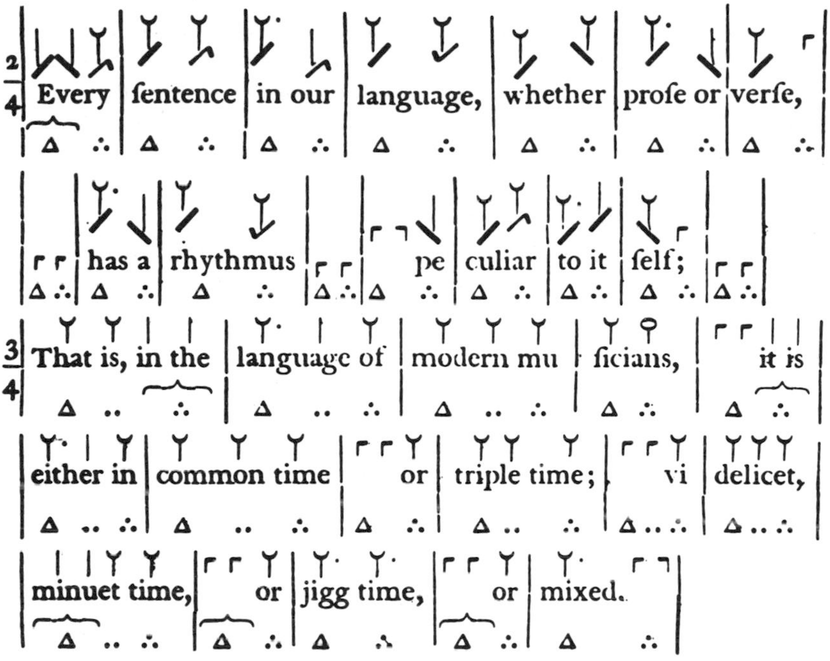

Figure 1. Steele's system of notation for representing the prosodic features of speech.

Neither would the Greek feet under all their various names, answer in any suitable degree to the rhythmus of our language; for the commentators have told us, their long and short syllables were in proportion to each other, only as 2 to 1; whereas in our rhythmus we have the several proportions of 2. 1. $\frac{1}{2}.\frac{1}{4}.$ and 3. 1. $\frac{1}{3}.\frac{1}{6}.$[23]

but also, by recognizing what in recent years has come to be known as "silent stress", he anticipated the theorists who claim that pauses or periods of silence are an essential feature of English speech rhythm: "They [the pulsation of emphatic and remiss] must be continued, by conception in the mind, during all measured rests or pauses, as well as during the continuance of either uniform, articulated, or modulating sounds."[24] As we shall see, there has been considerable experimental research on isochronism in recent years and the results of some of these studies refute Steele's observations. Nevertheless, the implications of his theory are especially pertinent to the acquisition of English speech rhythm by the foreign learner, and, as such, have been vital as a starting point for this present investigation.

Steele's observation that, despite the regularity of pulsation in English, monotony is generally avoided as a result of the recurrence of pauses and the wide variation in the duration of syllables is a practical point all too rarely considered in the planning of English language teaching programmes, yet I believe that it alone would be sufficient to place him in a unique position among speech rhythm investigators and teachers of prosodic features. Before Steele, the pause was merely regarded as a caesural division, but he saw it as an integral part of the bar contributing to the measure or timing of the whole utterance. He convinced Monboddo of the importance of the pause in English rhythm, but it was centuries before his profoundly original teaching was widely accepted by English prosodists.

Our next prosodist of note in the temporal tradition is Walter Young, a Scottish clergyman, who, independently of Steele, also undertook an investigation into the nature of the English speech rhythm in the latter part of the eighteenth century. According to Sumera,[25] the main value of Young's work lies in his psychological observations which, she says, "seem to foreshadow the gestalt approach and some of the conclusions that Paul Fraisse arrived at on the basis of experiments."[26] Young stresses the principle of subjective patterning in English, explaining that the impression of patterning is maintained even when the sound is discontinued for a short period since silences must be reckoned as part of the measured movement. Like Steele, he observes that regular rhythm can be varied by introducing some irregularities both in the combinations of bars and within the bars themselves, and, very perceptively it seems to me, points out that "[in English] the syllables are arranged less according to their real quantity than according to the accent with which we are accustomed to pronounce them."[27] However, as Sumera observes,

> he fails to see the demarcative function of stress in rhythm in English and, moreover, . . . the implications of his own statement: 'We can sometimes articulate three, perhaps even four syllables, in our own language, in longer time than we employ in expressing one syllable in the same sentence. It would be rash, however, upon perceiving this, to assert, that the one syllable was in quantity triple or quadruple of the others, as in different occurrences, or in different arrangements of the same syllables, the proportions might be varied'.[28]

In statements such as this, Young anticipates in quite a remarkable way the conclusions of William Thomson at the beginning of this century, and of André Classe who in the pre-World War II years advanced our understanding of the theory of isochronism in English prose rhythm through his kymographic investigations.

The early 19th century saw little original advance in rhythm studies, most phoneticians preferring to follow Steele. Nevertheless, two theorists merit our attention here—if not for their originality, at least for their emphasis on issues he had already raised. The first of these was James Odell who in *An Essay on the Elements, Accents and Prosody of the English Language* accepts without reservation most of Steele's views but says he must dissent on the question of "the ancient and natural distinction between prose and verse."[29] This leads him into a discussion of the function of the pause in verse structure and the organization of rhythmical cadences in prose. Referring to Steele's assertion that

> a discourse in prose as well as in verse or a tune will give some uneasiness or at least not be satisfactory to nice ears if its whole duration be not measured by an even number of complete cadences, commensurable with and divisible by two or three, that is, of cadences either in common or triple time[30]

Odell points out that although in the sentences of prose presented by Steele to accompany his notes on quantity and emphasis "the cadences appear indeed to the eye to be equal, and rhythmus correct . . . this appearance is not realized when the sentences are pronounced in an easy natural manner, and as . . . they would be by a correct speaker."[31] He also disagrees with Steele's distinction between force and poise, pointing out that "a cadence, of which the emphatic place is filled with a syllable both short and unemphatic, is not unfrequent in the most polished versification,"[32] and with Steele's eight degrees of quantity:

> Mr. Steele assumes eight different subdivisions of quantity, corresponding to the musical notes from a quaver to a dotted semibreve. It therefore cannot be difficult with such a variety of notes, and equivalent pauses, or even with the first six of them (which are all that he uses on this occasion) to give the semblance of equal cadences to almost any subdivisions of a sentence that chance might suggest: but no measures, whether of sound or silence in prose or verse can be regulated by arbitrary computations: nor can such diversities of measure as Mr. Steele assumes be ever realized in practice.[33]

Odell says[34] while it is true that long syllables are occasionally extended beyond, and both long and short syllables respectively contracted within their usual dimensions, the longest, compared with the shortest, is never in a proportion greater than four to one. Nature, he points out, puts a limit beyond which a long syllable cannot be protracted, unless it be either in a *drawl* or a *monotony* and conversely, the shortest syllable must have the time requisite for distinct articulation. On the question of pauses, Odell makes some valuable observations. Whereas Steele had believed that pauses ought to be accounted as parts of the metre both in verse and prose, Odell says ". . . no pauses can, with propriety be reckoned *parts of the metre* except those which accompany a short syllable when it occupies the place of a long one,"[35] These he says he would distinguish by the name of *metrical pauses*. However, there are other pauses of a non-metrical nature which are significant in the speaking of verse. He goes on,

> All other pauses should indeed, be made to conform to the rhythmical pulsation, and their respective quantity or duration must therefore be proportioned accordingly. But though they must increase the number of cadences in the *recitation*, they have no effect whatever on the *structure* of the verse.[36]

Odell explains that in a regular rhythmus it is requisite not that verses of the same denomination should all be sung or said in the same time, but that the several cadences in any verse should be respectively equal. He emphasizes that this equality must not result from "any artificial conformity of utterance"[37] in the speaker but must proceed from the natural drift of current pronunciation in reading or speaking plain prose.

Thus Odell was prepared to accept the original and perceptive theory of Steele at a time when many of his contemporaries were ignoring it—but at the same time he did not hesitate to dissent in those areas in which he believed the master had erred. Not so the Reverend James Chapman who unhesitatingly adopted Steele's views in their entirety. Chapman[38] was a teacher who evidently saw the need to organize the somewhat unsystematic arrangement of Steele's tracts for the benefit of his students, and from this point of view he holds a significant place in our historical survey. However Sumera believes that we cannot afford to underestimate the importance of such remarks as the following: "Thesis or pulsation is not peculiar to a long syllable, nor the Arsis or remission to a short one but may be upon either."[39] "Whether a cadence begins with a long or a short syllable or note, or with a rest in silence, is quite indifferent to rhythmus; but the syllable, or note, or rest, must invariably carry with it the heavy poise or Thesis."[40]

In statements such as these he clearly anticipates some of the relatively recent observations of Abercrombie[41] on verse structure. However, generally speaking, he did not add significantly to contemporary knowledge of speech rhythm, many of his explanations and definitions being drawn directly as Omond[42] points out, from Thelwell's "Definitions of the Rhythmus of Verse and Prose".[43]

The middle of the century saw the publication of Coventry Patmore's *Essay on English Metrical Law*[44] which, according to Omond, ranks very high among English studies of prosody and is, in his opinion, one of the few papers of abiding value which the subject has elicited."[45] Another temporal theorist, Patmore asserts that metre, in the primary degree of "a simple series of isochronous intervals, marked by accents,"[46] is as natural to spoken language as an even pace to walking and argues that "verse is but an additional degree of that metre which is inherent in prose speaking."[47] Metre itself implies something measured, he points out, and that something is the time occupied in the delivery of a series of words. That which measures it, being in his opinion itself unmeasured, is an 'ictus' or 'beat', actual or mental. By this means speech is divided into "equal or proportionate spaces". However, Patmore cautiously maintains that

> the equality or proportion of metrical intervals between accent and accent *is no more than general and approximate*[48] and that expression in reading, as in singing or playing admits, and even requires, frequent modifications, too insignificant or too subtle for notation of the nominal equality of those spaces.[49]

According to Omond,[50] Patmore attaches too much importance to delivery, and rejects the Patmorian claims that metre exists in all speech when adequately rendered, and that prose and verse, when properly delivered, have the same temporal foundation, pointing out that Patmore does not discriminate sufficiently between word accent and metrical beat or ictus. However, in Omond's opinion, the chief defect of the *Essay* is its non-recognition of minute intervals of pause, and he points out that, in concentrating his attention on syllables, Patmore failed to give sufficient consideration to silent intervals. Taking the statement of Patmore that "in music played *staccato* on the pianoforte, the actual duration of sound in crotchet or quaver note may be the same,"[51] Omond argues that it is not the duration of sound but the interval between the beginning of one sound and the beginning of the next which is identical—and that "that interval is partly occupied by silence."[52] Recognition of these silent spaces, says Omond, "is essential to just prosody and often revolutionizes our ideas of a line's actual structure."[53]

However, not only is the pause an integral part of verse structure. As we shall see,[54] failure to use the pause correctly contributed to the rhythm anomalies which characterized the utterance of the non-native subjects in the study reported in this book. Native speakers are themselves rarely aware of this essential constituent of rhythmicality, yet intuitively they use it frequently to supply the ictus or beat which normally falls on the stressed syllables of their utterance.

During the second half of the 19th century through the first decade of this century there was a proliferation of rhythm studies, most of little consequence—but some few of significance. These will be considered briefly here in view of the influence they have had on later investigations. It has been said, for instance, that experimental work on the rhythm of speech virtually began with Brücke[55] who in 1871 concluded that metrical feet are isochronous. According to Patterson,[56] however, this finding should be disregarded on the grounds that Brücke's equipment and methods were unsatisfactory.

After a lapse of some twenty years two other German scholars presented some highly significant statements on rhythm although, in Patterson's opinion, they did not always recognize the implications of their own conclusions. Both Meumann[57] and Sievers,[58] he says, speak of two antagonistic rhythmic tendencies—one toward freedom and variety, the other toward equal "Sprechtakte". For Meumann, "rhythm is a mental process by means of which we group sensations of sound into a system of images arranged on a temporal basis,"[59] and because intellectual processes are at work, he contends, organic phenomena are only accompaniments. Thus breath, for instance, adapts itself to the rhythm. Although doubtful of Brücke's equal bar theory, Meumann concedes that there is a tendency in speech "to slow up or to hasten the number of elements in a group in order to make the group fit the natural attention period."[60] Yet for all this, says Patterson, Meumann failed to appreciate the implications either of acceleration and retarding on the one hand, or of syncopation on the other. According to Sievers, it is prose which tends to be divided into sections of approximately equal duration. These sections, he says,[61] can appear even when the separate "Sprechtakte" seem of unequal duration. Patterson is critical of Sievers for what he regards as Sievers' inconsistency in defining rhythm from the point of view of the "timers" but applying it from the point of view of the "stressers".[62] According to Sievers, "time-organization and stress gradation" are by far the most important among the factors in rhythm, but as Patterson points out, in its application, Sievers' two-beat theory for Old English verse actually falls back on the assumption that time is not so important a factor as we imagined. Patterson says that even Sievers' supposition that Old English poetry was meant to be recited freely in no way removes the inconsistency. Schipper,[63] some years later, also accepted the two-beat theory for the alliterative lines of Old English. According to this view,

> The structure of the alliterative line obeys only the requirements of free recitation and is built up of two hemstichs which have a rhythmical likeness to one another resulting from the presence in each of two accented syllables, but which need not have . . . complete identity of rhythm, because the number and situation of the unaccented syllables may vary greatly in the two sections.[64]

However, in his definition of poetical rhythm generally he clearly recognizes the importance of the time element. He regards this rhythm as a "special symmetry, easily recognizable as such, in the succession of syllables of different phonetic quality which convey a sense, and are so arranged as to be uttered in divisions of time which are symmetrical in their relation to one another."[65] In prose, word order is determined almost entirely by the sense, he says, although even in prose "a certain influence of rhythmical order may be sometimes observable."[66]

According to Wallin,[67] however, it is often only the visual arrangement of language in schematic lines instead of a straight-forward succession of words that causes us to distinguish verse from prose. This observation, made as a result of his experiments at Yale is mentioned by Patterson in the course of his discussion of the view that one continuous text may lead to two different types of experience depending upon predominance of syncopation or predominance of coincidence in the relation between the speaker's pulses and his accented syllables. Patterson says that patterns of grammatical (that is, dictionary) accent have a decided influence on the speaker in suggesting to him whether he speak a passage as prose or verse.

When a prose attitude is instituted, he says, the delivery of a "timer" makes it quite clear that

> he is uttering his accented syllables in a comfortably irregular fashion—comfortably, because his ability to organize subjectively such irregularities completes for him, by means of syncopation, the easiest rhythmic experience that can be evoked by such conditions. If, however, the grammatical stresses . . . arrange themselves obviously in a repeated pattern he . . . utters the passage in question in harmony with his instinctive feeling that the predominating coincidence between accents and time-pulses is the easiest process whenever a sequence of some one stress-pattern is involved. Thus, both in the case of prose and verse, *he follows automatically the line of least resistance*. . . . The hearer, on the other hand, receives his suggestions no longer from mere dictionary accent, which is easily obliterated in rapid delivery, but from the particular rendering of the one who utters the words.[68]

Patterson believes that there are "only two ways in which a series of measuring time-units can be co-ordinated with a second series of sensations—syncopation and coincidence. Either syncopation predominates, in which instance we feel the stimulus as prose, or coincidence predominates, and verse experience ensues."[69] He insists, however that "there exists no actual arrangement of lines or of stress-groups in the words themselves which is capable of leading us invariably into a perfect balance between syncopation and coincidence,"[70] and points out that Wallin's experiments showed how easily passages of verse from both Tennyson and Browning could be read as prose, if so arranged. Wallin's unit of measure was the interval between centroids, and by using this system he dispensed altogether with the foot and bar as terms.

Another investigator of this period who advocated measurement according to the centroid system was Scripture.[71] Although the centroid theory is concerned with both time and stress, Scripture sees no possibility of division of speech into the several units of sounds, syllables, words, feet, etc., maintaining that speech is "a flow of auditory and motor energy."[72] Thus, he says, "the centroid will rarely coincide with the maximum of energy."[73] This, Patterson interprets as meaning that factors other than intensity must be taken into consideration when determining the position of centroids; a significant assertion, as we shall see when we consider some more recent studies on the acoustic correlates of stress.

For Verrier[74] the unit for speech measurement was the "vocal step". In contrast with the views advanced by many of his contemporaries, Verrier, Patterson says, maintains that the origin of rhythmical verse is to be found in the prose "segments" of every-day conversation. These segments which may be "short" or "long" are measured from strong vowel to strong vowel and, according to their average length, each person is accorded his "vocal step" or "natural rhythm". Longer segments, it seems, do not exceed three syllables or the length of a rather slow walking step. As a result of his experiments with three native English speakers Verrier reports that he found "an unconscious tendency to bring the consecutive rhythmic segments to an equal duration."[75] This, he says, results in "a relative shortening of sounds, according as the number of the syllables of the segments increases."[76] On the basis of this finding he concludes that English prose modulates incessantly from two to three-beat rhythm.

> Whether there is or not dependence between the rhythm of pronunciation and that of walking, they both have one single and same cause: the necessity of co-ordinating and regulating our muscular movements, in a word, of making them rhythmic, in order to diminish, the expense of energy.[77]

Whereas Scripture defines rhythmic movements as movements repeated at apparently equal intervals, Verrier regards the equality of time-intervals as an illusion. Nevertheless, according to Patterson,[78] he appears to believe that rhythm depends upon the illusion of equal time-interval for its basis, but nevertheless enjoys the introduction of a measure of irregularity, in much the same way as harmony enjoys dissonances.

Each of these prosodic theorists has contributed in some way to our understanding of the temporal view of English speech rhythm. However, it is to William Thomson we must now turn for what is probably the most comprehensive statement we have yet had on the subject. His first contribution appeared in 1904,[79] to be followed twenty years later by *The Rhythm of Speech*,[80] a volume of some 550 pages containing twenty-four Laws which he says are the concentrated if somewhat dry essence of all he has to say on the subject of the rhythm of speech.

Although he has a great deal to say that is pertinent, Thomson was probably less original than is sometimes imagined, since several of the issues he raised; such as, syllabic quantity, measurement, and notation, had been considered—as we have seen—by a number of his predecessors. He says in the Preface that although the book is "mainly an investigation into the nature and manifestations of speech rhythm in the verse and prose of existing languages, especially of English", his larger aims are:

1. To lift the whole subject out of the region of bookish learning with its appeal to the eye, and set it on a basis of scientific observation by means of the ear, verifying results by the application of tests open to all.
2. To encourage in schools and universities a rational analysis of verse-form resulting in a rhythmical synthesis. . . .
3. To devise a notation fitted to serve as a universal medium of communication, and thus do for the rhythm of speech what the symbols of the music-page do for the less complex rhythms of music.[81]

Such a system of notation which, he says, is necessary in order that the rhythm can be realized at a glance, should show:

The Time, as $\frac{3}{8}$; the measures by means of bars; the number of sounds or silences in each measure; the quantity of each sound, as 1, 2, 1$\frac{1}{2}$; and of each silence, as $\frac{2}{\wedge}$ or $^{(2)}$; the relative strengths of the accents, as ′, ″, ‴, etc., or *cres.*, *dim.*; the tempo, as *accel.*, *rall.*; the metre; and, if desired, the sound-grouping and the sense-phrasing.[82]

Excluded should be: absolute duration, absolute, or even measured accent, pitch, timbre, quality, consonantal burden, alliteration and meaning.

In answer to the critics of his *Basis of English Rhythm* who had objected that his methods were those of music, he maintains that his use of musical symbols for units of duration is rather a kind of arithmetic—not music at all—that in fact his methods of observing, analysing, testing, and recording, are the methods of scientific research. Nevertheless, at the beginning of his second book he states quite clearly:

In the notations about to be given I represents the commonest unit of duration introduced by a weak blow, and | I, one headed by a relatively stronger blow. A measure begins with a strong blow and ends at the next on a par with it. The notations |II|, |III [are] common examples.

Let us now suppose that a number of persons of normal faculty hear a fairly rapid series of "equal sounds" in twos, with the accents or stronger blows on every second sound, some, however, beginning their accents with the first sound, others with the second. Thus we have the rhythms,

   ∧ | I I | I I | I I | . . . .
   I | I I | I I | I . . . .

which, taken in pairs as they occur, yield the two phrasings shown by interlining in

   | I I | I I | I I | . . .
   I | I I | I I | I . . . .

But these are not exhaustive, for the first rhythm yields also

   | I I | I I | I I | . . .

where the pairs begin with the second sound; and the second yields also

   I | I I | I I | I . . . .

where the pairs begin with the fourth sound, or

   I | I I | I I | I I | . . .

where the pairs begin with the sixth sound. In all, as against two rhythms with *only one measure*, we have at least five phrasings built on three phrases. That no phrasing for the second rhythm is given with pairs beginning on the second sound is to be attributed to a well-established law which forbids a solitary unaccented sound. Such a sound, whether initial or final, goes with the nearest accented sound. This is a simple matter of experience, of which confirmation may be found in the frequent occurrence, in a verse, of a solitary accented syllable and the absence of a solitary unaccented one. *Now measuring, not phrasing, is of the essence of rhythm.* [83] Therefore a measure being defined as a portion of rhythm beginning with one strong accent and lasting up to, but not including, the next, the measures exhibiting the rhythm of our two accented series are as printed above, the bars marking the beginning of each accented sound. The accent is heard not at the end of that sound, nor in the body of it, but only at its rhythmical onset. Neither accent nor any subordinate blow has duration. It stands, as has been said, exactly on a par in relation to time with Euclid's point in relation to space. The mind measures from point of force to point of force in time, just as the joiner measures from point to point in space. [84] Moreover, just as, under the influence of accent, grouping in twos results in so many varieties of phrasing, so grouping in threes and fours gives rise to an ever increasing complexity. [85]

Thomson goes on to explain very fully combinations of time units, [86] and measures which remain equal while the unit changes. [87] He notes that Steele and a few of his successors knew of such measures but observes wryly that

20th century prosodists "still shy at them."[88] This brings him to the important issue of the necessity of accent in Rhythm and Time:

> Quantity without a basis of accent, and quantities without syllicts, are as unthinkable as environment where is no inheritance to be environed. The two are inseparable; the one is nothing without the other. You cannot have distances without points, nor points without distances. But, in practice, you must think first of the points. When you have fixed two points of time, you have determined one duration. With only one duration there can be no quantity.[89]

Of the distinction between Rhythm and Time he says:

> In | I I | and | 2 | we have the same Time, viz. $\frac{2}{4}$, and the same measure, period or total duration, but not the same rhythm; for rhythm takes cognisance also of the number of sounds. In | I I I | and | $2\frac{1}{2}\frac{1}{2}$ | we have the same Time, viz. $\frac{3}{8}$, and the same number of sounds, but still not the same rhythm: for rhythm embraces the distribution of time over the sounds. In I | I I | I and | I I | I I | we have the same Time, the same number of sounds and the same distribution of time over the sounds, but not the same rhythm: for rhythm implies the distribution of accents over the sounds. In I | I I I | I and I | I I | I I we have the same Time, the same number of sounds and the same distribution of time over the sounds, but not the same rhythm: for rhythm, in addition to other *distinguenda*, observes the duration, position and accentuation of rests.[90]

Thus for Thomson, unlike Patmore, rests are an essential part of the rhythm. Again, "Syllables, accented or unaccented, but especially the latter, may, without detriment to rhythmical continuity, be sparingly replaced by silences, called rests, having approximately the same quantities."[91]

However, like Patmore, he believes that the essence of rhythm consists in the measurement of intervals marked by accents. Indeed, for Thomson accent is indispensable in the creation of rhythm. But as he says, "In the creation of the effect of Time or rhythm, given suitable quantities, it is not the strength of the accent that counts, but its existence, even in the slightest recognisable form."[92] Nevertheless, he insists that nothing but an increase in loudness can determine the stress point in the syllable which in his terminology is the *syllict*, or onset of the vowel.

In addition to his *Laws*, Thomson sets out what he regards as the twelve outstanding principles of speech rhythm. Some of these, as Sumera[93] rightly observes, we would not find wholly acceptable. Nevertheless, they do summarize much of his thinking and are a succinct expression of the main tenets of the temporal theory of speech rhythm.

1. In the rhythm of speech the sounds that count are syllables; more specifically, syllabic points-of-force (onsets, accents, blows or ictuses); still more specifically, vowel points of force (onsets, etc.); briefly, what I have called syllics.

2. The phonetical material of a syllable counts only in so far as the vowel-sound with which it begins must be present in the minimum amount practically necessary to carry the syllict. Syllicts are the only events in a rhythmical phrase.

3. Syllicts vary in strength or loudness, some being specifiable as principal. A principal syllict acts both as a measure-ictus and thesis-ictus, and is usually called an accent.

4. Accents generally occur at equal intervals—in which case we have equal periodicity in its simplest form—but variety may be added by intervals related as the numbers 2, 3, 4, transition being possible from any one to any other.

5. The rhythmical material starting with one accent or principal syllict and extending to the next, constitutes a measure, replaceable by an equal measure, or, in cases of measure-variation, by an equivalent measure. The replacing of a measure in either way is called substitution.

6. A simple measure, by a natural division, consists of thesis and arsis, the ictus of the latter, called arsis-ictus, being, in cases of unit-sub-division, stronger than any other outside the thesis-ictus. If thesis is equal to arsis, we have the equal genus, and the Time is duple; if double, the double genus, and the Time is triple. A compound measure consists of two or more simple measures, the first part acting as thesis to the second's arsis.

7. Expressed in terms of a suitable unit or beat, the interval starting with one syllict and extending to the next is called the quantity of the syllable starting with the earlier.

8. Quantities range from $\frac{1}{2}$ to $4\frac{1}{2}$, and include at least $\frac{2}{3}$, $\frac{3}{4}$, 1, $1\frac{1}{2}$, 2, $2\frac{1}{4}$, and 3, subject to considerable limitations of possible transition. Here we have quantity-variation.

9. A syllable may occasionally be replaced by a silence of approximately equal quantity called a rest, and either may be slightly increased in duration by a pause. As the sound preceding a rest, strictly speaking, has no specific quantity, it is obvious that neither can the rest.

10. A measure is built on some distinct accentual plan applied to beats or units, latent or expressed, and called its Time. Beat-variation is common.

11. The rhythm of a measure includes the Time and the scheme of quantities.

12. It is possible to establish and verify an analysis of the rhythm of a speech-phrase by tapping beats, quantities or measures as required, the taps being simply reproductions of accents and other syllicts, or of beat-

ictuses, latent or expressed. All notations are verified by combining the four methods. The student should practise till he acquires confidence, remembering that, if he sophisticates a natural reading or his beating of time, he is lost. [94]

Such a summary is clearly of value to us as a statement of the temporal theorists' position. However, it would not be long before experimental evidence based on instrumental analysis would be used to complement the auditory observations of these early investigators. It seems to me that Thomson's most valuable contribution to our understanding of English speech rhythm in his insistence that the duration of English syllables is variable (as indeed Young had suggested)[95] whether due to length of vowel, or of consonants, or of the two combined, and that this feature is a consequence of interval isochronicity. He is extremely critical of the lexicographer's practice of marking out the length of vowels in their recommended pronunciations and of presenting the isolate-form pronunciation of words, when, as he shows, it is clearly the length of the entire syllable heard in relation to the other syllabic units of the whole phrase which is the important feature to be observed. He says:

A syllable is popularly supposed to be simply either long or short. The existence, or at all events, the wide extent of variations of length in both long and short syllables—in the same syllable, indeed, according to its setting—has generally not been suspected. . . . That such variations exist can be shown by a very simple experiment. Starting with a phrase, 'a long dress', one hears that the adjective is, speaking in a general way, a long syllable. If we substitute for 'long' its comparative, thus obtaining the new phrase, 'a longer dress', we observe, by tapping the accents, that the time elapsing between the sounds *long* and *dress* is just what it was before the addition, which shows that time has been deducted from the syllable *long* and transferred to the suffix *er*. If we now prefix *ad* to *dress*, our phrase becomes 'a longer address', which we perceive, in spite of its two additional syllables to be of the same duration as the original phrase. In fact, the three syllables *longer ad* now occupy the same period of time as the one syllable *long* did at first, the time taken to the syllables *er ad* being given at the expense of the syllable *long*. Thus it is clear that the syllable *long* has at least two different durations. Within certain limits, therefore, the insertion or omission of unaccented syllables does not affect the total duration of a phrase, and the length of accented syllables varies according to the character and number of unaccented syllables intervening before the next accent. [96]

Using his own system of notation, Thomson shows that in the following sentences no fewer than four different quantities exist for the syllable *long*.

Just as a lóng dress leads to a lón - ger dress,
| 1½ ¾ ¾ | 3   :   3 1½ ¾ ¾ | 1½ 1½   :   2 . ⌒

So a long ad-dress leads to a lon-ger ad-dress.
| 2 1 | 2 1 : 3 |1½ ¾ ¾ | 1½ ¾ ¾   :   2

The path lies   along a brook.
1 | 2 | 1½ ⅔ | 1 1 | 2   [97]

Thomson's observations regarding syllable duration have important implications for the teaching of all of the prosodic features of spoken English since, obviously, if the speaker does not make the necessary timing modifications, he cannot produce rhythm groups of equal periodicity, nor can he—though this is not relevant to our present discussion of rhythm—produce the pitch glides of intonation patterns with the appropriate durations. Using his own system of notation, Thomson sets out in some detail passages of verse and prose showing how speech phrases can be interpreted according to sound or sense grouping. His analyses are interesting although most professional readers of today would, I think, have some reservations about his sound-group interpretations since style in recitation has changed somewhat since the time of his writing.

The year after Thomson's monumental work appeared Sonnenschein published the results of an early kymographic investigation of syllable duration. "There is no generally accepted system of English syllable-measurement in existence. This yawning gap in our scientific literature, I greatly daring, have attempted to bridge over by some pioneer work."[98]

Until this time, as we have seen, phoneticians had relied almost solely on auditory observations for their pronouncements but as Sonnenschein points out, the rules which he had earlier drawn up on the basis of this technique were "subsequently developed, and to some extent modified in the light of experimental research."[99] Thus, as he says, "the rules have acquired a certain objective foundation to which they could otherwise have laid no claim."[100] His method of measurement differs from mine[101] in that he measured only the duration of (i) the vowel and (ii) the consonant sound or sounds which *follow* it in the syllable, and not the initial consonant or cluster, his reason being, he says, that

> any sound or sounds which may *precede* the vowel-sound of the syllable are negligible, so far as an effect upon ear is concerned; the effective part of a syllable from the psychological point of view is its vowel-sound and any consonant-sound or sounds that may *follow* this vowel-sound within the syllable . . . the explanation probably is that the initial consonant-

sounds of syllables (if any), though they occupy time in utterance and form part of the syllable, are thrown into obscurity by the superior sonority of the vowel-sounds that follow them, and so produce little or no effect upon the ear—i.e., upon the mind; whereas there is nothing within the syllable to weaken the effect of a consonant-sound that stands at the end of it.[102]

With Sweet,[103] he agrees that "length is not necessarily coincident with stress or shortness with the absence of stress."[104] He shows, for example, that an accented syllable may be short and an unaccented syllable may be long, as in the word *echoes* ($\acute{\smile}$–), a point stressed by Abercrombie in his classification of disyllabic feet,[105] and reminiscent of Chapman.[106] However, Sonnenschein adds that although a stress does not necessarily make a syllable long, stressing may be accompanied by lengthening.

Sonnenschein's interest in the duration of syllables is associated with his view that "quantity is a structural element in English verse, side by side with accent."[107] He points out, however, that in maintaining this view he does not commit himself to the position that English verse is quantitative in the sense that the syllables group themselves in feet and divisions of feet by reason of their inherent qualities, as do the syllables of Classical verse. Rather, English verse has both accentual and quantitative elements in its structure, and in addition is isosyllabic, so that "while the grouping of the syllables is mostly otherwise effected, our poets sometimes fall back upon the method of counting of a certain *number* of syllables to form a group, the number being determined by the question how many syllables the majority of the neighbouring groups contain."[108]

He asserts that "in so far as English ears are insensible to distinctions of quantity, any pair of syllables is actually felt to be equal in duration to any other pair."[109] Thus, he says,[110] we find that a foot containing two unaccented syllables is not necessarily defective in time as in, "extreme rage" (Shakespeare, *Two Gentlemen* II, vii, 22) where the length of the unaccented syllable *ex* justifies the foot *in ex* ($\smile$ –). But even where a foot is defective in duration—that is, where both the syllables are short, the defective duration of one group of syllables often finds compensation in the extra length of some adjacent group. For example, in the lines from *A Midsummer Night's Dream*,

The ploughman lost his sweat, and the *green corn*
Hath rotted ere his youth attain'd a beard

(II, i, 95)

the two short syllables "and the" are balanced by the two long syllables "gréen corn" in such a way that the two feet taken together have about twice the duration of a normal foot; for example, "the plough-".

Sonnenschein also suggests[111] that it is quite legitimate to place the foot division after "green" and to prolong the word, so that it fills the place thus left vacant in the last foot:

and the gréen córn

This, he reminds us, is often done in the ordinary recitation of the line; as it is in, "to the wild | sky"

In Memoriam, CVI, 1.

"of a lóng | clóud"

Morte d'Arthur, 10, 54.

"To the lást | sýllable of recorded time"

Macbeth, V, v. 21.

However, as he says, the prolonged syllable must be of sufficient importance to bear such prominence, and the next syllable to it must be accented.

These observations of Sonnenschein are extremely important in their application to conversational speech and to prose, both of which, according to Tempest,[112] possess prose-rhythm and cadence but lack the regular pattern which metre establishes, and thus fail to produce an expectancy of uniform periodicity. The fluent speaker, by intuition or experience, makes the necessary adjustments to the duration of his syllables in the course of utterance and by this means is able to maintain a credible rhythm, but the foreign learner has to be shown how to effect proportioned durations in the arrangement of his rhythm units, and from this point of view the implications of Sonnenschein's observations—albeit on verse rather than on prose rhythm—cannot be disregarded.

Sonnenschein argues that in all manifestations of rhythm what we are really concerned with is the psychological rather than the physical fact—that is to say, with the *impression* made by the physical fact upon the mind through the sense organs. The mind of man, he points out, is not an exact chronometer, and therefore it fails to distinguish ratios which differ from one another in a relatively small degree. Not only this. "Ratios which are recognized by the mind as . . . different may [in fact] be unified or identified as representative of or intended for one and the same ratio."[113] He shows that the absolute durations of sounds measured kymographically in his study represent periods which the ear may be incapable of taking cognizance of, and suggests that the actual durations of syllables in the Classical languages might likewise have been shown to vary quite considerably had modern instrumental measurements been made of them instead of the dichotonous classification as either "long" or "short". Further, says Sonnenschein, when Quintilian asserted that a long syllable contained two units of time and a short syllable one unit of time he was pointing to a reality in the structure of verse (acceptance as equal of syllables which varied considerably was a fundamental postulate of classical verse structure) but his rule needed interpretation from a psychological point of view. As we shall see, some investigators are still reluctant to accept the psychological fact. Yao Shen and Peterson,[114] for example, a little over a decade ago concluded on the basis of a spectrographic investigation of the postulated equality of time intervals that isochronism in English does not exist. While O'Connor reports[115] that his experiments failed to find physical isochronism present even in a limerick in which the metrical rhythm was strictly maintained. On the other hand, as recently as 1971, Uldall[116] reported "a strong tendency to isochronism in . . . [the] reading style [of David Abercrombie]." It would seem, then, that Sonnenschein's theory of "impression of proportion" is particularly pertinent to English speech rhythm.

According to Thomas Taig, who in 1929 published his *Rhythm and Metre*, both poets and musicians have found isochronous measures to be "an irksome limitation."[117] Somewhat impatiently he says:

> In spite of M. Verrier's warning, some of the advocates and many of the opponents of isochronism still assume that the sound material within the periods is actually produced in equal spaces of time. . . . With the exception of certain dances there is nothing in the arts to support such a view.[118]

However, Taig's main preoccupation was the issue of speech-rhythm notation. He is, I think, quite rightly critical of the use of musical notation for this purpose, since although, as he says, "it gives some clue to both time and stress, and . . . has the initial advantage of being in common use . . . its chief defects are . . . insistence on strict isochronism and the theoretical coincidence of accent and stress."[119]

He points out that, "compared with music, language presents a more rapid succession of waves, and on the whole, has more variety in its rate of progression. Its range of tempi is not greater, but the tempo is constantly changing."[120] Because of these variations in the tempo of speech, absolute time values cannot be given to the various notes, as in music, he argues, more useful would be some kind of graphical system by which accent could be represented on the ordinate axis and time-values on the abscissa.

Giving by way of example the sentence, "The curves are simply a convenient method," which, he says, has four accents separated by intervals of time felt to be equal, he explains:

> In the graph of that reading each syllable is indicated by a thickening of the line, upward and downward curves show increase and decrease of accent, and time-values are plotted on the horizontal plane below. . . .

The time of the first wave (between the crests) is divided into $\frac{2}{3} + \frac{1}{3}$, the second is approximately $\frac{1}{3} + \frac{1}{3} + \frac{1}{6} + \frac{1}{6}$, the third is $\frac{1}{2} + \frac{1}{2}$. In the same way changes of tempo can be shown by varying the spaces between wave-crests, and we may proceed to graph whole pages of prose provided our experience is sufficiently clear to let us analyse the relationships.[121]

The   curves   are   simply   a   conven-ient   method

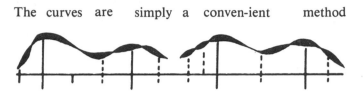

Figure 2.   Taig's system of notation for the representation of English speech rhythm.

Taig gives several examples of this proposed system and shows how common and triple time divisions which occur in most prose passages can be represented. It is, in my opinion, a more valid system for the representation of speech rhythm than musical notation, although one might well query his grounds for making these time divisions. He assumes, correctly I believe, that the waves are isochronous but it remained for our next investigator to examine by scientific techniques the extent to which English speech is objectively isochronous.

The investigator whose findings have probably been more widely discussed (and misinterpreted) than those of any other on the topic of isochronism in English is André Classe whose *Rhythm of English Prose* appeared in 1939. Classe concludes:

> An English sentence is normally composed of a number of more or less isochronous groups which include a varying number of syllables. These distribute themselves into different recognizable patterns. Two sets of factors, grammatical and phonetic, determine the degree of apparent equality of the groups [i.e., the duration of a speech unit from accent to accent] as well as the types of the patterns [i.e., the arrangement of the syllables composing such a group].[122]

He drew this conclusion on the basis of a series of experiments using kymography to measure the time intervals between accents in connected utterance. However, it is sometimes forgotten that Classe also says[123] that perfect isochronism can only be realized when very definite conditions—comparatively seldom met with in ordinary speech—are fulfilled. These conditions,

(a) Similarity of phonetic structure of the groups, including number of syllables

(b) Similarity of grammatical structure of the groups, and similarity of connection between the groups[124]

are clearly characteristic of verse and, as Classe points out, are a frequent feature of the more rhythmic type of prose, but they do not occur regularly in ordinary speech, the elements of which are constantly changing. We may well wonder, under these circumstances, whether we err in regarding English speech rhythm as isochronous, whether, in fact, the isochronicity of speech intervals is a myth. But the answer I believe is no—provided we recognize that this isochronicity is approximate, that it is a tendency only. It seems to me that many investigators who have sought to refute the theory of isochronism have overlooked this point in their search for absolute equality of intervals.

As Classe says: "that subjective isochronism forms the basis of English verse rhythm, nobody who has heard a child reciting *Mary had a little lamb* will feel tempted to doubt."[125] Nevertheless he quite rightly asks whether verse and prose have different rhythmic bases, whether there is a difference of nature between the two media. His own view is that "the first is but a stylization of the second, a systematic utilization of the natural features of the language."[126] He explains that if we consider any two consecutive stress-groups they may be *objectively* equal in duration or they may simply be *perceived* as equal, even though their actual duration in units of real time may differ. Verrier,[127] he points out, sees the groups as actually equal, whereas Patterson's theory[128] implies that under certain conditions we perceive the stress groups as approximately equal, even though their actual length varies. According to Classe:

> . . . in ordinary speech, or even in careful prose we seldom feel that the accents return at *rigorously* isochronous intervals. It is highly probable, of course, that we tend to equalize the groups we perceive and to minimize the differences. On the other hand, it is not less likely that we tend to place the stresses so as to facilitate the perception of groups as equal groups.[129]

The problem for him, then, is two-fold: (1) To what extent are the groups objectively isochronous? (2) Do they appear to be isochronous? His investigation is an attempt to answer the first question by way of measurement of the time interval between accents. In his first experiment using such sentences as:

He had a	biscuit, a	muffin, a	tea-cake and coffee[130]
[hi əd ə	biskit ə	mʌfin ə	ti:keik ənd kɔfi]

he found that for groups which did not differ too widely as regards the number of syllables included and the syntactical structure of the utterance, approximate isochronism seemed to be frequently realized. However, in sequences of unequal groups; for example,

He is an	*English*	*painter of con*	*siderable*	*fame*[131]
[hiːz ən	iŋgliʃ	peintər əv kn	sidrəbl	feim]

he found,

> it is very much more difficult to realize isochronism with a number of syllables varying considerably from group to group, even in enumerations than in the case of a continuous homogeneous sentence with more equal groups. There is a point where the elasticity of the pause ceases to compensate for inequalities.[132]

Clearly, series of groups containing a uniform number of syllables are comparatively rare in a language of such derivational complexity as English; however, as Classe explains:

> From the very nature of speech, it is obvious that, in the normal course of events, all the necessary conditions will generally not be present at the same time. But it does not follow that isochronism cannot be the *basis* of the rhythm of English. If we consider some of the less isochronous groups, we shall notice an interesting fact. Suppose in the first place that the duration of a group depends exclusively on the nature of the component syllables, their number, and the grammatical context of the group. If no other influence made itself felt we should then expect the duration of the group to be more or less proportional to the number of syllables and the importance of the 'cuts'. But this is not the case. . . . Whenever short groups are mixed with longer ones, the speaker minimizes the differences by changes in his rate of delivery. . . . It is not inconsistent with the facts to ascribe the acceleration, when it is present, to a desire on the part of the subject to equalize the groups, or to speak of *a tendency towards* isochronism.[133]

Nevertheless Classe points out that even if a speaker succeeds in making groups subjectively isochronous (a thing which he asserts can be done without difficulty) the rhythm thus produced is "of very inferior quality: the speaker ambles in some of the groups, then sprints in a very unnatural way."[134] He concludes, therefore, "that the conditions which make for *subjective* isochronism are those most favourable to objective isochronism."[135]

He asserts that there are three main elements which can make or mar the rhythm of an English sentence:

(a) The phonetic factor of number of units in the bar.
(b) The logical factor of grammatical connexion between bars.
(c) The phonetic factor of the nature of the units in the bar, especially accents.[136]

In ordinary speech these elements are always present and, as we would concur, their relative importance changes constantly. However, he points out that the reason normal speech and non-artistic prose are on the whole "rather irregular and arhythmic" is that even when two of the above elements happen to favour the rhythmic tendency, "the third may prove highly antagonistic."[137]

Following his examination of the rhythm of ordinary speech, Classe investigated the rhythm of a series of texts, representing several very different types of prose, from the markedly poetic *Song of Songs* to the familiarly conversational *Widowers' Houses*, with a view to determining whether the conditions which make for isochronism are more frequently present in prose of a highly rhythmical character than in more commonplace expression. The results of his statistical analyses show that a strongly marked rhythm cannot become established unless the series of stimuli—in this case, stresses—is sufficiently long. However, careful examination of the *Song of Songs* revealed that this selection, which had the shortest sentences of all, was nevertheless the most strongly rhythmical—a fact, says Classe, which suggests that a more regular distribution may compensate for a decrease in the size of the larger rhythmic unit.[138] He concludes that although prose and verse may utilize different rhythmic devices—for example, if the rhythm is mainly founded on syllabic equality it will more nearly approximate to that of verse—there is no sharp line of demarcation between the two media.[139] Prose rhythm, he asserts, is the more supple and varied, being unrestricted by the limiting nature of the traditional foot.[140] However, in the case of ordinary speech, "it is seldom that a conscious effort is made to achieve rhythm, and the various elements usually distribute themselves so as to create a rhythm with certain definite characteristics (which are those of the language) in the easiest possible way."[141]

The purpose of speech, he says,

is primarily utilitarian; so long as rhythm helps, or at least does not hinder the necessities of an easy articulation, or the clear perception of the meaning, isochronism is prominent, although still other factors may interfere (such as phonetic nature of the various groups and their grammatical structure). When isochronism is incompatible with logical or phonetic necessity, it must give way before them and disappear more or less completely.[142]

Nevertheless he is of the opinion, although he cannot prove it, that "many of the idioms and popular phrases of the English language have only been evolved and have remained because their rhythmic structure made them striking and easily remembered."[143]

According to Classe, the more we experiment, the more we are made to realize that "the rhythms of speech never have the monotonous accuracy of mechanically produced pianola rolls,"[144] and therefore it would be a mistake to look for rhythmic units of a perfectly definite type. We are aware of arrangements of longer and shorter syllables but, contrary to the views of earlier investigators, not of commensurability between syllables[145]—nor can we recognize any definite or fixed ratio between "long" and "short". Syllables are simply longer or shorter. As he truly says, "the study of the relative durations [of syllables] and of the factors that determine them, is one of the most interesting, as well as one of the most difficult aspects of the problem of the rhythm of speech."[146]

Classe extended considerably the boundaries of our knowledge of speech rhythm both through his own original investigations[147] and through his testing of the observations made by Daniel Jones[148] on the basis of subjective impressions. Those who follow him in the temporal tradition are pointed, I believe, in the right direction, while those who oppose his views have in his conclusions a valuable starting point for their own investigations.

In 1945 Kenneth Pike restated two postulates of Classe and popularized the concept of "stress-timed" rhythm. Classe, as we have seen, concluded among other things that "an English sentence is normally composed of a number of more or less isochronous groups which include a varying number of syllables,"[149] and that as a consequence of this fact "the length of the component syllables must vary within wide limits, according to the characteristics of the context."[150] However, according to Pike:

> The tendency toward uniform spacing of stresses in material which has uneven numbers of syllables within its rhythmic groups can be achieved only by destroying any possibility of even time spacing of syllables. Since the rhythm units have different numbers of syllables, but a similar time value, the syllables of the longer ones are crushed together, and pronounced very rapidly, in order to get them pronounced at all, within that time limitation. This rhythmic crushing of syllables into short time limits is partly responsible for many abbreviations—in which syllables may be omitted entirely—and the obscuring of vowels; it implies, also, that English syllables are of different lengths, with their length of utterance controlled not only by the lexical phonetic characteristics of their sounds but also by the accident of the number of syllables in the particular rhythmic unit to which they happen to belong at that moment.[151]

By way of example, Pike shows that in the pair of sentences

　　The ´ man's ´ here
　　The ´ manager's ´ here

we have similar timing and stresses, but a variant number of syllables. Because the length of the rhythm unit in English is largely dependent upon the presence of its one strong stress, rather than upon the number of its several syllables, he says, "it may conveniently be labelled a STRESS-TIMED rhythm unit."[152]

Whereas Classe asserts that perfect isochronism can only be realized when the phonetic and grammatical structures of the groups are similar, Pike, as can be seen, takes the view that the groups tend to be isochronous whatever their phonetic or grammatical shape. Pike goes on to explain that many languages other than English use a rhythm which is more closely related to the syllable, in that the syllables rather than the stresses tend to come "at more-or-less evenly recurrent intervals."[153]

Pike's observations on the distinction between stress-timed and syllable-timed rhythm are based on his very considerable experience in the teaching of English to native speakers of Spanish, and thus they are particularly relevant to the present study which has involved native speakers of some Asian languages with a syllable-timed rhythm. Very much concerned by the problem of a suitable system of rhythm notation, in 1962 he showed how rhythm units could be recorded as waves.[154] He says that what is necessary is a conceptual framework "which will allow training in the practical transcription of rhythm units."[155] His proposed system focusses on rhythm units as waves with initial margin, ascending slope, nucleus, descending slope, and final margin, each of these elements being treated in terms of stress, length, pitch, and their segmental components. It is a practical approach to the perennial issue of notation but does not add anything to his previously stated views on the theory of isochrony.

Actually, as Shen and Peterson point out,[156] Pike did not use the term "isochronous groups"—this, as we have seen, was Classe's terminology. Nevertheless, Pike's authoritative statements did much to propagate the belief that isochrony constitutes the basis of English speech rhythm, and for some years experimental work on this feature was eclipsed by research in other fields.

In the 'sixties a number of reports, often based on spectrographic analysis, were published, one of the most significant of these being the occasional paper by Yao Shen and Peterson already mentioned, *Isochronism in English*.

They conclude from their systematic investigation of a series of prose readings using spectrographic analysis: "We did not find isochronism in our limited data and therefore cannot say that there is isochronism in English."[157]

On the other hand, they apparently do not oppose the use of techniques based on this theory in the teaching of English as a foreign language. Observing that isochronism is a phonetic rather than a phonemic feature—that when it is mentioned it is not in contrast with any other feature of English but rather "in contrast with the isosyllabism of a foreign language,"[158] they ask the leading question: Is isochronism then a useful teaching device? It is, I think, with considerable insight that they go on to suggest that "the description of a language and the way to teach it as a foreign language are not always one and the same thing."[159]

They point out[160] that four types of factors are involved in isochronism: *three essential factors*,—these being two primary stresses, one terminal juncture, and a time span; *three variable factors between the two primaries*—the location of the terminal juncture which can be anywhere, the number of segmental phonemes which can vary from two up, the number of plus junctures which can vary from zero up; *a possible variable factor*; that is, the duration of pause which may follow or accompany a terminal juncture; and finally, what they call *a questionable factor*, this being the duration of the plus juncture.[161]

According to Shen and Peterson,

A more precise description of isochronism then is the tendency toward equal time lapse between stretches of speech which occur between two primary stresses with one and only one terminal juncture between them, irrespective of the number of phonemes, the number of /+/s, and the location of the terminal juncture between the stresses, as well as the possible cessation of speech 'following' or 'accompanying' the terminal juncture.[162]

A few years later, J. D. O'Connor[163] in London also set out to test the isochrony of groups of syllables between stresses. On the basis of measurements made of the durations of stress groups in five sentences containing an equal number of syllables (7) he found that

(a) there was no physical isochrony between the four groups in each line, whether the measurements were taken from the beginning of the stressed syllable or from the beginning of the stressed vowel.

(b) the phonetic structure of the word influenced the duration of the stress groups.[164]

He showed furthermore that even in a limerick in which the rhythm was as strict as possible, physical isochrony was not present. Following this test he proceeded to investigate how accurately a listener can judge isochrony. The results are interesting and, I think, seem to support one of Patterson's general conclusions; namely, that to the aggressively rhythmic person "no series of impressions exist that cannot in some way be conceived as rhythmic,"[165] whereas it is uncertain to what extent an observer whose rhythmic proficiency is less than moderate can develop the characteristics of an aggressive "timer". Patterson suggests nevertheless that such a person may surprise himself "when assisted by the harmless magic of a drum-beat tune."[166]

Using a device to produce electrically generated clicks, O'Connor recorded 37 sets of clicks, the intervals varying in steps of 5 ms. between 340-260 and 340-460 ms., and passing through equality at 340-340 ms., and asked his subjects to judge whether the intervals were isochronous. He reports:

> [The] results suggest that about 50% or more of the subjects judged the intervals to be equal anywhere between 340-320 ms. and 340-375 ms. . . . When the intervals are 340-345 ms., i.e., almost equal, a sudden drop occurs in the equal judgments; and at 340-395 ms. there is an even greater rise in equal judgments, 33 subjects out of 36 (91%) judging the intervals to be equal. Both these results suggest sequence effects: on the tape the item 340-345 ms. followed the item 340-375 ms. which 27 subjects judged equal; the shortening of interval 2 to 345 ms. in the succeeding item seems to have influenced the judgments. The item 340-395 ms. followed immediately after two rather obviously unequal items, i.e., 340-430 ms. and 340-255 ms.[167]

Three years later, O'Connor[168] complemented this study on the perception of isochrony with an experiment designed to determine whether the duration of the rhythmical foot was at all dependent in performance upon the number of sound segments composing the foot. Using the frame "Take _____ Park", the items /ses, sets, sekts, seksts, speksts, spreksts, spreiksts/ were successively inserted. O'Connor hypothesized that

> if the effect of isochrony—i.e., equal duration of successive feet in the utterance—were absolute, the duration of the variable would not alter in relation to the frame items. This would be achieved in two basic ways: either the frame could be lengthened in proportion to any duration increase of the variable necessitated by its segmental structure, or a fixed duration of the variable could be maintained through the set by varying the duration of component segments in more or less inverse proportion to their number.[169]

He concludes:

> 1. There is no evidence that the frame items accommodate their duration to that of the variable.

2. The variable has a clear tendency to greater duration as segmental length increases.

3. The duration is . . . not directly proportional to the number of segments; there is therefore a compressive tendency which might correspond to the tendency to isochronism mentioned in phonetic literature.[170]

As we have already seen, Elizabeth Uldall[171] found "a strong tendency to isochronism" in the reading style of David Abercrombie, but points out that "4-syllable feet do not follow this tendency."[172] Her material for the investigation consisted of spectrograms of a reading by Abercrombie of the fable "The North Wind and the Sun". The reading, she reports, was of 45 seconds' duration, in moderately slow "news reading" style, and divided by Abercrombie himself into rhythmic feet consisting of intervals from the beginning of a syllable marked "strong" and continuing through segments of the strong syllable and any weak ones until the next marked "strong" syllable.

Abercrombie,[173] who is probably the leading advocate of isochrony among contemporary phoneticians, in the course of a series of lectures on rhythm at Edinburgh in 1971,[174] made a number of authoritative statements on the question as follows:

1. The rhythm of speech is essentially muscular.[175]

2. There are two series of muscles producing speech movements:

(a) the series producing chest pulses (i.e., the syllable-producing process)

(b) the series producing abdominal pulses (i.e., the stress-producing process)

3. Speech rhythm is based on the periodicity of one of these two trains of pulses.

4. In speech there can be two different kinds of rhythm—*stress-timed*, in which the stress pulses are isochronous, or *syllable-timed*, in which the syllable pulses are isochronous.

5. Usually a language has one or the other type of rhythm but not both since the two types are incompatible. If one train of pulses is isochronous the other train cannot be.

6. English has a stress-timed rhythm which manifests itself in all modes of spoken expression: verse, prose, monologue, conversation, although in the last it can be interrupted. Three stresses are necessary before it can be said that an utterance is stress-timed. Hesitations do not usually upset periodicity since the tendency to stress timing is constantly trying to assert itself.

7. In English, syllables are of uneven length, being contracted and extended to maintain isochronicity.

8. Sometimes the isochronous beat falls on silence—in which case we say

the stress is silent. Silent stresses are completely integrated in the phonology of English and can be structurally predicted.

9. Non-recognition of silent stresses (which can be obligatory or optional) is the reason for the denial by some people that English is stress-timed.

10. The fundamental unit in rhythm is the syllable, but in stress-timed languages a unit longer than the syllable—the foot—occurs. The foot, a unit which does not occur in syllable-timed languages, includes a stressed syllable and whatever follows it up to but not including the next stress. Each foot is the same length and thus the syllables which comprise it must be variable in length. The length of an English utterance depends not upon the number of syllables but upon the number of feet it contains; for example, in the line,

> _I_ | _don't think it_ | _matters_

there are three feet but interpreted with a lengthened _don't_

> _I_ | _don't_ | _think it_ | _matters_

there are four feet.

From my own auditory observations of Abercrombie's utterance in conversation, in recorded speech, and in lectures,[176] I would agree with Uldall's conclusions regarding his own pronunciation. Furthermore, I am of the opinion that fluent native speakers, generally, show a tendency toward subjective isochrony. At the same time, I accept the conclusions of those investigators who can present evidence based on experimental research to show that _absolute objective isochrony_ does not exist in English. As recently as 1967, for instance, James Duckworth[177] was able to report as a result of his reinvestigation of the validity of isochronism:

> In the sample studied, the only conclusion can be that the notion of stress timing or isochronism which has persisted for a number of years, could not be defended. The number of syllables per segment seemed to be a much more powerful determining factor in the duration of a segment than the placement of stress.[178]

On the other hand, George D. Allen,[179] who in recent years has conducted a number of experiments on English speech rhythm, is of the opinion that a succession of _nearly_ equal intervals is sufficient to "promote in listeners, both native speakers and foreigners alike a feeling of rhythmicalness about the language."[180] Nevertheless, he does point out that since isochronism goes beyond this feeling to the notion of _exactly_ equal intervals, "we must look for a mechanism within English phonology that enhances the probability that exactly equal intervals occur, some rule that allows speakers of English to either move a stress around in time so that it occurs at the right place or suppress stresses that come at the wrong time.''[181] He suggests that one such mechanism may well be that which was mentioned by Pike;[182] namely, the suppression of stresses in subordinate positions in the sense group. ''The location of neighbouring stresses can not only change the location of stresses within a word'', Allen points out in concurrence with Bolinger,[183] but ''it can also promote and suppress the rhythmic accent on stressed monosyllables . . . here at least is a phenomenon that not only is clearly at work in English but also is strong enough to produce iso-chronism.''[184]

In 1970 Allen reported the results of a further experimental study on the location of rhythmic stress beats in English, concluding (a) that the beats of English speech are the stressed syllables, and (b) that the beats are strongly associated with the onsets of the nuclear vowels of those syllables.[185]

In his survey of some of the more recent research on the ''tendency toward equality of interstress intervals [in English]''[186] he observes that many researchers have been disappointed at not finding it in their data because they had not established in advance a criterion for deciding when there was a ''tendency'' and when there was not—they could see only strict equality or none.[187] Thus, he contends, failure to prove that English is stress-timed ''may be blamed as much on inadequate conceptions of what stress-timing can be and improper tests for its existence as on its non-existence in English.''[188]

Taking for granted the validity of the notion of ''syllable beat'' he says he proceeded to investigate the location of the beat within the syllable by means of finger taps and click matches. Both techniques had been used in previous studies, he points out,[189] and were used by him in order that the results of his experiments could be compared with those of the earlier investigations ''for mutual validation''. He reports, however, that in his experiment, the subjects' tapping behaviour was used to investigate both the degree to which a syllable was a rhythmic beat and the location of the beat in the syllable:

> The measure of 'rhythmicalness' was the reliability with which a subject tapped; i.e., the more of a down beat (stressed) a syllable is, the easier can a subject tap to it and the more tightly clustered will his taps therefore be; the measure of beat location was the average tap location.[190]

According to Allen, the results of his experiments combine those of two earlier investigators: Classe,[191] who found the rhythmic beat in speech to be located at the onset of the nuclear vowel of the stressed syllable, and Newcomb,[192] for whom the beat location was found to be the point of release of the last consonant before the nuclear vowel. ''The present study combines these results, showing that the beat location precedes the vowel onset by an amount positively correlated with the length of the initial consonants.''[193]

In his discussion, Allen points out that not only do his results describe the locations of rhythmic stress beats in ongoing speech, but they also ''illustrate the nature of stress in English as an element of a performance or speaking grammar as opposed to a competence grammar of English.''[194] The implications of this statement for the acquisition of normal stress and rhythm patterns by the non-native speaker are, I think, obvious. As Allen notes,

> A competence grammar of a language deals with what a speaker knows intuitively about how to compose and understand sentences in that language. A performance grammar is concerned with the speaker's knowledge about how to produce and perceive actual utterances in the language.[195]

Now, since speech rhythm—as part of the performance grammar of English—is rule-governed, it seems to me that, given assistance in learning the rules and adequate opportunity for practice, the foreign learner should be able to acquire satisfactory rhythmic patterns with no more trauma than he would experience in learning any other system of the language. The rules, as Allen says, are relatively simple, the sequential production of the stressed syllables being organized so that most of the patterns are merely *successions* and *alternations*, the ''rhythms of succession'' consisting in the main of arrangements of monosyllabic content words all of which receive a certain degree of stress in any sentence in which they occur; for example,

Those ballpoint pens write quite well,

and the ''alternating rhythms'' deriving either from arrangements of monosyllabic function and content words such as occur in the sentence, *I had a glass of milk and a roll for lunch*, where most of the function words are invariably unstressed, or from the alternation of stressed and unstressed syllables in polysyllabic words: for example, *exami'nation*.

According to Allen,[196] the pressures of rhythm and syntax on each other keep these successions and alternations of stress in close alignment and, as a result of this, much of the time it is difficult to separate them. A number of phoneticians, notably Daniel Jones[197] and Bolinger[198] have drawn attention to the kinds of accentual changes that occur when rhythm and syntax conflict but none, to my knowledge, has shown quite so explicitly as Allen[199] the high degree of correlation between lexico-grammatical stress and rhythmic stress which exists in English. By so doing, he has added considerably to the data currently available on stress-timing in English speech rhythm.

We have seen that from the 16th century to the present time there has been a fairly sustained interest in the related subjects of rhythmic stress and metre in English, and we have noted during this span the work of some selected scholars who, it seems to me, have contributed significantly to our understanding of one of the main theories of the nature of rhythm, the *temporal* view, which holds that time is the basis of English rhythmical structure. There are other theories as Crystal[200] shows—the *quantitative* approach which was extremely popular until the early 18th century and, as we noted in Chapter I, has found support in recent years in the work of Sheridan Baker (1960),[201] and the *non-temporal* approach which postulates an accentual rhythm—that is, a rhythm based on the regular recurrence of a stress or accent. Barkas,[202] as he says, distinguishes three subdivisions of this theory, the *isosyllabic* theory (the lines being equivalent because they contain the same number of syllables), the *accentual* theory (the lines being equivalent because they contain the same number of accentual syllables), and the *syllabic-accentual* foot theory (lines being equivalent because they contain the same number of groups of syllables of both kinds, accented and unaccented). This general accentual approach, it will be recognized, is that which during the 19th century became the traditional view and has since then been taught in the schools.

However, Barkas[203] also distinguishes several subdivisions of the temporal view—these being, the *isochronous foot* theory (lines are equivalent because they contain the same number of groups of syllables, equal in duration; the *isochronous interval* theory (lines are equivalent because they contain the same number of equal intervals between points of accentuation; the *quantitative foot* theory (lines are equivalent because they contain the same number of feet, the constituent syllables having simple ratios of duration to each other within each foot); and the *quantitative interval* theory (lines are equivalent because they contain the same number of intervals, the parts of which, measured from some identifiable points within the syllables, have simple ratios of duration to one another within each interval).

Yet, in Crystal's opinion, the temporal thesis is untenable. He says:

There were no objective measurements put forward in support of the temporal theory when it was propounded, and when these did come to be made it was readily demonstrable that great variations in terms of temporal length existed between prominent and unprominent syllables. Occasionally, even, the latter could be longer than the former . . . [further], syllabic relations are not as exactly definable as musical notes, a point long since made by Steele. . . . But most important, recent research has shown that it is facile to expect that such a phenomenon as stress can be identified with a single phonetic feature.[204]

One could hardly disagree with any of these contentions. Nevertheless, the temporal theory is the one upon which this study was undertaken and the one upon which the learning experiences were based. The longer I am involved in speech rhythm studies, the more am I convinced of the correctness of Quintilian's assertion, *Rhythmi, id est, numeri, spatio temporum constant* (Rhythms, that is, numbers, consist in the measure of time). But as so many of our investigators have pointed out, intervals of time, in order to be measured, must first be marked. According to Tempest, for instance, space of time is not even comprehensible to the mind unless there is some mark by which it may be recognized, "this mark, in the case of auditory rhythm, being a time-occupying sound",[205] and he goes on to argue that it is the sound segments which make rhythm possible. Certainly it is in the permutations and combinations of *stressed syllables* that we have the key to English speech rhythm, for is not every vocalized sound, stressed or unstressed, characterized by quality, intensity, frequency, and duration?

Clearly, as Crystal[206] suggests, then, if we would understand rhythm we must first determine what it is that constitutes stress—more particularly what it is that distinguishes stressed from unstressed syllables in the stream of speech. Although, as we shall see, stress has been one of the most widely investigated of linguistic systems in recent years, consensus of opinion regarding its phonetic correlates is sadly lacking. It is nevertheless, to some of these studies that we must now turn in order to take cognizance of the background to the investigation of stress which forms the nucleus of this work.

CHAPTER THREE

(a) The Work of Some Experimental Phoneticians on Stress

Although, as we have seen, the relationship between stress and rhythm has been recognized for centuries and the function of stress as marker of the rhythmic impulse accepted for quite as long, it is only in comparatively recent years that the nature of stress has come to be examined. However, when investigators did begin their search for the correlates of stress, most concentrated their attention on lexical or word stress in preference to the grammatical or sentence stress which is so intimately associated with speech rhythm.

By so doing, they delayed even further establishment of the factors which influence the production and perception of the phenomenon in the process of ordinary speech communication, for while disyllabic words spoken in isolation do in fact create the impression of a rhythmic unit which is associated with a particular pattern of stress variation, they cannot produce the overall effect of periodicity which characterizes every whole utterance of normal English.

Certainly until the middle of this century lack of suitable instrumentation precluded exact measurement of some of the physical parameters associated with stress. However, it seems to me that for far too long investigators have been hampered by two other related obstacles: misconceived assumptions originally made on the basis of auditory observations in the days before rigorous scrutiny and interpretation of instrumental records of acoustic and physiological phenomena could be undertaken, and inexact use of terms of strict definition, correctly belonging to other disciplines, which, over the years, have been loosely applied to stress, and are in this context peculiarly susceptible of misinterpretation.

The whole issue of stress has been complicated further, as Lehiste[1] points out, by the fact that the points of view of the speaker and the listener have often been confused in stress definitions. Whereas Jones[2] had described stress as "the degree of force with which a sound or syllable is uttered, . . . a subjective action, [involving] a strong 'push' from the chest wall [which] gives the objective impression of *loudness*,"[3] Bloomfield[4] defined it as "intensity or loudness, [consisting] in greater amplitude of sound waves."[5] Both phoneticians evidently believed the stronger force involved in the production of stress to be associated with the more than usually energetic action of the muscles of the respiratory, phonatory, and articulatory systems, but in their definitions emphasized either the role played by the speaker in producing it, or the listener in perceiving it.

However, their respective followers in proposing their own explanations have not always maintained this dichotomy, and thus we find descriptions of the production aspect given in terms of perception and *vice versa*.[6] This obviously, has exaggerated the elusive character of stress and, as Wang[7] has pointed out, of the proliferation of descriptive labels attached to both aspects of stress, some have suggested physical dimensions; some, psychological interpretations; and others, relations with the physiological mechanism of speech production.

According to Crystal,[8] a physiological definition of stress has been by far the most common, those who support this view generally seeing the phenomenon from the standpoint of the speaker and thus emphasizing its production aspect. However, he says that "the main difficulty with any theory of stress based on production is that it only provides a partial explanation of the phenomenon, and does not help in explaining how it is we perceive stress when someone else is speaking."[9]

A similar criticism could be levelled against theories of stress based on perception. The school which regards stresses as "differences in loudness . . . found to be consistent in [the] relative strengths [of the vowels]"[10] in no way explains how stress is produced, while those who contend that the several degrees of stress which constitute this system are caused by "an increase in tension and energy in the whole of the vocal apparatus"[11] may add quasi-physical dimensions to an essentially psychological explanation, but they still do not adequately define what Crystal[12] has called the 'Janus-faced' nature of stress.

However, Lehiste[13] suggests that whereas psychoacoustic investigations of loudness have at least been attempted, the inability of phoneticians until comparatively recently to measure expiratory muscular effort has impeded their attempts to establish the physiological correlates of stress. Thus impracticability of investigation would seem to have been a contributory factor to the failure of researchers to propose an adequate definition of the phenomenon from the speaker's point of view.

Nevertheless, during the last 20 years or so, improved experimental techniques deriving from the technological advances of recent years have led to renewed interest in the physical effort associated with the production of stress and encouraged re-examination of some of its supposed physiological correlates. Electromyographic investigation of muscle activity involved in respiration, and precise measurement of subglottic pressure by various techniques, are two of the means by which evidence has been obtained of the part played by the speaker in producing stress.

One result of these investigations is that definitions in terms of motor theory are now usually proposed when the phenomenon is considered from the point of view of the speaker, and psychoacoustic explanations presented when the standpoint taken is that of the listener. However, whether the investigations have been concerned with the production or the perception aspect of stress, most researchers have had as their objective the establishment of a one-to-one correspondence between stress in its function as a contrastive feature at the lexical level and a single physico-physiological parameter. It is now generally recognized[14] that there is no single mechanism to which the production of stress can be attributed and that the impression of prominence is in fact a composite phenomenon only to be understood by reference to several independent parameters.

These parameters, obviously, can be more readily investigated in the word in citation form than in the context of the sentence where various features vie for salience:

> The impact on an Englishman's ear and interpretative powers of the continuous flow of acoustic signals which constitute an utterance may, in fact, be analysed in terms of an everchanging pattern of sound qualities, . . . of a certain significant melody in word and utterance, and of apparently varying degrees of length of the syllables. In addition, he will be conscious of the emotive colouring which is superimposed upon the utterance by such means as variations in voice quality. He would appear to perceive certain segments as standing out from their neighbours on account of their having an apparent greater loudness, or a distinct change in pitch, or distinctive length. He will also have the impression that some sounds make in themselves a greater auditory impact than others, are 'inherently more sonorous'. Many of these phonetic prominences may be interpreted in his mind as features of semantic significance and related to the prominence of the important ideas of the utterance.
>
> There is, in addition, a more elusive feature which characterizes the whole utterance, a certain beat or rhythm, also related to what is known as stress which corresponds with the occurrence of at least some of the 'prominent' segments.[15]

Nevertheless, as a result of this empshasis on stress as a contrastive feature at the lexical level, there has been only limited investigation of stress in terms of the mental pulse or beat which, as already observed, is a significant feature of normal connected English utterance. This is unfortunate, since not only is this beat the stimulus for the subjective sensation of rhythm in spoken English and, as the basis for the rhythmic grouping of the words of the utterance, closely associated with programming but, realized by means of a complex of features, it also relates to the listener, by creating in his mind an impression of prominence which, as Gimson[16] has pointed out, may be interpreted as a feature of semantic significance. From this point of view, stress assumes extremely important dimensions for the foreign learner of English who, as Jassem[17] has suggested, experiences considerable difficulty in recognizing the rhythm units of connected speech, and, as I will show, demonstrates his inefficiency in programming by faulty phrasing and anomalous organization of rhythm groups.

Yet, by far the greatest number of investigations into the nature of stress have been concerned with the isolate word form. Even Stetson,[18] whose study may well be regarded as one of the most significant this century in terms of its influence on the work of other investigators, rarely used connected speech in his experiments, and, when sentence-like material was used, more often than not it was composed of nonsense syllables which certainly would not occur in normal English utterance. Indeed Twaddell regards as "most disastrous for linguistic purposes"[19] the kind of material used by Stetson, but makes the point that Stetson's main concern was the syllable and that "he was only incidentally interested in stress and transition phenomena."[20] Even so, he was very much interested in the train of syllables in the process of speech, and in the relationship between word accent and the accentual pattern of the phrase. "It is fundamental to the character of the syllable that it appears as a factor in the rhythmic pattern."[21] However, as he says in the Preface to his *Motor Phonetics*:

> . . . the processes of ordinary speech are far too elaborate for unaided analysis. For many years much study has been devoted to detailed recordings of actual speech, but little has resulted for phonetic theory. In other sciences it is necessary to simplify material, to delimit problems, to work under artificial conditions. So in phonetics experiments must be made with simple combinations under carefully controlled conditions before we can hope to attack the extremely complicated phenomena of ordinary speech.[22]

Actually Stetson's real interest was the analysis of skilled movements in the making and perceiving of rhythms, his physiological investigation of speech movements growing out of the application of this analysis to the process of speech. He postulates three fundamental types of skilled movements associated with the speech process: *the movement of fixation; the controlled or tense movement;* and *the ballistic movement.* The movement of fixation he says "occurs when opposing groups of muscles hold the member in position."[23] When a person is about to speak, the chest is partly inflated and is often held in that position for a short time before any syllable is uttered. Thus the chest is fixated or poised in readiness for the utterance.

For the controlled or tense movement, "at least two opposing groups of muscles work together in producing the movement. Both the antagonistic muscle-groups are contracted throughout the movement."[24] According to Stetson, the direction of the controlled movement can be changed after it is under way, since such movement is relatively slow; it is employed, for example, when one traces a curve slowly, or when air is slowly expired in a prolonged vowel.

In the ballistic movement, on the other hand, the entire movement consists of a single pulse, thus it is impossible to change the direction of this movement once its course has begun. It is started, he says, by a sudden contraction of the positive muscle-group which immediately relaxes, and is arrested as a rule by the contraction of the negative muscle-group. The movement is a movement by momentum, he says, and thus, during at least half of its course "neither of the antagonistic muscle-groups is contracted, so that the moving member flies free."[25] All rapid movements, according to Stetson, are of this type. "In speech, the rapid movements of articulation and the syllable pulse are ballistic."[26] In the simplest possible case, he says, the ballistic movement is started and stopped by the muscles themselves, but it can also be released and arrested by "accessory movements of articulation" (i.e., by releasing and arresting consonants).

For Stetson,

> the unit movement of speech is the pulse which produces the syllable, a pulse of air through the glottis made audible by the vocal folds in speaking aloud and stopped and started by the chest muscles or by the auxiliary movements of the consonants.[27]

He takes as his basic unit the syllable because, he says, "the syllable is the simplest utterance possible."[28] It is, he explains, "the unit which incorporates the syllable factors [i.e., the release, emission, and arrest of the pulse], and in turn is incorporated in the units of the foot and breath group."[29] It functions, he points out, as a unit for word- and syllable-stress, for the tones of tone languages, and for the feet of patterned verse. The actual production of the syllable is associated with chest pulses, "the quick strokes for each air pulse [being] made by the short muscles between the ribs."[30] These muscles (the intercostals), he says, "produce the syllables 'Oh, Oh, Oh . . .' as units included in the slower movement of the breath group which is made by the larger muscles of the chest and abdomen."[31]

He explains that just as no air pulse from the nozzle of the hand bellows can be made without inflating the bellows and maintaining the position of the boards of the bellows while the hands make the small strokes for the air pulse, no syllable can be uttered without inflating the chest and maintaining the chest-abdomen position while the intercostal muscles make the quick strokes that actually produce the syllable. Thus, a single syllable is part of the movement of a whole breath group.

"The air pulse for the syllable 'Oh' is released and arrested by the rib muscles but the supporting co-ordination involves the large ribcage muscles, the diaphragm, and the abdominal muscles for this one-syllable breath group."[32]

According to Stetson, the syllable pulse—like any other rapid movement—consists of two strokes, a *beat stroke* which releases the pulse with or without the help of a consonant, and a *back stroke* which, with or without auxiliary consonant movement, arrests the syllable pulse. Of the functions of the syllable factors called "releasing" and "arresting" he says:

> Syllables like '*a, Ah, I,*' are released by the chest; the rapid rise of pressure of the syllable is generated by the intercostal muscles of the chest. The pulse is arrested by the intercostal muscles which take up the momentum of the pulse.
>
> Syllables like '*pay, bay, die.*' are released by a consonant, and the process is more elaborate. The intercostals act as before, but the consonant constriction occurs at the same time, so that the air pressure develops behind the consonant closure; the syllable pulse is released when the consonant opens. Thus the 'release' is always due to the combined action of intercostals and articulation.
>
> Syllables like '*ape, Abe, ice, ire.*' are arrested by the consonant constriction which blocks the air flow and raises the pressure in the trachea and so takes up the momentum of the pulse. Thus the 'arest' may be due to the action of the articulation alone.
>
> In spite of this difference in function, the same consonant when releasing or arresting is essentially the same articulation: it is a commonplace for an arresting articulation to become a releasing articulation, e.g. '*up, up*' becomes '*u' pup*'; '*eat, eat*' said faster and faster becomes '*tea, tea*'.[33]

Stetson[34] says that it is possible to prolong a syllable at will if the syllable is open or if it ends in a voiced continuant; such as, /m, n, l/. Just as in beating time the movement may be prolonged after the pulse of the beat, the beat stroke of the syllable may be arrested by a back-stroke process which continues the movement in a slow, "controlled" form. However, when the syllable movement has a consonant arrest, the length of the syllable is conditioned.[35] The ballistic stroke of the syllable is arrested by the consonant movement and the syllable movement cannot be indefinitely prolonged into a controlled movement.

Stetson argues that, contrary to general opinion, the chest is not like the

wind chest of an organ, maintaining a steady flow under pressure throughout the breath group and interrupted only by the constructions of the consonants and coloured by the vowels. Rather, the chest muscles produce a
separate pulse of pressure for each syllable, and between the syllable pulses
the pressure falls. A slight pressure is generally maintained during the
breath group, Stetson says, but the chest-pulses of the syllables rise from
this level, "like the ripples on a wave". Between the breath groups the
pressure goes to zero although the overall posture and the chest volume are
maintained. If there is an intake between breath groups, the pressure
becomes negative.

Stetson contends that

> careful experimentation proves the breath group to be due to an
> abdominal movement with its culminations which mark the stresses of
> the constituent feet. One of these stresses constitutes the main stress of
> the breath group, while the syllable pulses are produced by the inter-
> costal muscles of the rib cage.
>   The 'foot' is the smallest unit group incorporating the syllables; it is
> due to an abdominal pulse which integrates a single stressed syllable or a
> few syllables grouped about a single stressed syllable.[36]

No matter how simple an utterance may be, Stetson asserts, it contains all
the essential movement units of the complete phrase. "The syllable or
syllables are components of a foot; the foot or feet are components of a
breath group; the breath group or breath groups compose a phrase."[37]

Thus Stetson establishes a hierarchy of constituents: *the phrase* (a group
of words bounded by inspirations); *the breath group* (a movement of
expiration involving the abdominal muscles and culminating in the main
stress of the utterance); *the foot* (an abdominal pulse containing one
stressed syllable); *the syllable* (a chest pulse—consisting of a rapid ballistic
movement of the intercostal muscles). The simplest utterance, he says, will
be a phrase of one breath group consisting of a monosyllabic foot, although
a breath group may be composed of 10-15 syllables. The organization of
both feet and breath groups is due, he maintains, to a single movement of
which the single syllables and the feet form a part,

> like the ripples on a larger wave. The notion of the stress as a single
> isolated peak rising from the plain, a mere marker for the breath group
> or foot, is inadequate. In reality, the primary stress is the climax of the
> single slow movement which underlies and constitutes the unity of the
> foot, and of the breath group.[38]

In his interpretation of Stetson's exposition of the controlled movement of the abdomen-diaphragm musculature, Twaddell says:

The breath group as a whole is characterized by dominance of abdominal driving over diaphragm retarding. This is a controlled movement; but it need not be a uniform continuous movement. There may be, within the overall net upward displacement of the diaphragm, SURGES during which the diaphragm is driven with more-than-average intensity.

. . . The coincidence of a surge with a chest pulse constitutes the culmination of a FOOT. If the breath group consists of a single foot, there is one and only one culmination. If there is more than one foot in the breath group, one of the culminations is the 'main stress'. . . .

If we need two degrees of abdomen-diaphragm surges to differentiate between the signal 'breath-group main stress' and the signal 'foot stress', the mechanism is thus available: extra intensity of abdominal action or momentary reduction of the diaphragm's opposing action or both. The nature of the muscles involved in this 'controlled' movement would seem to permit such a more-or-less intensity of diaphragm lifting, resulting in two distinct degrees of compression of the thoracic cavity antecedent to intercostal activity.[39]

Twaddell says that he can find no explicit discussion of this but believes that Stetson's distinction between "stress of the foot" and "the main stress of the breath group" seems to imply it. He assumes that Stetson accepts the American English system of four distinctive degrees of relative stress: *primary*, *secondary*, *tertiary*, and *weak*, represented / ´ ˆ ` ˘ / respectively, but as Stetson does not specifically discuss the last two Twaddell can do no better than speculate on his model. According to Twaddell:

Stetson's abdomen-diaphragm model provides for two degrees of surge superimposed upon the overall controlled movement of the breath group: a 'foot-stress', apparently / ˆ/, and a 'main breath-group stress', apparently / ´/. The model calls for as many feet as there are / ´ /s and / ˆ /s in a breath group, and as many/ ´ /s as there are breath groups in a 'phrase'.[40]

Twaddell believes that there are three possibilities in determining the nature of these / ´ / and / ˆ / surges: (1) extra intensity of abdominal contraction: (2) momentary relative relaxation of diaphragm resistance; or (3) both. However, he says that he cannot read from Stetson's book any clear indication of a choice among the three. He suggests, nevertheless, that extra-abdominal action is present in both / ´ / and / ˆ /, and that / ´ / also has diaphragm relaxation.[41] He also speculates that both / ´ / and / ˆ / have diaphragm relaxation, and that / ´ / also has extra abdominal action. In terms of Stetson's model, he says that / ˘ / would correspond to a chest pulse, but, as Stetson postulates several models of chest-pulse activity, he is uncertain as to which could be most properly associated with / ˘ / stress. Twaddell is likewise concerned with determining the physiological correlate of / ˋ / stress. He speculates that / ˋ / may result from some kind of abdomen-diaphragm action, different from that of / ˋ / and / ˆ /, but says "a more attractive possibility would be to regard / ˋ / and / ˘ / as different kinds of chest pulses: / ˋ / distinctively stronger, in some way, than / ˘ /."[42] Stetson does not discuss this possibility but Twaddell suggests that / ˋ / could correspond to a controlled movement, and / ˘ / to a free ballistic movement.

> Inherently, a controlled chest pulse, with the external intercostals acting throughout, but so as to yield somewhat to the dominating action of the internal intercostals would be a prolonged pulse;[43] the continuing contraction of the internal intercostals would result in a 'stronger' speech segment at least impressionistically because of greater length, perhaps objectively as well.[44]

Twaddell wonders, however, whether it would be possible to pronounce a / ˘ / with artificial prolongation without replacing it with / ˋ /, since as Stetson states explicitly,[45] a characteristic of the stressed syllable is that it is lengthened in the breath group.

Twaddell suggests the following 'Stetson-model' scheme for the so-called stress phonemes of American English:

> / ´ / maximum: an abdominal surge accompanied by momentary relative relaxation of the opposing diaphragm musculature; / ˆ / major: either an abdominal surge or a momentary diaphragm relaxation; / ˋ / minor: a controlled chest pulse, with dominance of internal intercostal over external intercostal action throughout the pulse; / ˘ / minimum: a ballistic chest pulse, with the motion of the chest wall checked, braked, stopped toward the end by various mechanisms.[46]

Such a scheme, as Twaddell[47] himself admits, represents only one person's guesses as to the most promising possibilities to be tested in a project to specify the articulatory model of the several so-called stress phonemes, while Lehiste[48] is of the opinion that it is still not possible—even using modern techniques—to establish the physiological correlates of different degrees of stress.

However, it would be impossible to try to understand Stetson's model of stress other than in the context of his theory of motor phonetics. For Stetson, as we have seen, the essential unit was the syllable, and so his main interest in stress was its effect on the factors of the syllables on which it falls and the breath group in which they occur. He asserts, for instance, that in the production of a stressed syllable, ". . . all the auxiliary movements tend to increase in amplitude. Added breath pressure increases the intensity; increased opening of the jaw modifies the quality of the vowel toward the maximum opening of 'ah'. Added stress on the consonants increases the duration of the consonants."[49] He gives as examples of the changes due to increased air pressure, the tendency of the stops to become continuants; of a surd phase to appear in the production of sonants; and of consonants generally to be aspirated as a result of the accumulating mouth pressure. Extreme stress on the syllable, he says, leads to diphthongizing of the vowel—an extremely common modification in languages with heavy word stress.

The role of stress in the breath group is likewise related to the syllable, since the dynamic pattern which constitutes the breath group in English is produced by means of the word stresses, the several syllables of each group having—as we have seen—varying degrees of stress. Stress, according to Stetson, affects both the rate and the grouping of syllables, and thus, in any utterance consisting of feet and breath groups, the stressed syllables both mark the beat or impulse which is the basis of the rhythmic grouping of the words, and determine the timing of the utterance. The two great causes of phonetic modification, Stetson says,[50] are changes of rate and of stress—and these two factors are both involved in rhythmic grouping.

"Rate forces movements to coalesce or drop because the rate determines the duration of the individual movement in the movement series."[51] The stressed syllables are most resistant to such changes, he says, and the arresting consonants of unstressed syllables, the least resistant. However, although the vowel is conserved despite increased rate of utterance, its quality changes and it is possible, Stetson remarks, "to note a regular series of reduced 'values' of the vowel, which ends in shwa. With the increase in rate all vowels in unstressed syllables arrive at the common shwa."[52] Native speakers of English other than Americans would probably dispute this last statement of Stetson, arguing that the unstressed syllable in English may also be uttered with /ɪ/ or indeed with several other indeterminate vowel qualities. However, the important point is that the unstressed vowel is neutralized and, as Stetson points out, "The breath group tends to maintain its rate and therefore the unstressed syllables within the group are shortened in compensation for the lengthening of the stressed syllable."[53]

Twaddell is especially critical of Stetson's "lack of crucial experiments, of realistic linguistic material, [and] of adequate transcription of utterances",[54] asserting that "these lacks forbid any claim that a particular supra-segmental phoneme has been correlated with particular muscular behavior".[55] I would agree. Nevertheless, largely as a result of this early work of Stetson, researchers over the last twenty years or so have directed their attention not only to the relationship between the activity of the respiratory muscles and the "movements of speech", but also to the respiratory system as the place of origin of stress.

However, at the time when Stetson was pursuing his inquiries, much of the instrumentation necessary for accurate recording was unavailable or, at best, relatively crude[56] and it was almost 30 years before his theories were appropriately re-examined by means of more satisfactory techniques.

In the late 1950's electromyography came to be more widely recognized as a possible means of investigating the relationship between speech and respiratory activity, and, within a year of each other, a group of British researchers led by Peter Ladefoged,[57] and Iván Fónagy,[58] the Hungarian phonetician, independently published their first results. The British team could find no direct correlation between intercostal activity and the syllable, and in fact demonstrated that every syllable is not necessarily accompanied by a separate burst of muscular activity, as Stetson had asserted—that sometimes there are two separate bursts in a single syllable. However, according to Ladefoged, many of their records showed an increase in the degree of muscular activity immediately before syllables perceived as being strongly stressed. Fónagy likewise concluded that the activity of the internal intercostal muscles increases with the utterance of stressed syllables, adding that a return to the original physiological conception of accent classically formulated by Otto Jespersen was unavoidable, "since accent is simply not to be defined on an acoustic level."[59]

As a means of further testing Stetson's theories, Draper, Ladefoged and Whitteridge also conducted a series of experiments designed to measure subglottal (tracheal) pressure during speech. Again, their findings differed from those of Stetson:

> . . . we could find no correlation between subglottal pressure and syllables. It is clear . . . from hundreds of [records] that Stetson (1951) is wrong in claiming that there is a relation between respiratory activity and the syllable. . . . In our opinion there is certainly insufficient basis for a chest pulse theory of the syllable in normal speech.[60]

Nevertheless, they did find a relationship between subglottal pressure and *stressed* syllables, and on the basis of this they also affirm that "stress is best described in physiological rather than acoustic terms."[61]

Ladefoged points out that because of the "trading relationships"[62] between intensity, frequency, and duration, "there is no single, simple, acoustic event that always occurs in all stressed syllables in spoken English."[63] But he says, "it is apparent that every stress is accompanied by an extra increase of subglottal pressure."[64]

Ladefoged shares Twaddell's view that Stetson's writings are "full of unsignaled transitions and other hazards",[65] asserting that in reading Stetson there is always "the difficulty of deciding whether Stetson is making a statement based on reliable evidence or whether he is propounding a hypothesis."[66]

Furthermore, he says, Stetson confuses the situation by his use of particular terms; for example, his use of the expressions "ballistic" and "controlled" in relation to the movements of the chest muscles. In Ladefoged's opinion, "the major part of Stetson's work should be considered as a theory attempting to explain how the respiratory muscles are involved in speech, rather than an account of the observed action of these muscles."[67]

By way of contrast, Ladefoged and his co-workers have given us in their strictly empirical studies a great deal of accurate information regarding the relationship between the activity of the respiratory muscles and speech phenomena, their work on the physiological correlates of stress being among the most interesting and productive in the field of experimental phonetics in recent years. Their evidence derives principally from their electromyographic studies and their experimental investigations of changes in subglottal pressure.

Electromyography is a technique for detecting and recording the electrical discharges which are produced by contracting muscles. Every muscle is composed of a large number of *motor units* which are the smallest functional units of striated muscle, consisting of a motor cell, its axon process, and a group of muscle fibres innervated by this one nerve cell. As a result of the chemical reaction which follows a nerve impulse the muscle cell releases an electrical charge and this causes muscular contraction. By virtue of the attachments of muscles, shortening of the fibres resulting from their contraction produces movement.

In electromyography, muscular contractions are registered by means of an electrode which picks up *action potentials*—that is, the electrical discharges—of some of the individual muscle fibres of a single motor unit. A non-contracting muscle cell has a *resting potential*, but when a nerve impulse reaches the neuromuscular junction a chemical change occurs; the cell releases its electrical charge and the fibre contracts. When they are amplified[68] and displayed, the action potentials appear as a series of spikes. Increased muscle activity shows as an increase in the number of spikes and, to a certain extent, the greater amplitude of new spikes.

The electrode used to record action potentials can be placed on the skin surface above the muscle or inserted into the muscle. In either case it will record the potentials which are being conducted through the surrounding tissue. Whereas Stetson used surface electrodes, in most of the more recent experiments concentric needle electrodes have been inserted into the muscles, the insertion of needle electrodes generally being considered essential for the accurate examination of the activity of muscles which do not lie immediately below the skin—such as the deep internal intercostals.

Although various techniques have been developed for the measurement of subglottal pressure, two methods are generally used: direct measurement of air pressure by means of a hollow needle inserted into the trachea; and indirect measurement by means of the insertion of a small balloon into the oesophagus. The latter method, based on the assumption that subglottal pressure can be estimated from oesophageal pressure, is said to provide fairly accurate measurements, and was the one used by Ladefoged and his co-workers. He says:

> The balloon [1.5 cm. diameter and 2.5 cm. long] was passed through the nose into the oesophagus until it was just above the bifurcation of the trachea. . . . When the balloon was filled with 2 ml. of air an approximate sphere of air was held between the thin posterior membrane of the trachea and the vertebral column. Thus any pressure changes in the trachea were transmitted to the air in the balloon.[69]

This method, he says,[70] was criticized by Kunze on the grounds that it did not take fully into account the effect of changes in lung volume on the pressure in the oesophagus, and Ladefoged subsequently took measurements of tracheal and oesophageal pressures at a given lung volume immediately before and after utterance. Comparison of the two pressures enabled him to prepare curves in which the tracheal pressure was calibrated in terms of the oesophageal pressure. He says that from a series of other curves derived from these two, he and his colleagues could make for each point in the utterance "a reasonably accurate estimation of the tracheal pressure from the recorded oesophageal pressure."[71]

The impetus for the investigations of Ladefoged and his co-workers came, as Ladefoged acknowledges,[72] from study of the work of Stetson, particularly his conclusions that

(i) Every syllable is accompanied by a 'ballistic chest pulse' produced by the action of the internal intercostal muscles.
(ii) In 'open syllables' (e.g. *tea, spa*) the collapse of the lung is checked by an active inspiratory effort of the external intercostal muscles.
(iii) In a stressed syllable the action of the internal intercostal muscles is reinforced by the abdominal muscles.

Ladefoged says that although they were able to substantiate a number of points in Stetson's theory, they disagreed with all of these conclusions, and suggests that in view of the technical inadequacy of Stetson's recordings it is doubtful whether they did in fact show the activity of the muscles indicated in the legends.[73]

It is Ladefoged's belief that Stetson oversimplified the situation by considering the activity of the intercostal muscles in terms of a series of "ballistic movements". According to Ladefoged,

> Not only can the tension of the intercostal muscles be varied over a large range, but also there can be variations in the rate of change of tension. Sometimes a single increase in tension spans a group of articulations including two vowels separated by a consonant closure . . . [e.g., such disyllabic words as *pity* and *around*]; and sometimes there are two separate bursts of activity in what is normally regarded as a single syllable (e.g. in *sport*, *stay*, and other words beginning with a fricative followed by a plosive). It is quite clear that there is no simple correlation between intercostal activity and syllables.[74]

He says,[75] however, that there are two other phenomena which can be correlated with bursts of intercostal activity: the increase in the rate of air flow from the lungs which occurs in some voiceless consonants; and stress variation. His records of an utterance consisting of several repetitions of a single stressed syllable show that there is a general increase in the amount of muscular activity as the utterance proceeds, and that the muscular activity occurs in bursts which immediately precede each syllable.

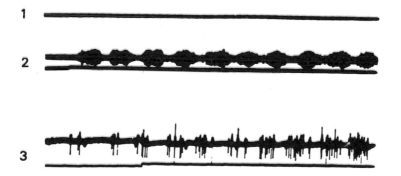

Figure 3: Internal intercostal activity during the repetition of a single stressed syllable recorded on a cathode-ray oscilloscope.
(1) Time marker, 1/10 seconds. (2) Microphone record showing the wave form of ten syllables.
(3) Internal intercostal action potentials.
(from Peter Ladefoged, *Three Areas of Experimental Phonetics*, p. 21.)

According to Ladefoged,[76] the general increase in muscular activity can be correlated with the decrease in the volume of air in the lungs which occurs during the utterance, and the localized bursts can be correlated with phonetic stress. He says that bursts of internal intercostal muscle activity associated with stressed syllables were also evident in recordings of connected speech. Of the first part of the sentence, *He agreed that he was very sorry for everything*,

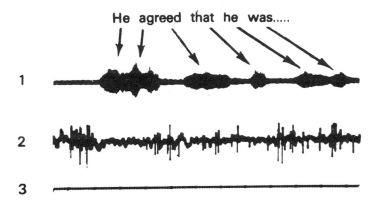

Figure 4:   Internal intercostal activity during continuous speech. (1) Microphone record. (2) Internal intercostal action potentials. (3) Time marker, 1/10 and 1/100 seconds. (from Peter Ladefoged, *Three Areas of Experimental Phonetics*, p. 22.)

Ladefoged says:

> There are striking increases in the muscular activity immediately before the first word and before the second syllable in *agreed*. But the latter syllable is also accompanied by a further burst of activity in the middle of the vowel (a pattern of activity . . . often observed during long vowels). The last two words are also preceded by bursts of activity.[77]

Ladefoged emphasizes that in the majority of the conversational utterances recorded there was no action of the external intercostal muscles. Thus, he says, "we could not find any evidence for Stetson's statement that English syllables with a certain kind of phonetic structure are always checked by the action of the external intercostals."[78] Nevertheless, he reports[79] that recordings taken from the external intercostal muscle showed this muscle to be active during the inspiratory phase of respiration when the pressure of the air in the lungs was less than that of the outside air, and also towards the end of monosyllabic words spoken in isolation. However, these bursts, he says, occurred whether or not the word ended in a consonant closure. (It will be remembered that, according to Stetson, active inspiratory effort by the external intercostals occurs in open syllables.) Ladefoged does not speculate on the possible reasons for his finding that whereas the word *tea* was checked by inspiratory activity after the first inspiration, when it occurred later in the utterance there was no burst of activity, although the word *teak* in the second breath group was arrested by inspiratory activity.[80] We might, therefore, be tempted to regard these bursts as random activity without any particular significance.

Ladefoged and his co-workers could find no evidence in their data to substantiate the statement of Stetson that the abdominal muscles reinforce the action of the internal intercostals in stressed syllables. Ladefoged concedes that the rectus abdominis may be active in cases of "very emphatic stressing, when the pressure in the lungs may be unusually high."[81] However, he says: "Our observations are that in normal conversational English the abdominal muscles are in action only at the end of a very long utterance. In most utterances the air pressure is regulated solely by the intercostals."[82]

He investigated the relationship between subglottal pressure and stress by means of a comparative study of noun and verb pairs which completed the expression, *That's a* . . . and *He didn't* . . . read with both rising and falling intonation patterns such as might be heard in declarative statements and questions. He reports[83] that the recordings showed each of the disyllabic test words to have only one peak of pressure. In the statements; for example,

(*That's a*) sɜveɪ (*He didn't*) sɜˈveɪ a clear distinction was made between the noun form and the verb form, the former having peaks of subglottal pressure during the first vowel, and the latter having them during the second vowel. These distinctions were less evident in the questions,

(*That's a*) sɜveɪ? (*He didn't*) sɜˈveɪ? according to Ladefoged, although the peaks still occurred earlier in the nouns than in the verbs. It seems that a large increase in subglottal pressure accompanied the greater intonation rise used by some of his subjects, and, as a result, the final unstressed syllable in questions had a higher subglottal pressure than the preceding stressed syllable. Thus, in these cases, the highest peak of subglottal pressure did not necessarily fall on the syllable with the greatest degree of stress. Nevertheless, he says it was still true that even in these question forms the nouns could be distinguished from the verbs by variations in the subglottal pressure.

He says that as might be expected from their electromyographic studies, he and his colleagues could find no correlation between subglottal pressure and individual unstressed syllables.

Thus whereas Stetson had claimed an identifiable chest pulse for every syllable, Ladefoged could find no such one-to-one relationship, and contends that bursts of intercostal activity and peaks of subglottal pressure occur in association only with stressed syllables.

However, Lehiste[84] says that inferential evidence against the presence of chest pulses as physiological correlates of both stress and syllabicity is provided by the results of Peterson[85] who concluded that quite normal syllabification patterns occur in the speech of some iron lung patients with essentially complete paralysis of the respiratory musculature. Peterson's subjects were in fact only able to speak during the exhaust cycle of the respirator and obviously required the aid of some special technique to increase their breath pressure during phonation but even with this limitation, according to Lehiste, their stress patterns were apparently normal.

Another phonetician who has reservations about the correlation between stress and thoracic and/or abdominal pulses is Yvan Lebrun,[86] who concludes that "the regular occurrence of abdominal and/or diaphragmatic stress pulses in conversational speech remains to be proved."[87] He says further that while the electromyographic investigations of Fónagy, Ladefoged, Draper, and Whitteridge point to a correlation between stress and increased contractile activity in the internal intercostal muscles, "this correlation . . . appears to be less constant and less universal than has been assumed by the 4 investigators."[88]

Lebrun drew this conclusion on the basis of his electromyographic experiments with French-speaking subjects. He cautiously points out that because his observations seem to justify his conclusion that neither the diaphragm nor the abdominal muscles play a significant part in the production of stress in French, it must follow that there is no other language in which they do. However, he says that the only way in which the diaphragm could produce a stress pulse would be to increase its relaxation suddenly so as to jerk upwards.

> This stress mechanism would require that the diaphragm should not relax completely until the last stressed syllable of an utterance is pronounced . . . Ladefoged and coll. found, however, that 'in 9 out of 11 [English] subjects the diaphragmatic activity ceased during the first two or three seconds of an utterance after a maximal inspiration. . . . In two subjects, the diaphragm did not relax for a considerable time'. These findings are in keeping with the observation made by various physiologists that the electrical activity of the diaphragm tapers off to zero during the first part of quiet expiration.[89]

Of the correlation said by Fónagy to exist between stress and the internal intercostal muscles, Lebrun is sceptical, pointing out that some of the recordings reproduced in *Elektrophysiologische Beiträge zur Akzentfrage* "are equivocal: they do not show an undoubted increase in the contractile activity of the internal intercostal just before the stressed syllable."[90] He is likewise critical of Ladefoged and his co-workers, pointing out that they have "only 6 short fragments of the recordings they made of the activity of the internal intercostals during speech. . . . It follows that the reader of the papers by Ladefoged and coll. cannot see for himself that in English stress correlates with an increase in the contractile activity of the internal intercostals."[91]

Lebrun also argues that Ladefoged's statement, "sometimes a single in-crease in tension spans a group of articulations including two vowels separated by a consonant closure (our records show that words such as *pity* and *around* may be spoken in this way",[92] amounts to saying that "a burst of action potentials was sometimes found to occur before the unstressed syllable *a-* instead of before the stressed syllable—*round*"[93]—that is, that action potentials may occur before *un*stressed syllables. In his own investigation of the action of the 8th internal intercostal during the utterance of nine French disyllabic words, some of which were repeated, he found that in only one case was the muscle more active before the stressed than before the unstressed syllable. In two cases, he says, there was apparently no difference between the stressed and the unstressed syllable as regards the activity of the internal intercostals; "in the remaining 9 cases, the internal intercostals were more active before the unstressed than before the stressed syllable."[94]

It would seem, then, that although the motor theory of stress has attracted considerable attention and support, the attempts of experimental phoneticians to present actual evidence of a distinct correlation between physiological parameters (in particular, respiratory muscle activity and subglottal pressure) and stress have met with variable success.

The alternative is the establishment of an acoustic theory. Yet, according to Fónagy,[95] who within the last ten years has investigated both electro-physiological and acoustic correlates of stress and stress perception, "It seems to be justified to define stress on the physiological rather than on the acoustic level. Stress and stress perception is closely related to increased activity of the phonatory apparatus, especially of the inner intercostal muscles."[96]

While in full agreement with Jones, in regarding as essential a distinction between the production of stress—the subjective activity of force of utterance—and the perception of stress—an objective activity—Fónagy finds difficult of interpretation[97] Jones' distinction between "prominence by intonation", and the pioneer phonetician's statement that in "stress-languages" prominence of the syllables is due to the coexistence of stress and pitch, if these features belong to different levels—one to the subjective physiological level, the other to the objective acoustic level.[98] Accordingly, Fónagy has investigated the projection of stress on the acoustic level. Using an EEG device, he registered the internal intercostal muscular activity and simultaneously recorded for spectrographic analysis the utterances of two subjects speaking a series of Hungarian one-word sentences. Analysis of the spectra of stressed and unstressed syllables revealed that greater effort was reflected in different ways:

> In most cases . . . the formants of the vowels in stressed syllables had higher amplitudes and a broader bandwidth. Especially sharp was the divergence in the higher frequency ranges. In these cases, the stressed syllables took a higher level and were longer and had a higher pitch. The saturation of the spectrum indicated stress even when the greater effort was not indicated by relatively higher sound pressure levels. Compared to the unstressed syllables, in stressed syllables the levels of the second and third formants were raised 1.8 and 2.3 dB.[99]

He concludes: "These results seem to be in good agreement with the acoustic theory of speech production."[100] And he quotes Fant: "A reduction of voice effort . . . leads to a decrease of the level of harmonics which is more prominent in the higher frequencies . . . due to a more steeply falling slope of the source spectrum envelope normally accompanying the lowering of the voice level."[101]

Fónagy points out that stress can also be marked (for example, in emotive speech) "by the loss of saturation, and by pale and harsh vowel color, reflecting an irregular voice production."[102] However, it must be remembered that stress in Hungarian is generally considered very strong,[103] and on this account there is some danger, as Lebrun has suggested,[104] in generalizing from Fónagy's results to other languages.

The influence of vowel quality upon stress in English was investigated by Lehiste and Peterson[105] about the same time as Fónagy was conducting his earlier electromyographic experiments. They also regard stress as a basically physiological phenomenon and propose that the perception of linguistic stress is based upon judgments of the physiological effort involved in producing vowels.

They argue that the physical properties of speech are organized into a symbolic code, the several components of which may be analysed and described at the physiological, the acoustical, or the perceptual level. It is the acoustical signal which is primarily available for study, and in attempting to interpret it, the investigator might transform it into a series of auditory correlates, such as pitch, loudness, and duration, or he might attempt to derive information about the processes of speech production from the acoustical signal itself. They say that it is this latter procedure which will provide information which more directly corresponds to the judgments of the listener about speech.

. . . . We assume the acoustical signal to be a representation of the positions and movements of the physiological mechanism relative to the distribution of air pressures within the mechanism. . . . It is our belief that the interpretation of the speech signal by a listener is based on a very complicated set of auditory parameters by means of which he makes an interpretation of the speech production. Thus we seek to describe speech in terms of such factors as (a) physiological effort, (b) rate of vocal fold vibration, (c) mode of laryngeal vibration, (d) pharyngeal and oral articulation, (e) palatopharyngeal closure, and (f) duration.[106]

According to Lehiste and Peterson, stress is a physiological phenomenon which in English is reflected in at least four acoustical parameters: speech power, fundamental voice frequency, phonetic quality, and duration. Fry,[107] they point out, had earlier investigated the effects of two of these parameters, amplitude and duration, while Fairbanks[108] and his co-workers had shown that phonetic changes normally affect vowel amplitudes. It was their aim, then, to study the inter-effects of amplitude and phonetic quality on stress perception: "We suggest that a listener will interpret sounds produced with equal effort as being in some respects similar with regard to stress."[109]

Pointing out that in everyday linguistic experience, for instance, the words CONvict and con'VICT appear to be stressed either on the first syllable (noun) or on the second syllable (verb), the degree of stress on the stressed syllable being subjectively felt to be the same, they argue: "If the acoustical energy of the syllabic sounds is measured, however, the first syllable appears to have considerably more energy in both instances. There must, then, be other factors besides energy which influence our judgments about stress in English."[110]

They hypothesized that amplitude changes due to changes in phonetic quality should not significantly influence the perception of phonemic stress since the listener associates a certain intrinsic relative amplitude with each vowel spectrum and applies a corresponding "correction factor" to the incoming signal. In order to test this theory, they analysed the vowel amplitudes of a series of noun/verb pairs distinguished by means of contrastive stress placement, the native English speaker who recorded the utterances being instructed to try to use the same degree of effort in the production of each test word which was carried in the frame "Say the word . . . again".

According to Lehiste,[111] spectrographic analysis of the syllable nuclei showed that the only pair in which vowel quality remained fairly constant in both productions was 'PERvert—per'VERT, the amplitude difference between the stressed and the unstressed syllable in this word pair being approximately 2 dB. She says that this was considered to reflect the difference in input energy. The difference for the two syllables of ¹ɪɴcline was shown to be zero dB. According to her scale of the intrinsic intensities of the syllable nuclei in American English,[112] the intrinsic amplitude of /ɪ/ is 78.1 dB and that of /aɪ/ is 80.2 dB. If the correction factor of approximately 2 dB is applied, she says, "the difference between the stressed and unstressed syllables of ɪɴcline equals that observed in the production of ᴘᴇʀvert."[113]

The results of the Lehiste and Peterson experiments suggest that correction factors are at work in stress perception, and support the view long ago expressed by Daniel Jones: that stress perception involves knowledge of the language in which the utterance is spoken. If—as the data suggest—correction factors can be applied to the amplitudes of vowels according to their phonetic quality, as these investigators point out, "it seems reasonable that similar correction factors might actually be applied for pitch as well as for duration."[114] However, the very notion of "correction factors" if valid, as Lehiste[115] argues, presupposes a certain amount of learning.

She says that it was only during this investigation in which she and Peterson tried to correlate observed differences in vowel amplitude with the perception of stress that she became acutely aware of the difference between the perception of loudness and the perception of stress. In casual auditory observation of vowels uttered with subjectively equal effort, the sounds appeared to be equally loud; yet acoustic analysis revealed differences in intensity which should have resulted in perceived differences in loudness, she says, if the listener were basing his judgment on the same physical differences in the perception of psychoacoustic stimuli and the perception of normal speech.

On the other hand, when vowels were produced with equal pressure level as measured by a ᴠᴜ meter but with unequal effort, listeners identified them as louder than those actually having greater amplitude but produced with normal effort. A suggested explanation of this phenomenon, she says,[116] would be to assume that the listeners were not reacting to the actual intensity differences but were responding to differences in effort. If this were so, a listener might well identify a syllable as stressed even if the average or peak power of that syllable were less than that of an adjacent unstressed syllable containing a more open vowel. These findings, she believes,[117] provide additional evidence for the so-called motor theory of speech perception postulated by Liberman.

According to Liberman and his co-workers,[118] the perception of speech is tightly linked to the feedback from the speaker's own articulatory movements, and thus a learned activity. They say that results of studies using synthetic speech as a means of achieving stimulus control suggest "that distinctiveness is not inherent in the acoustic signal but is rather added as a consequence of linguistic experience."[119]

This could account for the recent finding of McEntee[120] that the non-native speaker of English actually perceives syllable stress differently from the native speaker, presumably because different expectancies developed within the framework of his own language-culture group impose certain limitations on his perception of speech generally. As Miller[121] has said in reference to the concept of expectancy in regard to speech perception, "in normal discourse the range of alternatives that the listener expects is determined by his established verbal habits."[122]

The notion of "correction factors", then, would seem to apply only to those thoroughly familiar with the language, so that instead of perceiving sounds and prosodic features objectively from the physical stimulus, they would perceive them, rather, in a subjective way calling to mind their own manner of producing them. As Lehiste and Peterson point out, it *is* probable that "phonetic variation in the pitch level associated with a certain phonemic stress may be influenced to a considerable extent by the intrinsic amplitude of the nucleus of the syllable carrying the stress, higher pitch compensating for lower intrinsic amplitude",[123] but I doubt that such compensation could be achieved by any other than a native speaker or a listener with near-native competence.

According to Lehiste,[124] intensity plays an ambiguous part in the perception of stress and this constitutes a problem in interpreting its physiological and acoustic correlates. She says, "While there is a direct link between increases in respiratory effort, subglottal pressure, and the amplitude of the sound wave, intensity seems to provide a rather weak cue for the perception of stress."[125] On the other hand, frequency, she asserts, is intimately connected with stress, higher fundamental frequency providing a strong cue for the presence of stress in many languages.

The third phonetic correlate of stressedness—duration—has no such physiological basis as intensity and frequency, but as a language-determined phenomenon it appears to be a general cue to stress in several Western European languages which have been analysed by instrumental means.

In English it appears to have received less attention than either fundamental frequency or intensity, despite the fairly extensive research which has been undertaken during the last two decades in the search for the psychoacoustic correlates of stress. The one British phonetician who early recognized its significance in the perception of stress is Dennis Fry.

Like Lehiste and Peterson, Fry used as his test material English words in which a change of function from noun to verb is commonly associated with a shift of accent from the first to the second syllable. However, instead of natural speech he used stimuli produced on a pattern-play-back synthesizer.[126] According to Crystal, research using speech-synthesis techniques has probably been the most valuable in clarifying the nature of stress as they allow unambiguous reference to the dimensions of a specific sound stimulus and maximum control by the researcher over all the physical variables.[127]

And of Fry's work in particular he says, "[it] has been the most stimulating, comprehensive and balanced in this area."[128]

Certainly for over a decade (1955–1965) Fry published the results of a number of investigations each designed to test different aspects of his general view that stress differences are perceived as variations in a complex pattern circumscribed by the four perceptual dimensions (pitch, loudness, length, and quality) of the physical parameters we have been considering. He says it is probable that the listener's kinaesthetic memories also play a part in his reception of the speech of others and, "if this is so, it is likely that the contribution will be particularly strong in the case of stress judgments since rhythm of all kinds has a powerful motor component."[129]

Under normal conditions of communication the listener has a number of cues that he can use as the basis of any single judgment of stress and these are provided by variations in any or all of the perceptual dimensions. However, for a specific judgment he may be more dependent upon one cue than upon another. Fry points out that a sound stimulus may be varied along several physical dimensions, and such variations, provided they fall within certain ranges, will give rise to changes in the perceptual dimensions. "Thus it is possible to present to a listener sounds which he will judge to be different in pitch but the same loudness, quality and length, or different in quality, but the same pitch, loudness and length, and so on."[130]

In his 1955 study[131] he synthesized five disyllabic noun-verb pairs on monotones, and varied the relative duration and intensity of both syllables as a means of determining the influence of these physical parameters on the perception of stress. The synthesized words, recorded on tape, were introduced into a carrier sentence, also in synthesized speech, so that the test items came to the listeners in the form:

"Where is the accent in *OBject*", "Where is the accent in *conTRACT*", etc . . Fry says the results of his experiments indicate that

(1) duration and intensity ratios are both cues for judgments of stress,

(2) the vowel segments show the major differences in duration and intensity with a shift of stress, and

(3) duration ratio is a more effective cue than intensity ratio.[132]

It seems that when duration and intensity were operating together, there was excellent agreement among the 100 subjects as to which syllable was stressed; for example, when a vowel was long and of high intensity, the listeners agreed that the vowel was strongly stressed. However, when the effects of the two parameters were studied separately, duration was shown to be more important than intensity. As Fry points out, "It has generally been accepted that variations of intensity are most closely linked with stress differences in English but the results of this experiment indicate that the duration ratio has a stronger influence on judgments of stress than has the intensity ratio.[133]

In a subsequent study[134] Fry again tested duration and intensity as cues for the perception of stress but added fundamental frequency. The results confirmed Fry's earlier findings for both duration and intensity,

> The importance of the duration ratio is confirmed by the fresh data presented here; it seems that in English in a considerable variety of conditions, changes of vowel duration ratio can swing listeners' perception of strong stress from the first to the second syllable in the type of disyllable[135] that has been considered.[136]

He continues,

> There seems no reason to doubt that this factor operates in stress judgments in other rhythmic contexts. Intensity ratio has a similar influence but it is somewhat less marked. The data show no case in which change of intensity ratio caused a complete shift of the stress judgment from first to second syllable.[137]

Fry found that fundamental frequency, unlike duration and intensity, tends to produce an 'all-or none effect"—that is to say,

> the magnitude of the frequency change seems to be relatively unimportant while the fact that a frequency change has taken place is all-important. The experiments with a step-change of frequency show that a higher syllable is more likely to be perceived as stressed; the experiments with more complex patterns of fundamental frequency change suggest that intonation is an over-riding factor in determining the perception of stress and in this sense the fundamental frequency cue may outweigh the duration cue.[138]

Nevertheless, in the belief that formant structure, his fourth physical parameter, might prove to be one of the most powerful factors of all in determining stress, he next proceeded to investigate the effect of the phonetic value of the vowel on stress judgments.[139] Keeping the fundamental frequency of the periodic sounds constant at 120 Hz, and regulating the intensity of both syllables of the test words so that they had equal maximum intensity, he maintained a constant difference between formants 1 and 2.

He certainly introduced variations in the vowel duration ratio in order to estimate "the weight to be assigned to the changes in formant structure", [140] and admits the difficulty of comparing the changes in duration ratio and formant position, but the results of this experiment, he reports, [141] show quite clearly that the weight of the duration cue was considerably greater than that of formant structure, which was even less effective than intensity as a cue to stress perception.

Fry acknowledges that experiments such as those conducted in the course of his investigations require "drastic simplification" of the conditions in which the judgment is made, and points out that the perception of stress in natural speech actually depends upon the interaction of a number of cues. However, he says that the close control necessary to study the variables of speech is generally not possible with live or even with recorded utterance and, for this reason, the most satisfactory method is to synthesize the required speech sounds in some way.

Several other investigators [142] using both synthesized and natural speech appear to support Fry's finding that fundamental frequency provides a stronger cue for the presence of stress than any other of the basic physical parameters, but it must be noted that in practically all of these studies the focus has been on the nature of stress as manifested in the disyllabic word— rather than in the context of the sentence. The most notable exception is Dwight Bolinger [143] who, over a number of years, has investigated the phenomenon of stress at both word and sentence level.

One of Bolinger's most important contributions to the search for the phonetic correlates of stress must surely be his conclusion that the primary cue to stress is pitch prominence. [144] Length, he says, is simply an "auxiliary and residual cue," while intensity is for him "negligible both as a determinative and as a qualitative factor in stress'. [145]

He believes that in order to avoid unwanted associations it is better to speak of "pitch accent" than stress at the level of utterance, the term *stress* being more appropriate to specify prominence at the lexical level. For Bolinger, accent is a pitch movement involving a departure from some reference line. This movement may be a rise or a fall since all that is needed for pitch prominence is "a rapid and relatively wide departure from a smooth or undulating contour." [146] The differences of form respond to differences of meaning, he says, thus giving the accents a morphemic status. "Differentiating them often calls for a repertorial cue (the user's knowledge of the morphs of his language, and what syllables have the *potential for pitch accent*) [147] or a gradient phonetic cue (length of syllable and grade of vowel)." [148]

But not only has Bolinger investigated the perception of stress vs. non-stress. In view of the structure of English words—particularly that of compounds—having two levels of stress, he felt that the relative importance of intensity should be tested in more complicated surroundings.[149] Taking the well-examined expressions *lighthouse-keeper* and *light housekeeper* he tried to determine whether intensity differences are effective under two sets of conditions:

(1) with disjuncture differences going counter to intensity differences, which may be called the extreme case;

(2) with intensity differences carrying the burden alone and unopposed, which may be called the neutral case.[150]

He concludes:

All the modified patterns went in the direction of the modification, not only in an absolute sense but, in most instances, in proportion to the *degree* of modification. Neither in the extreme case of disjuncture opposing intensity nor in the neutral case of disjuncture relatively balanced, did intensity appear to have the slightest influence in making the distinction.[151]

As we shall see, Bolinger has made some interesting observations on what he calls "the struggle waged by pitch accent to arrange the phonetic bulk of utterances in a way that will serve its needs",[152] in his study of the relationship between pitch accent and sentence rhythm but, as an experimental phonetician, his support for frequency and his criticism of the value of intensity as a cue to stress, must be regarded as his more notable contributions to our knowledge of this feature. Nevertheless, Lehiste[153] points out that he appears to have ignored differences in intrinsic intensity in evaluating his experimental results, and suggests that some of his findings might lend themselves to reinterpretation if intrinsic intensity differences were taken into account.

Another researcher who did not introduce a correction factor to account for the differing intrinsic intensities of the vowels in the syllables he used for his experiments is Philip Lieberman.[154] Lieberman investigated the acoustic correlates of stress in American English by analysing the fundamental frequency, envelope amplitude, and duration of 25 contrastive noun-verb pairs recorded by 16 different speakers. He found that

(1) higher fundamental frequencies and envelope amplitudes were the most relevant of the unidimensional acoustic correlates of stressed syllables;

(2) envelope amplitude was more important than duration.

Comparison of the two syllables of the test words revealed that the stressed syllable had a higher frequency in 90% of the cases, a higher peak envelope amplitude in 87% of the cases, and a longer duration in 66% of the cases. The stressed syllable, compared with its unstressed counterpart in the other word of the stress pair, had a higher frequency in 72% of the cases, a higher amplitude in 90% of the cases, and a longer duration in 70% of the cases.[155] Lieberman says that

> in no case did the stressed syllable have both a lower amplitude and a lower fundamental frequency than the unstressed syllable. Moreover, the stressed syllable in all but two cases had either, or both, a greater integral of amplitude with respect to time (over the syllable's duration) or a longer duration than the unstressed syllable of the same utterance.[156]

He points out that his results preclude any conclusions with regard to the most important *single* acoustic correlate of syllable stress since the array of acoustic events measured was by no means complete. However it is clearly possible, he says, "to make unequivocal stress judgments for many different speakers with a simple binary program that uses all the redundancies inherent in a restricted set of multi-dimensional acoustic events."[157]

It seems to me that Lieberman's results, although in one respect—duration—different from Fry's, do in fact illustrate the point made by the British phonetician that the listener is never concerned exclusively with one dimension but rather, in his perception of the sounds of speech, takes in continuous variations along all of the basic dimensions so that his linguistic judgments are determined by their interaction. This has in fact been shown by Lieberman in reference to the perception of the emotional content of speech. In an experiment undertaken in collaboration with Sheldon B. Michaels,[158] to examine the contributions of fundamental frequency and amplitude to the transmission of the emotional content of normal human speech, he found that there was no one single acoustic correlate of the emotional modes of the experiment; phonetic content, gross changes in fundamental frequency, the fine structure of the fundamental frequency, and the speech envelope amplitude, in that order, all contributing to the transmission of the emotional modes.

While some researchers, as we have seen, insist that frequency is the main cue to stress in English and even go so far as to assert, as Mol and Uhlenbeck have done, that "intensity cannot be considered as a factor, regardless whether this term is taken in an acoustic or in an articulatory sense",[159] others, such as Pike,[160] have concluded quite as definitely that it is intensity that carries the distinctive contrast between stress and non-stress.

Morton and Jassem,[161] having noted pitch to be the predominant acoustic parameter associated with stress in three rather distantly related languages—English, French, and Polish—considered it would be worthwhile to compare the nature of stress in a number of different languages at one level of description "by some kind of unified or even standard method so that results obtained for such different languages could be directly comparable."[162] Accordingly, they synthesized the nonsense syllables /sisi/, /sɔsɔ/ and /sasa/, ensuring that the vowel qualities in both syllables of each test item were identical in order to avoid the problem of different intrinsic intensities. The parameters of fundamental frequency, intensity, and duration were varied systematically and tapes of the test material presented to 60 native English speakers.

Morton and Jassem report[163] that within the ranges of variation used, fundamental frequency changes were by far the most effective in producing universally accepted stress-marking. A syllable was marked stressed if it differed at all from the standard or "context" fundamental, although a raised F_0 was shown to be more effective than a lowered one. Nevertheless, changes of 58% in the fundamental were shown to be no more effective than changes of 25% in producing consistent stress marking—a result which confirmed the "all or none" effect of fundamental frequency changes observed by Fry. They also found that the more intense and longer syllables were more likely to be marked as stressed although, curiously, when a syllable was reduced in duration by 40%, some of the judges consistently marked the shorter of the two syllables as being stressed.

A few years later, the same stimuli were presented to Polish listeners. When a comparison was made of the results for both English and Polish subjects, a striking similarity between the two groups seems to have been shown in the strong effect produced by fundamental frequency variations.[164] However, variations in duration are reported to have been more effective with the Polish than with the English subjects.[165] Intensity was found to be ineffective until a difference of 6 dB was reached,[166] although, as Lehiste points out, the effect of this difference could be outweighed by differences in duration.

I have not seen results of this experiment with French speakers, although Rigault[167] has reported that frequency was by far the most important physical correlate of perceived stress in his experiments. "Nous pouvons donc conclure . . . que la fréquence est, de loin, le facteur prédominant dans la perception de la proéminence de la syllabe."[168]

In Lehiste and Ivić's[169] study of accent in Standard Serbo-Croatian, on the other hand, the decisive cue for stressedness was found to be duration. Thus, as Lehiste points out, "In many languages, fundamental frequency combined with intensity provides the decisive cue; in others, duration is the most dependable correlate of stressedness."[170]

These are the results of some of the researchers who, by means of instrumental analysis, have in recent years investigated the nature of linguistic stress in English. There has been an appreciable move from the psychological definition in terms of production as proposed by Classe following his kymographic study, "Stress is essentially a psychological phenomenon normally accompanied by modifications of the physical characteristics of speech which serve to situate it.''[171] in the direction of a dichotomous explanation embracing both production and perception aspects of the phenomenon. To all of these investigators I am grateful for their studies have stimulated my interest in stress at the sentence level, and have inspired me to embark upon the comparative investigation of English speech rhythm, the report of which constitutes the Alpha and Omega of this study.

(b) The Characteristic Features of Stress-timed Rhythm

The assumption underlying the present study was that the rhythm of native English speech is stress-timed. Obviously all speech rhythm exists in time, but the speakers of different languages divide time differently, and thus even though some feeling of rhythm is experienced whatever the language spoken, the particular timing and organization of the rhythm units of a language determine a rhythmic succession which is an essential and distinctive feature of the phonological structure of that language.

Although every language has a characteristic rhythm, there appear to be only two general types of speech rhythm, "syllable-timed" and "stress-timed". Languages of the former class are based on a periodicity of pulses which synchronize with the even time spacing of syllables, the latter, on a periodicity of uniformly spaced stresses. These two trains of pulses—both isochronous—are mutually exclusive so that, when occasionally they coincide in a language, they do so only by accident. One recognized exception to this rule is Czech in which Daneš[172] maintains, the rhythm units are both syllable-timed and stress-timed.[173] According to Abercrombie,[174] there is some evidence that syllable-timed rhythm is a characteristic feature of the earliest speech of all language learners and that stress-timing, which appears a little later in the child's language development, is an extra feature which has to be learnt by speakers of such widely differing languages as English, Persian, Hebrew, Modern Greek, Mandarin Chinese, Scots Gaelic, and Scandinavian—to mention a few.

This would accord with the "six-per-second" hypothesis discussed by Lenneberg[175] who postulates that there is a basic periodicity of approximately six cycles per second in human speech which is due to physiological rather than to cultural factors. If the basic time unit in the programming of motor-speech patterns is 160 ±20 msec, it should be possible, he says, to make different use of the time units available, since there is most likely "more than one way of distributing a train of syllables over the rhythmic vehicles."[176]

Whether this is so or not, the two types of rhythm (syllable-timed and stress-timed) do not normally coexist in any one idolect, the rhythm of the mother tongue being acquired and established quite early in life, although, as Pike[177] has pointed out, a deliberate pacing of syllables to produce syllable-timing in English is a feature of a type of chant often used by children to signify triumph with both joyful and maliciously taunting implication. However, such utterance evinces other formalized features (such as non-normal syllable quantity and pitch variation) and cannot be regarded as in any way typical of normal native English pronunciation.

As we have already observed, in English the stressed syllables occur at perceptually regular time intervals, and thus the timing of rhythm units (that is, a phrasal group containing one strongly stressed syllable and one or more unstressed syllables interrupted by a pause) is achieved by the relative isochrony of the stresses which carry the rhythmic impulse. On the other hand, languages such as, French, Urdu, Hindi, Finnish, Hungarian, Cantonese, and the native languages spoken by the foreign subjects in this study, have a rhythm which is more closely related to the syllable, in that the syllables—rather than the stresses—are spoken at more or less uniformly recurrent time intervals. In these syllable-timed languages, the duration of an utterance is proportional to the total number of syllables it contains and, generally speaking, there is no modification, as there is in English, of the sounds which constitute each syllable—their duration is invariable.

However, according to Abercrombie,[178] it is a necessary consequence of the fact that English is spoken with a stress-timed rhythm that its syllables are of uneven length. The duration of a given syllable in English varies according to the context[179] and thus the actual number of syllables in a rhythm unit is no real index of the duration of the interval. The number of syllables in the several rhythm groups of an utterance may in fact vary quite considerably, but the impression of isochronous intervals is maintained as a result of normal qualitative and quantitative adjustment of the unstressed syllables in relation to the fully stressed hub of each rhythm unit.

In the main, it is this variability of syllable duration which makes the rhythm of English so exasperatingly difficult for the foreign learner, for while most non-native speakers have learned that in English the unstressed syllables are crowded together between the stressed ones, they invariably fail to recognize the significance of the timing of syllables in connected utterance and as a result, produce an anomalous rhythm which seriously impairs the total intelligibility of their utterance.

Furthermore, as I will show, they frequently misuse that other essential constituent of rhythmicality, the pause, and never, without specific instruction, do they seem to grasp the principle of what Abercrombie and others have termed "silent stress" but what I prefer to call *rhythmic disjuncture*. Very few native speakers are in fact aware of this phenomenon, although intuitively they are constantly using it to preserve the rhythmic impulse established by the more tangible manifestations of stress; namely, the variations of pitch, loudness, and length which in English are our principal cues to syllable prominence. Even though linguistic constraints require of the speaker of English a certain degree of conformity in his organization of the words of a phrase, it is possible for several speakers to divide a text in different ways according to individual interpretation[180] and, provided their rhythm units are organized so as to create an impression of proportion or equivalence resulting from the relative isochrony of the stressed syllables, they will produce and maintain a credible native rhythm pattern.[181] The reason for this is to be found, I believe, in the native speaker's intuitive feeling for the pulse or beat even in material not normally regarded as especially "rhythmical"; for example, the language of ordinary conversation.

As we have seen, the notion of the isochrony of stresses in connected English utterance has been a controversial issue for centuries—yet surprisingly few phoneticians have actually presented evidence for or against the existence of the phenomenon in this or in any other language. Thus, even Abercrombie, who is one of its strongest advocates, has to concede:

> Not everyone, by any means, believes or has believed in the theory . . . that English is a language of stress-timed rhythm. . . . But those who do not believe the theory, it should be noted, do not take account of silent stresses. If one looks for isochronism between stressed *syllables* only, it is fairly certain that, in a stretch of speech of any length, one will not find it. It is the *silent* stresses that keep the isochronous stress-pulse going in all but the shortest utterance.[182]

Abercrombie argues that these "silent stresses" are different from other speech pauses in that they do not involve interruption to the stream of speech—rather, they are part of it simply filling the gap in an utterance which would otherwise be filled by a stressed syllable. It seems to me, however, that these pauses can also occur in place of unstressed syllables, in which case they obviously do not carry the beat, although they perform the function of preserving the rhythm already established. In this study, therefore, no special attention was given to silent stress; pauses were regarded simply as being appropriately or inappropriately placed. In any case, as Abercrombie points out, "Silent stresses may sometimes take a form which is not, strictly speaking, silent; the final sound of the preceding syllable may be prolonged over the space they occupy. This prolongation appears to be in free variation with silence, though it is more common with some people than others."[183]

In this study, it was taken for granted that the speech of the native subjects was stress-timed and when deviations from this norm occurred in the utterance of the non-native subjects reasons were sought for the discrepancies. The essential nature of a time pattern consists in the underlying pulse or beat, and it soon became evident that the non-native subjects, generally speaking, were failing to maintain this pulse—thereby distorting the most simple rhythmic patterns—by randomly introducing additional pauses and stresses which, in upsetting the internal temporal relationships of the accentual groups, produced a somewhat staccato rhythm reminiscent of the syllable-timing of their first language.

To my knowledge there has been little experimental study of syllable-timed rhythm—certainly the reports published are minimal—and, despite the very considerable study of both rhythm and stress phenomena, only a limited amount of controlled experimental investigation of stress-timed rhythm. Duckworth,[184] who is one of the few phoneticians to have reported the results of investigation into the accuracy of the notion of stress-timed rhythm, says that the syllables seemed unquestionably to be the basic unit of the rhythm of English in the sample he examined, and the placement of stress, "merely incidental and relatively unimportant."[185] For all that, he does not deny that isochronism cannot be found in English—rather, that "it is probably not a general organizing principle of the rhythm of spoken English."[186]

On the other hand, Bolinger concludes:

Stress-timed rhythm is not entirely illusory. Its dominant position in verse would alone be enough to provoke some reaction in prose, if indeed its roots were not in prose to begin with. But to find it extensively we must look beyond offhand discourse toward speech that is aesthetically contrived or often repeated. A proverb or a prayer is apt to congeal in rhythmic form and every writer or public speaker at some time indulges in poetic prose.[187]

The test material used in the several experiments which constitute this study consisted of items which ranged in style from simple, well-known rhymes and verses, through colloquial-type sentences, to literary prose which verged on the poetic. Thus the subjects, native and non-native speakers alike, were given ample opportunity to demonstrate their ability to establish and maintain the rhythmic impulse in a wide variety of English speech forms, traditional and contrived. Although it was expected that the obviously stress-timed rhythm of the strongly metrical items would be realized by both categories of speakers, even if not actually recognized by them as such, the subjects were given complete freedom to interpret the material in any way they thought fit. However, the results of the study seem to point to the reality of two distinct types of speech rhythm—stress-timed as produced by the native English speakers, and syllable-timed as produced by the foreign subjects, every one of whom spoke the items with a periodicity of syllable pulses characteristic of the organization and timing of the rhythm units of his own syllable-timed first language.

PART II

Investigations

CHAPTER FOUR

Auditory Perception Test

We have seen that most of the stress research undertaken in recent years has been concerned either with the production or with the perception aspect of the phenomenon. In the investigations reported in this book account was taken of both production and perception in order that the "Janus-faced"[1] nature of stress could be seen in relation to the linguistic events linking speaker and listener in the actual process of speech communication. This double-pronged assault was made in view of the wider objectives of the study—examination of the phonetic nature of stress in relation to English speech rhythm, and investigation of the problems associated with the foreign learner's acquisition of stress-timed rhythm. These objectives, in my opinion, could be achieved only by determining in the first instance how the native speaker produces the cues by which the rhythmic impulse is marked; and, in the second, why the non-native speaker, if he can perceive these cues, is nonetheless unable to produce English speech rhythm adequately.

The first stage in the investigations was to ascertain which words in a series of test items consisting of meaningful connected speech were stressed.

Determination of the actual stress placement of two groups of speakers, one native English-speaking and the other, foreign, was made independently by ten adjudicators, themselves native speakers of English, most of whom were my colleagues in the University of Sydney Department of Education. They were asked to listen to readings of 12 test items recorded by the two groups of subjects and to indicate the words in each utterance which seemed to them to be stressed. They were non-linguists and therefore the concept of stress was defined simply as "prominence"[2] to cover their general impressions of the sound variations in the speech continuum which were to be interpreted as stress.

It was pointed out to them that although a particular syllable in a disyllabic or polysyllabic word might be accented and therefore have lexical stress it did not necessarily follow that that syllable would carry sentence stress in the whole utterance; for example, in the sentence,

She stepped into the room

the first syllable of *into* is accented, but although *in* receives lexical stress it does not carry the stress which would render it prominent in the utterance of the whole sentence. On the other hand, the second syllable of the word *return* in the sentence,

They had to return their books

receives both lexical and sentence stress because of its semantic significance in the utterance. Thus no special training in phonetics was necessary to enable the adjudicators to perform their task satisfactorily. It must be admitted, as Fry[3] has pointed out, that the untrained subject is less aware of stress than of phonemic distinctions and that because of this it is difficult for him to respond to stress differences. However, it should be noted that in my investigations natural connected speech was used rather than the synthesized isolate word forms used by Fry and several other investigators whose work we have considered. For my listeners, the main problem seemed to be their expectancy of prominence.

Since, as has been observed in Chapter III(a), the concept of expectancy[4] plays a major role in speech perception, procedures had to be taken which would ensure that the words judged as stressed were those which were actually given prominence by the speakers, and not simply words which the listeners thought *ought* to be stressed. It was decided, therefore, that a word would be accepted as stressed only if there were agreement by 7 or more of the ten judges.

In order to preclude the possibility of their attributing stress placement on the basis of their own kinaesthetic memory which, as we have seen,[5] contributes strongly to the perception of both stress and rhythm, the adjudicators heard each utterance twice only—the exceptions being items 3 and 4 which, because of their length, were replayed three times each—and were requested to judge the position of the stressed syllables on the basis of a first impression, wherever possible.

Of the 22 readers, aged from 21 to 60, the native subjects were all speakers of Australian English who used a spectrum of pronunciation ranging from Broad to Educated or Cultivated,[6] although most could be regarded as speakers of General Australian English. The 11 non-native subjects were speakers of several Asian languages, all of which were characterized by syllable-timed rhythm. The texts which they read included 2 nursery rhymes, 3 excerpts of verse characterized by a strongly metrical rhythm, 5 fabricated equivalents of these items, and one passage each of colloquial and literary prose. It was expected that the non-native subjects, although familiar with English verse and prose of considerable structural and conceptual complexity, would have had only limited experience in the speaking of English texts. In order, therefore, that they should not be disadvantaged, the test material selected featured reasonably basic structures and vocabulary, even the verse items being fundamentally similar to the stress profile of natural spoken English.[7] The arrangement of the test sentences was such that fabricated equivalent sometimes followed and sometimes preceded original material, as follows:

1. To market, to market, to buy a fat pig,
   Home again, home again, jiggety-jig.
2. "Will you walk a little faster?" said a
   whiting to a snail,
   "There's a porpoise close behind us, and he's
   treading on my tail."
3. In the breathless stillness of a tropical
   afternoon, when the air was hot and heavy,
   and the sky brazen and cloudless, the shadow
   of the *Malabar* lay solitary on the surface of
   the glittering sea.
4. When I asked her what she would have done if
   he had spoken to her in the street she smiled
   and said that as she seldom walked in that
   direction it didn't seem likely that he would
   have much opportunity ever to speak to her.
5. "Is there anybody listening?" said the chairman
   to the Board.
   "There's a rather urgent matter that I want to
   settle first."
6. The boys in our neighbourhood go to school in
   their families' brand new cars. As status
   symbol the car is essential, but smash it and
   who must pay?
7. The evening is always the best time to phone:
   Wednesday night, Thursday night—six or half
   past.
8. The Owl and the Pussy-Cat went to sea
   In a beautiful pea-green boat.
   They took some honey and plenty of money,
   Wrapped up in a five-pound note.
9. Humpty Dumpty sat on a wall,
   Humpty Dumpty had a great fall.
10. If she's leaving please let me know. Sixteen
    students still want a place.
11. Never leave the tap on. Always turn it off.
    Drought here is one of our greatest plagues.
12. Dreary lay the long road, dreary lay the town.
    Lights out and never a glint of moon.

It will be observed, for instance, that items 5, 6, 7, 10 and 11 are fabricated to correspond to the rhythm of the nursery rhymes and verse of items 2, 8, 1, 9 and 12 respectively. It had been thought that the non-native speakers' rhythm in these prose sentences might be influenced by the obvious beat of the strongly metrical items, but the order of presentation appeared to have no noticeable effect on the readings or on the listeners' judgments of them.

The test was administered in four sessions since it was considered that the listeners could not reasonably be expected to adjudicate accurately on more than six readers at one sitting. The recordings were presented to them on a good quality tape recorder in a seminar room in the Education building of the University. Some of the recordings had been made in the Phonetics Laboratory under studio conditions; some simultaneously with electromyographic recordings; and some in an ordinary seminar room; thus the levels of the original recordings lacked uniformity. To rectify this, all utterances were re-recorded through a programme control amplifier to an average level. It was this version of the readings which was presented to the adjudicators.

They were each issued with several test sheets which provided them with transcripts of the test items arranged vertically in a manner similar to that shown in Table 1. Space in columns was allowed for the recording of their judgments. In recent years, George D. Allen,[8] as we have seen, has conducted a number of experiments on the location of rhythmic stress beats in English, his subjects generally being required to indicate the position of the beat within the stressed syllable by tapping. I rejected this technique, which has also been used by several other investigators, among them Classe,[9] Verrier,[10] and Miyake,[11] because accuracy of beat location was of less importance for the purposes of my experiment than accurate perception and recording of stress placement. This in itself was no easy task since the listeners were required to make judgments on the utterance of two quite different groups of speakers. To have required the adjudicators to indicate the location of the precise point of the stress beat in the speech of subjects using a syllable-timed rhythm would have complicated their assignment unnecessarily.

They were given the following instructions:

This is an experiment in the perception of sentence stress. You will hear in all 11 native and 11 non-native speakers of English each reading 12 test items some of which will be very familiar to you. In this session 5 (or 6) readers will be presented to you. Listen carefully to each utterance, and then place a tick beside the word or words in the item which seem to you to be stressed. In some sentences you will find that a number of words are stressed; in others, very few might seem to be stressed. Again, some of the speakers might use stress more than other speakers. Try very hard to mark only those words which seem to be thrown into prominence by the particular reader. On no account mark words which you think *ought* to be stressed, that is, words which *you* yourself would stress in reading the items. The test is not one which involves a 'right' or 'wrong' answer. All I want you to do is to indicate the words which seem to you to be spoken with greater prominence than the rest of the sentence. You may record your judgments while the reader is speaking or, if you prefer, you may listen to the whole utterance and then tick the stressed words. You will hear each item twice. Have you any questions?

There was some brief discussion about the nature and function of stress, but the subjects agreed that it was probably better simply to record their quick impressions of prominence rather than try to reason the factors which influenced their perception. It was at this stage that the distinction between word and sentence stress was pointed out to them. They then heard a few examples of the test material read by a speaker whose recording was not included in the experiment, and were given time to record their responses. In the experiment, several of the adjudicators preferred to hear items in their entirety before marking the stressed words, although most recorded their judgments while the readings were in progress.

The results showed that the two groups differed quite considerably in the number of words which were stressed—the non-native speakers stressing almost twice as many syllables as the native speakers—and in the placement of stress. A significant feature of the utterance of the foreign subjects was that it was marked by numerous instances of misplaced stress at the lexical level. Although judgments were made on 22 readers, it was decided to analyse statistically the results of the sixteen—8 native and 8 non-native—whose oscillographic recordings[12] were considered most suitable for acoustic analysis.

The foreign subjects appeared to stress not only the words ordinarily thrown into prominence by native speakers but also a number of other words not normally emphasized in the stream of speech; for example, conjunctions, prepositions, and attributive adjectives. To these may be added a number of examples of misplaced syllable stress; for example, the accentuation of the second syllable in the following words:

> por'POISE, fas'TER, op'PORtunity,

all of which occurred frequently; and the use of strong forms, and full vowels in normally unstressed positions; for example,

> *When I asked* '*HER*
> *she would* '*HAVE done,*
> *to mar* '*KET,*
> *sixteen stu*'*DENTS.*

Examples of the differences between the stress patterning of native and non-native speakers may be observed in Figs. 5 and 6, in which the stressed syllables are marked off by vertical lines drawn through the several traces of the oscillographic recordings.

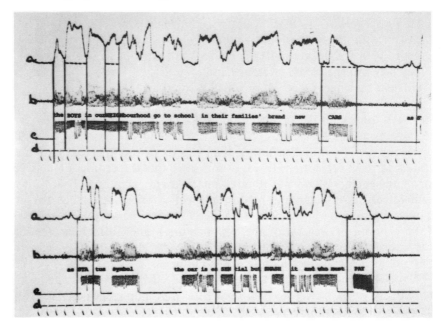

Figure 5.   Oscillographic recording of native English speaker's utterance of item 6. Stressed syllables (7) are marked off by vertical lines drawn through the several traces.
a = integrated intensity
b = duplex oscillogram of speech wave
c = fundamental frequency
d = time marker in 0.1 sec.

Reference may also be made to Table I which shows the differences in stress placement between native and non-native speakers.

The statistical significance of this discrepancy in stress placement between native and non-native speakers was tested by Chi square. The number of stress judgments for each syllable of the 12 items was calculated for both categories of subjects and the significance of the difference between the two groups was thus determined. The results of this analysis showed that there was a statistically significant difference between the native and the non-native speakers at both syllable and sentence level. Examination of the findings set out in Table 1 will show precisely where the discrepancies occurred. Whereas the foreign subjects were frequently observed to stress syllables which the native subjects did not, in no case was a native speaker

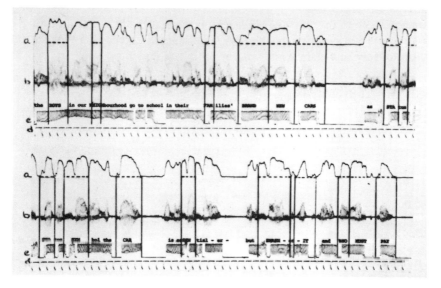

Figure 6. Oscillographic recording of non-native (Bengali) speaker's utterance of item 6. Stressed syllables (15) are marked off by vertical lines drawn through the several traces. Traces a–d as in Fig. 5.

observed to stress words or syllables which were not also stressed by his non-native opposite number.

The object of the perception test was to establish with reasonable accuracy which syllables in the several utterances were stressed by both categories of speakers. This was done as a preliminary to investigation of the factors which influence the listener's perception of stress. The knowledge that speakers of syllable-timed first languages carry over this characteristic of their language into English and that they stress more syllables in their utterance of English than do native speakers of English does not help us towards greater understanding of the phonetic nature of stress—or of how it is produced in English. The question then remains, what does a speaker *do* that causes the listener to receive an impression of stress?

Having accepted on the basis of the rigorous criterion noted above a considerable number of syllables perceived as stressed by the 10 adjudicators, I proceeded to examine these units of speech for any characteristics which might distinguish them from the unstressed syllables. My objective was to determine the physiological and/or acoustic correlates of stress by means of a comparative study of the phonetic characteristics of both stressed and unstressed syllables as produced by the two groups of speakers. In the first investigation electromyography was used.

TABLE 1

Comparison by Chi-square of the stress judgments made on the utterance of 8 native and 8 non-native speakers. A significant difference between the two groups of speakers is shown at both syllable and sentence level.

ITEM 1—21 Syllables			ITEM 7—21 Syllables		
Syllable	X^2	*Sig.*	*Syllable*	X^2	*Sig.*
TO	1.358		THE	1.157	
MAR	3.822		EVE	7.524	**
KET	34.502	***	NING	5.726	*
TO	3.303		IS	2.003	
MAR	3.508		AL	7.130	**
KET	34.502	***	WAYS	5.726	*
TO	1.415		THE	0	
BUY	12.564	***	BEST	4.535	*
A	1.415		TIME	9.717	**
FAT	31.901	***	TO	0.002	
PIG	1.113		PHONE	0.013	
HOME	1.415		WEDNES	13.412	***
A	0		DAY	17.431	***
GAIN	2.615		NIGHT	1.070	
HOME	1.415		THURS	9.341	***
A	0		DAY	7.707	**
GAIN	2.169		NIGHT	2.936	
JIG	25.306	***	SIX	5.843	*
GE	0		OR	1.157	
TY	0		HALF	13.316	***
JIG	0.290		PAST	0.084	

X^2 of whole item = 49.634*** X^2 of whole item = 59.351***

ITEM 2—30 Syllables			ITEM 5—31 Syllables		
Syllable	X^2	*Sig.*	*Syllable*	X^2	*Sig.*
WILL	25.931	***	IS	19.350	***
YOU	0.506		THERE	23.241	***
WALK	0.875		AN	5.639	*
A	0		Y	0	
LIT	9.762	**	BOD	3.303	

Syllable	X^2	Sig.	Syllable	X^2	Sig.
TLE	0		Y	0	
FAST	0		LIST	2.369	
ER	30.119	***	EN	0	
SAID	6.447	*	ING	8.640	**
A	0		SAID	15.625	***
WHIT	10.597	**	THE	0	
ING	6.447	*	CHAIR	12.050	***
TO	0		MAN	0	
A	0		TO	1.415	
SNAIL	0.049		THE	0	
THERE'S	10.579	**	BOARD	0.160	
A	0		THERE'S	13.228	***
POR	2.098		A	0	
POISE	56.100	***	RATH	9.917	**
CLOSE	18.962	***	ER	0	
BE	0		URG	2.225	
HIND	3.447		ENT	0	
US	2.903		MAT	5.656	*
AND	1.415		TER	23.241	***
HE'S	8.640	**	THAT	4.329	*
TREAD	18.960	***	I	0	
ING	0		WANT	32.615	***
ON	1.184		TO	0	
MY	0.960		SET	9.030	**
TAIL	0.178		TLE	0	
			FIRST	2.795	

X^2 of whole item = 60.502*** X^2 of whole item = 83.806***

ITEM 3—53 Syllables   ITEM 4—56 Syllables

Syllable	X^2	Sig.	Syllable	X^2	Sig.
IN	5.378	*	WHEN	9.657	**
THE	0		I	3.303	
BREATH	13.645	***	ASKED	2.700	
LESS	18.090	***	HER	40.672	***
STILL	6.696	**	WHAT	50.700	***
NESS	14.418	***	SHE	3.303	
OF	0		WOULD	21.925	***
A	0		HAVE	20.628	***

ITEM 3—53 Syllables (contd.)

Syllable	X^2	Sig.
TROP	13.358	***
IC	0	
AL	0	
AF	7.534	**
TER	0	
NOON	0.135	
WHEN	8.640	**
THE	0	
AIR	4.506	*
WAS	0	
HOT	0.542	
AND	0	
HEAV	0	
Y	16.849	***
AND	0	
THE	0	
SKY	15.872	***
BRAZ	14.964	***
EN	0	
AND	0	
CLOUD	2.695	
LESS	27.306	***
THE	0	
SHAD	4.919	*
OW	0	
OF	0	
THE	0	
MA	1.415	
LA	0	
BAR	8.640	**
LAY	6.447	*
SO	0.906	
LI	0	
TAR	0	
Y	0	
ON	0	
THE	0	
SUR	2.500	
FACE	34.502	***
OF	0	

ITEM 4—56 Syllables (contd.)

Syllable	X^2	Sig.
DONE	0.168	
IF	7.534	**
HE	1.358	
HAD	1.415	
SPOK	9.168	**
EN	0	
TO	1.415	
HER	14.418	***
IN	0	
THE	1.415	
STREET	2.851	
SHE	0	
SMILED	0.131	
AND	0	
SAID	30.440	***
THAT	21.925	***
AS	18.090	***
SHE	0.506	
SEL	9.141	**
DOM	0	
WALKED	4.450	*
IN	1.415	
THAT	9.762	**
DI	0	
REC	2.035	
TION	6.447	*
IT	0	
DID	34.359	***
N'T	0	
SEEM	16.849	***
LIKE	0.028	
LY	0	
THAT	18.090	***
HE	0	
WOULD	9.762	**
HAVE	9.762	**
MUCH	5.556	*
OP	0	
POR	6.447	*
TUN	0.666	

ITEM 3—53 Syllables (contd.)

Syllable	X^2	Sig.
THE	0	
GLIT	22.788	***
TER	0	
ING	0	
SEA	3.506	

X^2 of whole item = 73.450*

ITEM 4—56 Syllables (contd.)

Syllable	X^2	Sig.
I	0	
TY	0	
EV	0.900	
ER	0	
TO	0	
SPEAK	3.151	
TO	1.415	
HER	22.503	***

X^2 of whole item = 186.443***

ITEM 6—36 Syllables

Syllable	X^2	Sig.
THE	0	
BOYS	4.033	*
IN	0	
OUR	9.762	**
NEIGH	3.094	
BOUR	19.350	***
HOOD	19.350	***
GO	6.447	*
TO	0.506	
SCHOOL	0.911	
IN	1.415	
THEIR	1.415	
FAM	16.458	***
IL	0	
IES'	0	
BRAND	9.232	**
NEW	31.558	***
CARS	1.440	
AS	1.358	
STAT	0.027	
US	0	
SYM	5.032	*
BOL	15.625	***
THE	1.415	

ITEM 8—36 Syllables

Syllable	X^2	Sig.
THE	0	
OWL	10.625	**
AND	1.415	
THE	1.415	
PUSS	31.038	***
Y	0	
CAT	19.350	***
WENT	6.247	*
TO	0	
SEA	0	
IN	1.415	
A	0	
BEAU	32.405	***
TI	0	
FUL	0	
PEA	1.928	
GREEN	0.135	
BOAT	0.140	
THEY	0.506	
TOOK	13.645	***
SOME	8.640	**
HON	0.933	
EY	7.534	**
AND	0	

ITEM 6—36 Syllables (contd.)

Syllable	X^2	Sig.
CAR	36.000	***
IS	0.506	
ES	0	
SEN	2.443	
TIAL	15.625	***
BUT	1.358	
SMASH	1.415	
IT	33.166	***
AND	0.506	
WHO	0.917	
MUST	16.410	***
PAY	8.064	**

X^2 of whole item = 83.263***

ITEM 8—36 Syllables (contd.)

Syllable	X^2	Sig.
PLEN	12.367	***
TY	0	
OF	1.415	
MON	1.374	
EY	24.576	***
WRAPPED	41.561	***
UP	0	
IN	1.415	
A	1.415	
FIVE	9.116	**
POUND	2.878	
NOTE	2.401	

X^2 of whole item = 81.089***

ITEM 9—16 Syllables

Syllable	X^2	Sig.
HUMP	2.770	
TY	5.378	*
DUMP	7.368	**
TY	16.847	***
SAT	25.659	***
ON	1.415	
A	1.415	
WALL	0.351	
HUMP	1.643	
TY	0	
DUMP	3.770	
TY	6.447	*
HAD	27.056	***
A	1.415	
GREAT	42.449	***
FALL	5.297	*

X^2 of whole item = 52.777***

ITEM 10—16 Syllables

Syllable	X^2	Sig.
IF	22.900	***
SHE'S	31.558	***
LEAV	1.225	
ING	20.628	***
PLEASE	29.452	***
LET	3.303	
ME	2.307	
KNOW	0.369	
SIX	2.045	
TEEN	0	
STUD	0.407	
ENTS	2.307	
STILL	4.176	*
WANT	5.972	*
A	1.415	
PLACE	0.290	

X^2 of whole item = 42.412***

ITEM 11—20 Syllables   ITEM 12—20 Syllables

Syllable	X^2	Sig.	Syllable	X^2	Sig.
NEV	0		DREAR	0.261	
ER	0		Y	4.329	*
LEAVE	15.230	***	LAY	14.084	***
THE	1.415		THE	0	
TAP	1.600		LONG	9.116	**
ON	21.508	***	ROAD	0	
AL	13.776	***	DREAR	2.532	
WAYS	0		Y	0	
TURN	19.025	***	LAY	19.025	***
IT	4.329	*	THE	0	
OFF	0.152		TOWN	0.035	
DROUGHT	3.447		LIGHTS	3.697	
HERE	2.509		OUT	2.057	
IS	1.415		AND	0	
ONE	24.414	***	NEV	16.903	***
OF	0		ER	0	
OUR	6.447	*	A	0	
GREAT	19.440	***	GLINT	18.236	***
EST	18.090	***	OF	0	
PLAGUES	1.220		MOON	2.010	

X^2 of whole item = 65.606*** X^2 of whole item = 20.530

*   significance at 5% level
**   significance at 1% level
***significance at 0.1% level

CHAPTER FIVE

A Physiological View of Stress Patterning and Pause Placement

(a) *Electromyographic Investigation of Expiratory Muscular Activity*

Electromyography, it has been noted,[1] is a technique for detecting and recording the electrical discharges which are produced by contracting muscles—the only method in fact that provides completely reliable information about the activity of muscles cooperating in movement. It has been used quite extensively in recent years by researchers investigating the movements involved in articulation, but of particular interest to us in our search for the correlates of stress are the investigations of Ladefoged[2] and his co-workers who, as we have seen, in the late fifties re-examined Stetson's[3] theory of the syllable, and those of some few other phoneticians who have replicated Ladefoged's experiments. Ladefoged, it has been noted, demonstrated bursts of internal intercostal muscle activity synchronous with stressed syllables either when repeated in isolation or in simple sentences, and was supported by Fónagy[4] who reported similar findings, but criticized by Lebrun[5] on the grounds that inadequate evidence was shown to substantiate this claim. Nevertheless, on the basis of Ladefoged's results, it has been widely concluded that stress is associated with increased respiratory muscular activity.

Now, as I have already observed, most of the investigations into the nature of stress have been conducted at the lexical level, very little attention having been paid to the word in the context of the sentence. Examination of the reports of EMG investigations of stress likewise reveals that almost invariably the stimuli have consisted of isolate word forms and that scant consideration has been given to patterns of respiratory muscle activity occurring in the utterance of whole sentences of varying structure. Yet electromyography would appear to provide a ready means for the objective investigation of stress at the sentence level.

The results of the auditory perception test indicated, as we have noted, a significant difference between the stress placement of native and non-native speakers in connected utterance, and it seemed to me that a comparative analysis of the speech of the two groups using electromyography might confirm these different patterns and lead to insights into the characteristics of the speech rhythm of the foreign speakers, as well as bringing to light physiological facts relating to the nature of stress. Thus the EMG investigation was conducted with three objectives in view.

1. It seemed likely that the localized bursts of internal intercostal activity which had been found by Ladefoged et al.[6] to accompany stressed syllables repeated in isolation would be further demonstrable in the connected utterance not only of native speakers of English but also—and more noticeably—in the utterance of those native speakers of syllable-timed languages who retained their characteristic even time-spacing of syllables when speaking English.

2. It was considered possible, however, that the pattern of muscular activity produced by speakers of syllable-timed languages when speaking English—a stress-timed language—would differ from that produced by native speakers of English because of the inherently different organization of the rhythm units in the two classes of languages.

3. If it were found that the muscular activity pattern of a native speaker of a syllable-timed language speaking his mother tongue differed from that of a native speaker of a stress-timed language speaking his first language, it might be possible to assess L_1 interference on the basis of the speech rhythm used by the foreign speaker in his utterance of L_2.

Seventeen male subjects were used in the investigation. These included 4 native speakers of English aged 21–37 and thirteen non-native speakers aged 28–39. The foreign subjects were native speakers of Vietnamese (7), Cambodian (2), Bengali (2), Indonesian (1), and Pilipino (1). All the non-native speakers were graduate teachers of English who had been engaged in this work for an average of 7.5 years. When tested, all but two had been living in an English-speaking community for approximately three months, although in their respective countries each spent only an average of a little over 3 hours daily speaking English. The two subjects excepted were Vietnamese speakers who had been living in one of the University of Sydney residential colleges for approximately 8 months when tested and had also received 20 hours of class instruction in spoken English.[7] As a result, their speech, although still obviously foreign, was considerably more fluent than that of the other non-native subjects. As a means of making possible the further comparison of internal intercostal muscle activity in the utterance of speakers of stress-timed and syllable-timed languages, and indeed in order to assist me in determining whether increased activity could be associated with connected utterance in a monosyllabic language, they prepared and read test material in their native Vietnamese which corresponded in character to the English texts which, as noted above in connection with the auditory perception test,[8] were read in the following order:

Test Material

1. To market, to market, to buy a fat pig,
   Home again, home again, jiggety-jig.

2. 'Will you walk a little faster?' said a whiting to a snail,
   'There's a porpoise close behind us, and he's treading on my tail.'

3. In the breathless stillness of a tropical afternoon, when the air was
   hot and heavy, and the sky brazen and cloudless, the shadow of the
   Malabar lay solitary on the surface of the glittering sea.

4. When I asked her what she would have done if he had spoken to her
   in the street she smiled and said that as she seldom walked in that
   direction it didn't seem likely that he would have much opportunity
   ever to speak to her.

5. 'Is there anybody listening?' said the chairman to the Board.
   'There's a rather urgent matter that I want to settle first.'

6. The boys in our neighbourhood go to school in their families' brand
   new cars. As status symbol the car is essential, but smash it and who
   must pay?

7. The evening is always the best time to phone: Wednesday night,
   Thursday night—six or half past.

8. The Owl and the Pussy-Cat went to sea
   In a beautiful pea-green boat.
   They took some honey and plenty of money,
   Wrapped up in a five-pound note.

9. Humpty Dumpty sat on a wall,
   Humpty Dumpty had a great fall.

10. If she's leaving please let me know. Sixteen students still want a
    place.

11. Never leave the tap on. Always turn it off. Drought here is one of
    our greatest plagues.

12. Dreary lay the long road, dreary lay the town.
    Lights out and never a glint of moon.

The Vietnamese items included 3 traditional nursery rhymes, 3 poems of
varying style, and 2 prose passages, one being an excerpt from a modern
novel and the other an example of colloquial dialogue.

Nursery Rhymes
1. Chị lấy chồng
   Em ở giá
   Chị ăn cá
   Em mút xương
   Chị nằm giường
   Em nằm đất.

2. Lây trời mửa xuống
   Lây nước tôi uống.

3. Con mèo trèo lên cây cau
   Hỏi thăm chú Chuột di dâu vắng nhà
   Chú Chuột di chợ dường xa
   Mua mắm mua muối giỗ cha chú mèo

Poems
4. Dêm mửa làm nhỏ không gian
   long run thêm lanh nỗi hần bao la.

5. Lá dào rời rác lối thiên thai
   Suối tiễn oanh dửa lương ngậm ngùi.

6. Ta sống mãi trong tình thường nỗi nhỏ
   Thửo tung hoành hống hách những ngày xủa.

Prose
7. Hàng năm củ vào cuối thu khi lá ngòai dường rụng nhiều và trên
   không có những dám mây bằng bạc long tôi lại náo náo với những
   kỷ niệm hoang mang của buổi tựa trường.

8. Mẹ tôi gọi Tâm lại bảo khẽ: "Thế nào, việc học hành thi củ dã xong
   chửa? Tôi xem dao nầy cậu có vẻ gầy di một it dây." Tâm mỉm
   cười nhìn tôi ngụ ý nhỏ tôi trả lời hộ. Tôi vội dáp "Thửa mẹ anh
   Tâm dã dậu rồi dây ạ."

The EMG machine used was a 3-channel DISA Electromyograph (No.
13A69), the channels being recorded by a camera incorporated in the unit.
The film (speed 19.4 msec/mm) was developed and fixed by standard
photographic procedure.

Concentric needle electrodes (DISA 13K51), 30 mm in length and 0.45
mm in diameter, were used in this investigation; they were inserted into the
intercostal muscles following a preliminary intradermal injection of
Xylocaine.

Recordings were taken from the internal intercostal muscle in the right
sixth intercostal space in the mid-axillary line and from the external inter-

costal muscle in the right eighth intercostal space just medial to the angles of the ribs. (Fig. 7.)

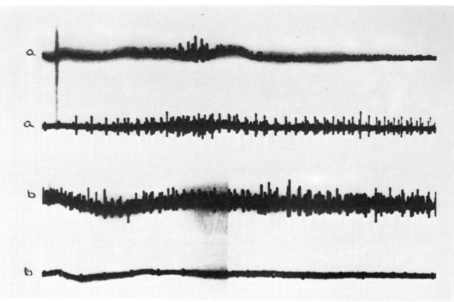

Figure 7.   Intercostal muscle activity in inspiration (a) and in expiration (b). In each case the upper trace is from the internal intercostal muscle and the lower one is from the external intercostal muscle.

The correct positioning of these electrodes was verified by the recording of marked activity in deep expiration and inspiration respectively. A microphone (Shure 545), placed some 25 cm from the subject, was used to record the speech wave on the remaining channel.

Simultaneously, certain acoustic phenomena were registered by means of a pitchmeter and intensity meter (Frøkjær Jensen) and recorded on four channels of a liquid jet oscillograph (Siemens Oscillomink E):

1. integrated intensity
2. speech/silence intervals[9]
3. a duplex oscillogram of the speech wave
4. fundamental frequency.

In addition, time of utterance was marked in 0.1 sec. (Fig. 8.)

The fact that speech is a combination of continuous and discrete characteristics[10] is clearly observable in instrumental analysis and, even in lieu of spectrographic recordings, a reasonably effective basis for the segmentation of an utterance can be provided by the duplex oscillogram because higher frequencies (that is, above 800 Hz) are converted into negative dips of the zero line on the oscillogram. Thus plosive and fricative sounds, for example, become useful reference points for the interpretation of sequential segments of speech. In cases during this investigation where the continuous characteristics of an utterance were more dominant than the discrete ones, it was found useful to analyse separately shorter segments of the item and at a later stage to examine the sense group as a whole. When the sections were joined, extreme care was taken to ensure correspondence with the original oscillographic recording of the utterance. This was essential, as we shall see, in the pause placement investigation where accurate measurement of silent intervals was a crucial feature of the experiment.

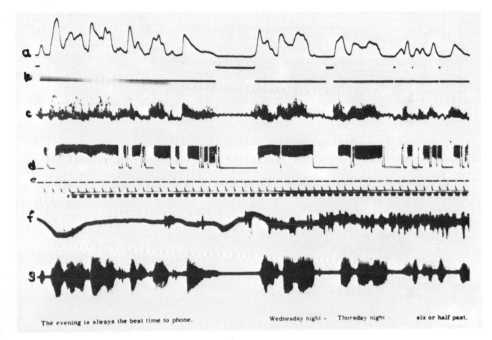

The evening is always the best time to phone.   Wednesday night -   Thursday night -   six or half past.

Figure 8. Oscillographic recording of acoustic parameters and electromyographic record of the internal intercostal muscle activity during native English speaker's utterance.
a = integrated intensity
b = speech/silence
c = duplex oscillogram of speech wave
d = fundamental frequency
e = time marker in 0.1 sec.
f = EMG of internal intercostal muscle.
    The amplitude of the EMG trace in this and succeeding figs. is 150 μV/cm.
g = microphone trace

The fundamental frequency extraction was made by means of high- and low- pass filters which, for most subjects were set at 120 and 60 Hz.

The amplitude envelope of the sound as measured on a Frøkjær Jensen intensity meter was recorded in dB relative to the background, since in measuring the intensity of speech sounds it is the relationship between the sounds which is of interest, rather than the absolute sound level.

Examination of the electromyographic (EMG) records of the internal intercostal muscle activity of all native speakers during connected utterance revealed a characteristic pattern which occurred regularly whether the subject were a native speaker of English speaking the English test items (Figs. 8, 9) or a native speaker of Vietnamese speaking the Vietnamese test items (Fig. 10).

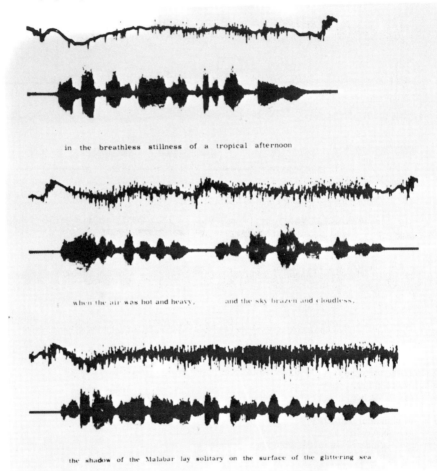

in the breathless stillness of a tropical afternoon

when the air was hot and heavy,   and the sky brazen and cloudless,

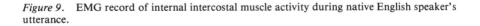

the shadow of the Malabar lay solitary on the surface of the glittering sea

Figure 9.   EMG record of internal intercostal muscle activity during native English speaker's utterance.

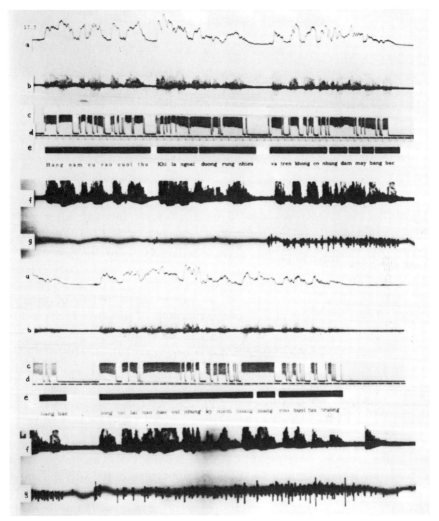

Figure 10. Acoustic parameters and EMG of internal intercostal muscle in native Vietnamese speaker's utterance;

a = integrated intensity
b = duplex oscillogram of speech wave
c = fundamental frequency
d = time marker in 0.1 sec.
e = speech/silence intervals (diagrammatic)
f = microphone trace
g = EMG of internal intercostal muscle.

Note that the EMG pattern is similar to that shown in Figures 8 and 9.

The pattern is represented diagrammatically in Fig. 11.

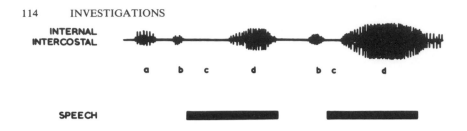

Figure 11. Diagrammatic representation of the EMG activity of the internal intercostal muscle during the utterance of a sentence.

Internal intercostal muscular activity ('a' in Fig. 11) which is apparently associated with a preliminary inspiration occurs prior to the commencement of speech; this activity is followed by a quiescent interval, after which activity again occurs in the form of a localized burst ('b') immediately preceding the onset of speech. [11]

TABLE 2

Means ($\overline{X}$) and standard deviations (SD) of the intervals (in msec) between the onset (A) and termination (B) of the localized bursts of internal intercostal muscle activity and the commencement of speech in each phrase.

	A		B	
	$\overline{X}$	SD	$\overline{X}$	SD
Phrase 1	204.7	56.4	60.0	58.7
Phrase 2	155.1	50.8	18.2	42.3
Phrase 3	198.5	54.4	52.4	28.8

During the first part of the utterance, muscular activity is minimal or absent ('c'), but after a variable period of time, activity ('d') can be observed, progressively increasing until the speaker reaches a point towards the end of his first phrase. Between successive phrases a period of internal intercostal inactivity occurs. Although corresponding in general with the linguistic pause, the EMG pause slightly precedes the former, both at commencement and termination. In subsequent phrases of the·utterance, the EMG activity ('d') is essentially similar to that of the initial phrase except that amplitude and frequency of the action potentials are greater, and the period of relative inactivity ('c') following the preliminary localized burst becomes progressively shorter.

The type of test item apparently had little effect on the EMG responses given by the native subjects, a similar pattern of activity being shown whether the item spoken were nursery rhyme, fabricated equivalent, verse, or prose (Figs. 8, 9, 12, 13). It was also noted that the amount of muscular activity recorded at the end of each item was relatively constant for a given subject despite the varying length of the items.

Other characteristics of the native pattern of internal intercostal muscle activity which were of particular interest in view of the objectives of the experiment include:

(i) a general progressive increase in activity throughout the entire sentence (Figs. 8, 9, 12, 13);

(ii) a progressive decrease in the length of the interval between the commencement of speech and the start of muscular activity until, by the third and subsequent phrases, this interval was usually observed to have disappeared altogether (Figs. 8, 9, 12, 13);

(iii) its reproducibility—repetition of the item by the subject yielded a record remarkably comparable to the original;

(iv) the obvious similarity between the EMG responses to the verse items and their fabricated equivalents (Figs. 12, 13);

(v) the absence of localized bursts of internal intercostal activity associated with the utterance of stressed syllables (Figs. 8, 9, 12, 13).

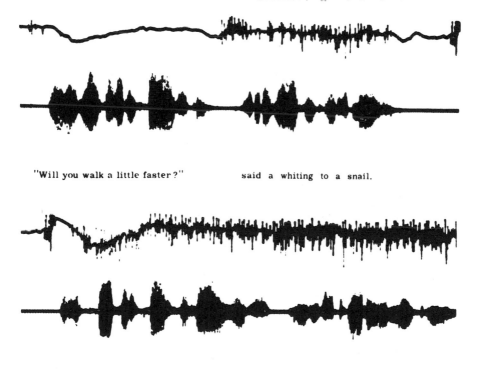

"Will you walk a little faster?"   said a whiting to a snail.

There's a porpoise close behind us,   and he's treading on my tail.

Figure 12.   EMG record of internal intercostal muscle activity during native English speaker's utterance of verse. Note the initial bursts of muscle activity before each phrase and the progressively increasing activity as the sentence proceeds.

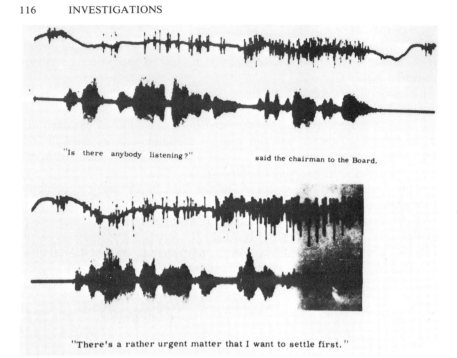

"Is there anybody listening?"   said the chairman to the Board.

"There's a rather urgent matter that I want to settle first."

Figure 13.   EMG record of internal intercostal muscle activity during native English speaker's utterance of item 5, which was fabricated with the same rhythm as the verse illustrated in Fig. 12. Note the similarity of EMG pattern in the two items.

Non-native internal intercostal muscle activity

The EMG pattern of internal intercostal activity used by the non-native subjects, although basically similar[12] to that described above for the native speakers of both English and Vietnamese, exhibited considerable variability. This variability of pattern occurred in the records of all foreign subjects when speaking English.[13] Sometimes, the activity, instead of increasing progressively in the successive phrases of an utterance, remained relatively uniform (Fig. 14).

Such repetitious patterns were most striking in the verse passages and their fabricated equivalents, where "duplications", "triplications", and so on, of the pattern of the first phrase were frequently observed (Fig. 15).

Sometimes, less activity was found in later phrases than in earlier ones. Thus, in an item which a subject divided into three or four parts, more activity might occur in the second, or even in the first part, than in the later parts of the utterance. This feature of non-native internal intercostal activity tended to occur particularly in the prose passages (Figs. 16, 17).

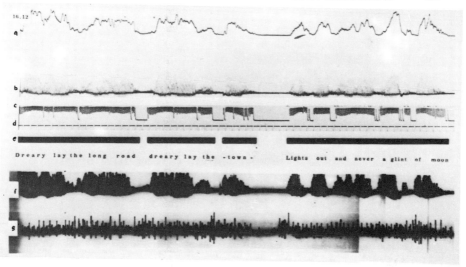

Figure 14. Acoustic parameters and EMG of internal intercostal muscle during non-native speaker's utterance of verse. Traces a-g as Figure 10. The internal intercostal muscle activity is relatively uniform throughout the utterance.

Even within a phrase the activity pattern varied occasionally. At times the greatest activity was seen not at the end of the phrase but at the beginning. Such waxing and waning of activity and repetition of the pattern of the initial phrase in duplicate or triplicate are features which were not observed in any of the records of the native speakers. Although variation of the "native" EMG pattern was observed in the records of the various non-native subjects, it was not possible to relate specific characteristics of EMG patterning to subjects having any particular mother tongue, although characteristic differences might have been revealed had the sample been larger.

It should be emphasized, I think, that in no case—either native or non-native—were localized bursts of activity of the internal intercostal muscle found to correlate with the incidence of stressed syllables.

The effect of pauses on the EMG trace of the internal intercostal muscle appeared to depend upon the duration of the silence. Short periods of silence appeared not to affect the EMG trace (Table 3) which usually continued without even minor interruption (Figs. 8, 10, 12, 14, 15, 16). With longer pauses, however, the EMG pattern showed either decrease or cessation of activity (Figs. 8, 9, 10, 12, 13, 14, 16, 17). Following cessation during a long pause, the resumption of activity in the ensuing phrase was usually heralded by a preliminary burst of muscle action potentials.

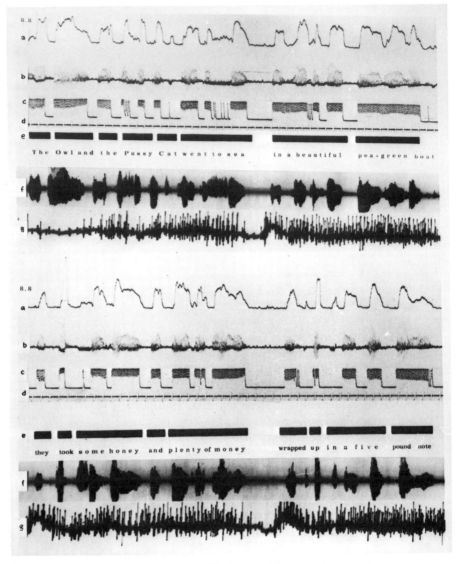

The Owl and the Pussy Cat went to sea   in a beautiful   pea-green boat

they   took s o m e h o n e y   and p l e n t y of m o n e y   wrapped up i n a f i v e   pound note

Figure 15. Acoustic parameters and EMG of internal intercostal muscle during non-native speaker's utterance of verse. Traces a–g as in Figure 10. Note that the pattern of intercostal muscle activity is repeated in successive phrases.

Figure 16. Acoustic parameters and EMG of internal intercostal muscle in non-native speaker's utterance of prose. Traces a–g as in Figure 10. The activity of the internal intercostal muscle does not increase progressively throughout the utterance (see records of native speakers in Figures 8, 9). Pauses are shown in positions which would be abnormal for a native speaker.

In the breath--less s t i l l n e s s of a tropi-cal afternoon   when the air was h o t and h e a v y

a n d h e a v y   and the sky brazen   and cloudless   the shadow   of   the   Malabar   la

the   shadow   of   the   Malabar   lay   soli- - - tary on the sur face of the gli ttering sea

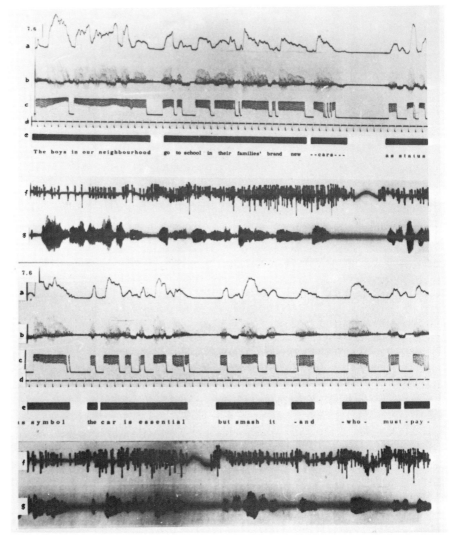

Figure 17. Acoustic parameters and EMG of internal intercostal muscle in Cambodian speaker's utterance of prose.

a = integrated intensity;
b = oscillogram of speech wave;
c = fundamental frequency;
d = time marker in 0.1 sec.;
e = speech/silence intervals (diagrammatic);
f = EMG of internal intercostal muscle;
g = microphone trace.

The EMG activity is variable throughout the utterance. Pauses are shown in positions which would be abnormal for a native English speaker.

TABLE 3

Duration of pauses associated with (A) cessation of EMG activity and (B) no change in activity of the internal intercostal muscle in the speaking of the test items

	A			B			
	N	X̄	SD	N	X̄	SD	t
Native speakers	43	380.5	173.1	47	171.1	115.9	6.7
Non-native speakers	190	287.1	241.5	289	74.4	49.3	14.5

N   = number of observations
X̄   = mean (in msec)
SD = standard deviation of mean

The difference in the means between (A) and (B) is significant in native and non-native speakers at the 0.1% level by t-test.

External intercostal muscle activity

In both native and non-native speakers a somewhat uniform degree of activity was observed from the external intercostal muscle. Some decrease was observable at the end of the longer test items but, by contrast with the internal intercostal muscle, phasal activity producing a distinctive pattern related to speech was not observed in any of the EMG records.

The findings of the EMG investigation will be discussed and related to pause placement following the presentation of results of the pause interval investigation in the next section.

(b) *Pause Interval Investigation*

Differences between native and non-native speakers shown in the EMG recordings were manifested to an even greater extent in the associated oscillographic recordings of the speech/silence intervals.

For the pause interval investigation there were two groups of 11 members each. The native group consisted of the 4 native subjects who had participated in the EMG investigation and 7 additional native speakers—mainly colleagues from the Department of Education University of Sydney—who brought the average age of the native speakers to 38.5 years. The composition of the non-native group was as described in the preceding section for the EMG investigation.

The duration of the pauses was measured from the speech/silence traces. The speech wave was rectified and the rectified output was applied to a comparator. One comparator input was set to a predetermined level to compensate for background noise, the other input of the comparator being connected to the rectified speech wave. When the speech wave input exceeded the reference level an output indicating speech was obtained. Thus intervals of speech and silence were recorded on one of the channels of the oscillograph.

It was arbitrarily decided that periods of silence 50 msec and longer should be regarded as pauses, since 50 msec was the shortest period recorded by any native speaker to mark a phrase boundary. Usually these intervals were confirmed by auditory observation of the recordings. However, occasionally it was found that there was insufficient energy in some of the high-frequency sounds to overcome the attenuation of background noise on the tape, and "silences" were shown on the oscillographic recordings which auditory observation could not verify. It was therefore considered necessary to recheck all pause duration measurements. This was done by re-recording the utterances at 38 cm/sec. (15 ips), playing back at 9.5 cm/sec. (3¾ ips), determining the word boundaries, and then measuring the pause intervals between them. Unconfirmed "silences" were rejected.

Analysis of the pause-interval data revealed certain characteristic features in the utterance of the non-native subjects which constituted a major obstacle to their proficiency in reading aloud. Foremost among these were the large number of pauses made by them,[14] and the relatively high ratio of pause interval time to total duration of utterance in the case of these speakers—differences which were shown by analysis of variance to be statistically significant.

In Table 4 can be seen
1. the mean number of pauses made by each of the subjects;
2. the mean ratios of pause duration to duration of whole item for each subject.

Comparison of the total period of silence in relation to the utterance time for each item by the individual members of both groups may be made by reference to Tables 5 and 6. Marked differences between the two categories of subjects can be seen in their utterance of both prose and verse items.

It will be noted that all the non-native speakers had more mean pauses[15] than any of the native speakers and that on the whole the mean pause-duration ratio was higher in the non-native speakers than in the native speakers. These differences between the two categories of subjects were found to be statistically significant (Table 4).

Qualitative analysis of the pause-interval data revealed that many of the pauses made by the non-native speakers were also inappropriately placed. By contrast with the native speakers' systematic organization of sense groups, the phrasing of the non-native subjects was erratic and in some cases quite haphazard.

TABLE 4

Mean number of pauses and mean ratios of duration of pauses to duration of test item in 11 native speakers of English compared with the corresponding parameters in 11 non-native speakers of English

Subjects	Mean number of pauses		Mean pause/duration of item ratio	
	native speaker	non-native speaker	native speaker	non-native speaker
A	1.2	4.8	0.03	0.13
B	1.7	5.1	0.05	0.16
C	2.6	10.2	0.12	0.19
D	2.7	3.0	0.15	0.07
E	2.3	4.1	0.10	0.10
F	2.0	7.2	0.07	0.13
G	2.3	4.0	0.08	0.10
H	2.3	5.7	0.12	0.12
I	0.8	7.3	0.03	0.17
J	1.3	3.0	0.04	0.11
K	2.3	4.8	0.05	0.12
	21.5	59.2	0.84	1.40

Analysis of variance—Native and non-native speakers

$F = 26.8$
Upper limit $F_{1.10} = 10.04$
$(P = 0.01)$

$F = 7.87$
Upper limit $F_{1.10} = 4.96$
$(P = 0.05)$

TABLE 5

Duration of time of utterance (in sec.) of test items as spoken by 11 native and 11 non-native speakers

NATIVE SPEAKERS

ITEM	A	B	C	D	E	F	G	H	I	J	K
1	4.5	4.1	4.7	4.4	4.9	4.1	4.3	4.5	3.6	4.9	4.4
2	5.8	5.4	6.6	6.1	6.7	5.8	5.9	6.9	5.2	5.8	5.4
3	10.1	8.5	10.1	11.4	11.5	11.5	10.4	10.6	8.8	9.7	8.9
4	9.8	9.5	12.2	10.2	11.3	12.8	10.6	11.4	8.9	9.6	10.0
5	5.6	4.7	5.9	5.1	6.5	6.6	5.4	5.9	4.7	4.9	5.2
6	8.0	7.5	7.4	6.5	9.3	8.3	7.7	8.1	7.0	7.9	7.8

Table 5 (contd.)

ITEM A	B	C	D	E	F	G	H	I	J	K
7	5.2	4.6	5.5	4.2	6.1	6.4	5.1	5.4	4.6	5.6	5.1
8	8.0	5.8	7.2	6.0	7.8	7.4	7.5	7.9	6.3	7.2	6.7
9	3.5	3.0	3.8	3.0	3.8	3.4	3.2	3.8	3.1	3.5	3.5
10	4.2	3.3	4.2	3.5	4.2	4.5	3.9	4.1	3.5	3.9	3.8
11	4.9	4.1	4.9	4.3	6.0	5.8	4.4	4.9	4.0	4.8	4.3
12	5.3	4.2	5.1	4.6	6.2	6.2	4.8	4.6	4.3	5.0	4.4

NON-NATIVE SPEAKERS

ITEM A	B	C	D	E	F	G	H	I	J	K
1	4.9	5.5	5.2	4.8	4.7	5.1	5.6	5.0	5.9	5.3	4.5
2	7.8	7.0	8.0	6.8	7.2	7.7	9.1	8.5	7.8	6.5	7.5
3	13.3	11.7	13.4	11.1	10.8	11.0	11.9	12.0	11.4	10.6	12.9
4	14.2	13.7	15.0	11.9	12.5	11.0	12.4	14.9	13.1	11.0	14.9
5	7.8	6.4	7.5	6.5	6.1	6.5	6.9	7.1	8.2	5.7	7.3
6	9.8	8.8	10.4	8.8	8.5	9.3	9.2	9.7	10.9	7.4	10.6
7	6.3	6.2	7.1	5.4	5.7	5.4	6.4	5.5	6.6	6.2	6.7
8	9.3	8.0	10.6	7.7	8.5	8.3	9.0	9.4	9.9	8.8	9.8
9	4.2	3.5	4.4	3.8	3.6	3.7	4.1	3.7	4.2	3.7	3.9
10	4.5	4.3	5.5	3.8	4.1	4.2	4.7	4.7	5.4	4.2	4.7
11	5.8	5.2	5.3	5.1	5.0	5.6	6.4	6.2	5.8	5.6	6.5
12	5.6	5.3	5.9	5.3	5.4	5.7	6.2	6.3	5.5	5.1	6.1

TABLE 6

Total duration of pauses (in msec) in each item as spoken by 11 native and 11 non-native speakers

NATIVE SPEAKERS

ITEM A	B	C	D	E	F	G	H	I	J	K
1	0	150	800	825	175	400	450	75	0	350	325
2	0	625	925	1275	575	450	550	175	0	325	100
3	375	75	625	2050	1085	440	1500	1300	0	150	200
4	400	175	1700	1675	725	550	1420	1735	0	0	480
5	200	300	625	675	825	425	650	1200	450	300	200
6	400	425	925	950	1350	640	0	725	375	400	310
7	175	340	710	450	850	600	600	1175	375	315	400
8	425	390	700	725	500	430	615	750	450	250	625
9	0	50	225	260	150	0	0	125	0	125	100
10	175	50	350	250	200	325	225	620	100	75	75
11	225	350	925	750	50	575	175	1150	50	250	200
12	250	150	625	775	535	190	575	1185	0	225	150

NON-NATIVE SPEAKERS

ITEM A	B	C	D	E	F	G	H	I	J	K
1	500	1200	1175	200	485	850	425	650	1500	450	325
2	840	1085	1705	600	800	865	1140	1315	1225	350	750
3	1625	1995	2730	805	875	815	1135	1475	1175	1275	1250
4	2245	2085	3205	720	950	765	1310	2205	1775	1050	2125
5	950	1400	1230	475	555	1050	845	760	1625	700	1375
6	1585	1525	2020	1110	875	1900	985	1270	2800	650	1560
7	750	1015	1505	360	575	800	760	675	1050	1050	925
8	2090	760	2115	640	885	1075	900	1275	1825	2135	1400
9	325	350	555	⁻75	200	250	0	225	325	50	100
10	535	475	1270	50	440	350	300	380	1150	450	275
11	1145	975	865	680	700	1000	1040	875	875	350	1000
12	605	650	960	495	480	600	425	760	600	450	850

TABLE 7
Number of pauses made by 11 native and 11 non-native speakers in each item

NATIVE SPEAKERS

ITEM A	B	C	D	E	F	G	H	I	J	K
1	0	1	4	4	1	1	2	1	0	2	3
2	0	3	3	3	3	1	2	1	0	1	1
3	1	1	2	4	4	3	4	4	0	2	1
4	2	2	7	5	2	3	5	6	0	0	5
5	1	1	1	2	2	2	3	1	1	1	1
6	1	1	3	2	4	2	0	2	2	2	2
7	3	3	3	3	3	3	3	4	2	2	4
8	1	2	2	3	2	2	2	1	1	1	5
9	0	1	1	1	1	0	0	1	0	1	1
10	1	1	1	1	1	2	2	2	2	1	1
11	2	2	2	2	2	2	1	1	1	1	1
12	2	2	2	2	3	3	3	4	0	1	2

NON-NATIVE SPEAKERS

ITEM A	B	C	D	E	F	G	H	I	J	K
1	3	5	8	2	4	5	4	6	6	2	4
2	4	4	8	4	3	6	4	9	10	3	3
3	6	9	20	4	7	12	5	8	8	4	6
4	7	14	24	5	7	11	9	13	12	4	8

Table 7 (contd.)

ITEM A		B	C	D	E	F	G	H	I	J	K
5	3	4	4	1	2	7	3	3	9	1	4
6	6	7	12	5	5	12	5	7	10	3	11
7	4	3	7	4	3	6	3	5	5	3	4
8	12	4	16	4	5	10	4	6	13	9	5
9	1	2	5	1	1	2	0	1	3	1	1
10	3	3	7	1	5	3	2	3	3	2	2
11	5	4	5	3	3	7	5	4	4	2	4
12	4	2	6	2	4	5	4	3	5	2	6

Examination of the pause placement used in the following interpretations of items 3 and 4, for instance, shows that the subjects concerned failed completely to observe the principle of constituent structure in their utterance of these passages:

(3) In the / breath / less / stillness / of a / tropi / cal afternoon / when the air was / hot / and heavy / and the sky brazen / and / cloudless / the shadow of the *Malabar* / lay soli / tary on the sur / face / of / the / glit / tering sea. /.

(4) When I asked / her / what she / would have done / if he had spo / ken to her in the street / she / smiled / and said / that / as she seldom / walked / in that direction / it didn't seem like / ly that / he / would / have much / oppor / tuni / ty / ever / to speak / to her. /.

It will be observed that determiners are separated from noun phrases, attributive and predicative adjectives from their constituent noun and verbs, nominative pronouns and oblique pronouns from their verbs, and conjunctions from their related clauses. This kind of indiscriminate pausing resulted in the grouping of words regardless of their syntactic function, and division into such nonsensical phrases as: *In the, and the sky brazen, lay soli-, tary on the sur-, when the air was* (Fig. 16).

Even in the verse items in which it might be expected that the strongly metrical rhythm would serve as a cue to appropriate phrasing, pause placement was found to be faulty in the utterance of the non-native speakers. Examples such as the following were common:

(2) Will you walk a li / ttle faster / said a whi / ting to a snail. / There's a / por / poise / close behind us / and he's / treading on my / tail. /.

(8) The / Owl and / the / Pussy / Cat / went to sea / in a beautiful / pea green boat. /. They / took / some honey / and / plenty of money / wrapped / up / in a five / pound note. /. (Fig. 15.)

Pauses were also misused at the phonological level. Whereas the native English speaker establishes word and syllable boundaries by means of subtle phonetic differentiation; such as, lengthening and reducing of segmental phonemes, stress and pitch change, several of the non-native speakers in this investigation used short pauses to signal *open* and *close* juncture. The term *pause* is used here, therefore, to subsume both the intervals of silence separating speech groups and the transitional phenomena used to catenate the smaller linguistic units.

An example of a Vietnamese subject's strategy in coping with transition features is shown in Fig. 18. This subject took 5.2 seconds to utter the 21 syllables of the rhyme. Characteristically, he used abnormally long junctures between syllables; for example, /ma + ket/-/ʒi + ge + ti +ʒig/, so that the auditory impression given was of a series of discrete linguistic units rather than of smooth transitions from sound to sound at the syllable boundaries. Typically, his release of voiceless plosives was delayed, and, when release did occur, the sound was uttered as the first phoneme of an extra syllable which was followed by a pause. In positions where the native speaker would use an unreleased plosive; for example, *fat pig*, there was often omission of the sound altogether.

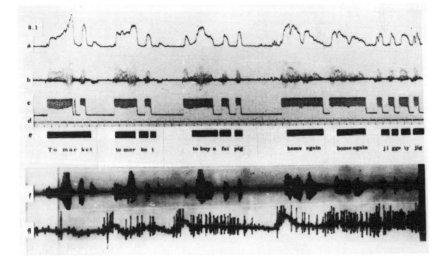

Figure 18. Acoustic parameters and EMG of internal intercostal muscle in non-native speaker's utterance of nursery rhyme. Traces a–g as in Figure 10. Unusual pause placement is shown at syllable and word boundaries. Major linguistic pauses are associated with decreased EMG activity; minor pauses have no effect. Duration, 5.2 sec.

Interpretations of the same item by two native speakers are shown for comparison in Figs. 19 and 20. The subject whose oscillographic recording is given in Fig. 19 made only one pause (of 150 msec.) between the two intervals of the obviously bipartite item, but the second, (Fig. 20) in addition to making this typical binary division, adjusted the length of the pauses between his rhythm groups to produce two completely isochronous sub-sections in the first interval. The duration of the second phrase was 1.9 sec. and of the first, 2.0 sec. However, the subject paused for 100 msec. after *market* within the first interval, and by this means marked the equal time period taken to say each section of the interval. Duration of the medial pause was 350 msec.

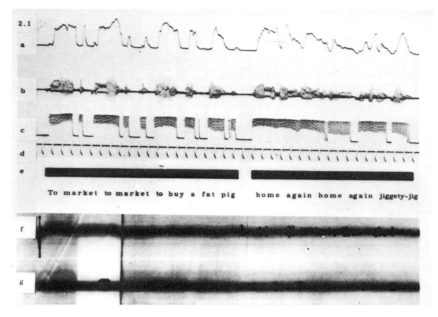

Figure 19.   Acoustic parameters and EMG of internal intercostal muscle in native speaker's utterance of nursery rhyme. Traces a-g as in Figure 17. This (native) speaker has made only one medial pause (cf. Figure 18). Duration, 4.1 sec.

The short pause was also used by the non-native speakers where sounds were elided: thus *she smiled* (item 4) frequently became *she smi'; lights out* (item 12) became *li' out*, etc. In the medial position also, frequent elision was observed; for example, *whiting* (item 2) became *whi'ing; likely* (item 4) became *li'ly*; and *sixteen* (item 10) became *si'teen*. Where homorganic clusters included a nasal consonant, the nasal was often articulated and the final consonant omitted; for example, *want* (item 10) was often uttered as *wan'*.

From the linguistic point of view, the numerous pauses made by the non-native speakers are of considerable interest because they were used not only to delimit sense groups and rhythm groups, but also to replace at times the linking mechanisms ordinarily used by native speakers to indicate word and syllable boundaries in connected speech.

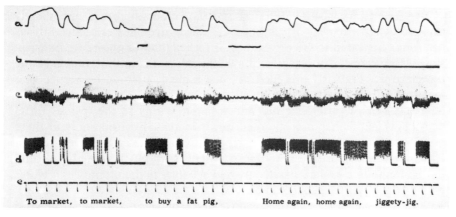

Figure 20. Oscillographic recording of acoustic parameters in native speaker's utterance of nursery rhyme. Traces a-e as in Figure 8. This speaker has made a typical binary division and, in addition, has equalized the two sub-sections of the first interval by means of a short pause. Duration, 4.3 sec.

(c) *The Relationship Between Expiratory Muscular Activity and Pause Placement*

The function of the intercostal muscles in man has been disputed over the centuries by opposing schools of anatomists,[16] some of whom have regarded both the internal and external muscles as inspiratory, while others have believed both sets to be expiratory. The most popular theory, however, seems to have associated the external intercostal with inspiration and the internal intercostal with expiration (this view, as we have seen, was held by Stetson), but few authorities have supported the reverse view. An alternative and more recent suggestion has been that both sets of muscles serve not to move the ribs but rather to regulate the tension in the intercostal spaces. However, following the work of Taylor,[17] it is now fairly definite that the external intercostal and the parasternal part of the internal intercostal muscle are inspiratory in man, while the remainder of the internal intercostal muscle is expiratory.[18]

In the investigation reported here, the posterior electrode was inserted into the intercostal space medial to the angles of the ribs, a site at which the internal intercostal is not present, and therefore it is known for certain that the activity recorded was from the external intercostal muscle (Fig. 7). The reciprocal results obtained with the two recording electrodes and the technique of insertion of the lateral electrode likewise suggest that the lateral electrode was recording from the internal intercostal muscle (Fig. 7).

The discovery of a characteristic "native" pattern of internal intercostal activity during connected speech and of the deviations from this pattern made by non-native speakers of English is of considerable physiological and psycholinguistic interest.

The preliminary localized burst of activity commonly found immediately prior to commencement of speech in the successive phrases of the various test items appeared to be physiological rather than linguisitc in function since, irrespective of the degree of syllabic stress, the initial syllable of the utterance was regularly preceded by such a burst. It could be argued that localized bursts synchronous with stressed syllables might be present in the later parts of the utterance but not apparent owing to the overall EMG activity which, as has been pointed out,[19] increased considerably in these positions. It must be noted, however, that even in the early phrases, when EMG activity was usually minimal or absent, such bursts of activity could not be found in association with stressed syllables in the utterance of either native or non-native speakers.

Even in the records of subjects whose first language was syllable-timed, it was still not possible to relate localized bursts of internal intercostal activity to particular syllables—either when these subjects spoke in English or in their mother tongue. It would seem, therefore, that there is a fundamental distinction between the internal intercostal activity associated with repeated isolated stressed syllables[20] and that which occurs in connected speech.

These findings indicate that the preliminary burst is associated with the onset of speech rather than with the degree of stress on the initial syllable. It is suggested that this burst of activity may be related to the necessity of the speaker to raise his intrathoracic pressure to the level required to overcome the resistance of the glottis preparatory to commencement of speech. The progressive overall increase in activity throughout the whole item is interpreted as an indication that greater expiratory muscular activity is required to maintain the intrathoracic pressure at an appropriate level for speech despite the steadily decreasing lung volume. Moreover, the minimal internal intercostal muscle activity observed in the initial phrases of the utterance ('c' in Fig. 11) would be explained if the expiration associated with the speaking of this part of the sentence were passive and due to elastic recoil of the lungs.[21]

It has been shown that long pauses in the utterance of both the native and the non-native speakers were accompanied by diminution or cessation of internal intercostal muscle activity, whereas shorter pauses usually had little or no effect on the EMG trace. It is possible that some degree of inspiration normally accompanies such long pauses, and this would account for the decreased internal intercostal activity when speech recommenced. If that were so, the progressively shorter period of muscle inactivity in the early part of successive phrases suggests that these inspirations might boost the lung volume to a progressively lower level as the item proceeded. In addition, it has also been observed that the degree of internal intercostal muscle activity was more or less uniform at the end of all the items spoken by a given subject, despite the considerable variation in the length of the items.

This may indicate that the lung volume by the end of each item uttered by the subject was relatively constant.

These interpretations of expiratory muscle activity on the basis of respiratory physiology must be regarded as entirely tentative, since no qualitative or quantitative estimations of air flow were performed. However, if the explanations suggested in the previous paragraph prove to be reasonably accurate, it would follow that the native speaker subconsciously plans in advance the depth of preliminary and subsequent inspirations in relation to the length and, presumably, the volume level of his utterance. At the same time, linguistic constraints require of the speaker a certain degree of conformity in his organization of words. Thus, although as Pulgram[22] shows, different speakers may divide a text in different ways according to individual interpretation and still maintain a credible native rhythm pattern, if their interpretation is the same it follows that their organization of the several units of the sequence must be identical. The native speaker's linguistic competence therefore implies a detailed cerebral programming of the utterance.

It may further be postulated that many of the abnormalities observed in the EMG records of the non-native subjects speaking English may be associated with a difficulty in programming the utterance—presumably as a result of their relative unfamiliarity with the language. Thus, the tendency of some of the non-native subjects to duplicate successive phrases suggests that the inspiration taken during the longer pauses boosted their lung volume to the level present at commencement of the utterance. This could mean that such speakers were treating each section of the item between the longer pauses as a totality, rather than as a segment of the whole utterance.

The frequent failure of the internal intercostal muscle activity to increase progressively throughout the phrase and the whole utterance (a feature which was so marked in the EMG records of the native speakers), as well as the overall variability of the non-native speakers' traces, might further suggest a degree of uncertainty in their interpretation of the items, particularly of the more complex prose ones in which they were not assisted by the linear arrangement of the item. In this way, comparison of the relative ability of the native and non-native speakers to adjust their respiratory action according to the requirements for effective utterance disclosed the inchoate psycholinguistic implications of the investigation.

In connection with a possible relationship between programming of respiratory function and efficient performance in speech, it may be significant that the subject whose EMG records exhibited the longest periods of initial internal intercostal muscle inactivity (a native speaker) was both a trained singer and an experienced public speaker whose breath control and phrasing would be expected to be of a high order. This greater degree of expiratory control during speech may be assumed to be associated with more economical use of the expired air and, possibly, with a deeper preliminary inspiration—both resulting from more efficient cerebral programming.

On the other hand, the unusual (by the native English speaker's standards) placement of pauses and inept phrasing by the non-native speakers suggest that they had not grasped the principle of unitizing sequences of words in conformity with the rules of the language—an indication of their less efficient programming. As teachers of English, they must certainly have been aware of the hierarchical structure of the texts, yet frequently their performance did not attest to their knowledge of the rules, since by their use of numerous and inappropriately placed pauses, they failed in many instances to demarcate the several sense groups of a given item and, as a result, were likewise unsuccessful in conveying the single idea contained in each.

It is very likely that the subjects whose records showed such unsatisfactory phrasing had learned English on the basis of isolate word forms. This, I believe, could account for their tendency, when faced with unfamiliar material, to emphasize the separable identity of both word and syllable; for, despite their knowledge of the structural patterns of English, at the spoken level they were obviously unable to mark catenation features by the usual phonetic cues—nor were they able to modify the isolate-form identity of words in context according to the conventions of the spoken language. Thus, whereas *open juncture* and *close transition* are accomplished in native English pronunciation without any break in the flow of speech, the non-native subjects tended, as we have seen, to use short pauses to mark both word and syllable boundaries (Figs. 17, 18).

It may further be noted that in no case was a non-native subject able to equalize the duration of the two sections of a traditional nursery rhyme—as was the native speaker whose interpretation of *To Market, To Market* is shown in Fig. 20. Whereas the native speaker effects this balance by adjusting the length of his pauses between word groups,[23] the foreign speaker's inability to control these intervals suggests influence exerted by a syllable-timed first language.

Not observable in these recordings are the subjects' use of strong forms in unstressed positions; for example, /ænd/-/tu maket/. The very common failure of the non-native speakers in this investigation to apply the principle of *gradation* to their utterance was, in large measure, responsible for their inability to produce anything like native-sounding rhythm groups in which the rhythmic pattern is achieved by means of qualitative and quantitative adjustment of unstressed syllables about a fully stressed hub syllable. In particular, the lengthening of syllables normally unstressed contributed markedly to an impression of syllable-timed rhythm—a further instance of L_1 interference.

The considerable delay between the utterance of vowel and final voiceless plosive in such words as *market* (Fig. 18) could have been associated with the desire of some subjects to pay special attention to aspiration of the fortis series /p,t,k/, especially if aspiration of these phonemes were not obligatory in their native language—not perhaps realizing that the native English speaker frequently produces either unreleased or weakly aspirated plosives in the final position in free variation with the fully released variety.

It is also possible that the non-native speakers' difficulty with voiceless plosives in the medial position could be traced to L_1 interference. In the first language of some of the foreign subjects, the glottal stop is regularly used both in this and in the final position. However, aware that glottal plosives are not phonemically distinctive in English, it is quite likely that confusion led them to substitute not the glottal stop for /p,t,k/ but the short pause.

Yet another example of L_1 interference may be cited. Consonantal clusters are non-existent in the first language of several of the subjects used in this investigation, and being unused to managing the articulation of sequences of contiguous consonants, they tended not merely to elide them (as indeed a native speaker might do in rapid colloquial speech) but to pause briefly before going on to produce the following syllable—by this means breaking the unity of the rhythm group.

Conversely, clusters were sometimes characterized by insertion of a transitional sound between two successive consonants—a Svarabhakti vowel—which frequently occurred in non-native subjects' utterance of *please*, [pəliz]; *close*, [kələʊs]; and *school*, [səkul]. The effect of this additional vowel was to produce an extra syllable, thus further complicating the speakers' rhythmic patterns.

It would seem, then, that the non-native subjects' faulty organization and timing of rhythm groups which resulted in the anomalies discussed above could be attributed to several factors:

1. the nature of the subjects' first language;
2. the subjects' method of learning English;
3. the subjects' lack of experience in speaking English.

Since the first language of a number of the non-native speakers was characterized by open syllables, uniform syllable duration, and phonemic distinctions which in English constitute only allophonic variation, these subjects experienced difficulty in producing consonant clusters, aspirated plosives, and syllables which varied in duration according to their position in the rhythm group.[24] While the duration of the vowel nucleus was usually responsible for syllable uniformity, it sometimes happened that consonantal substitutions also contributed to this effect; for example, the use of plosives for fricatives (substitution of /d/ for /ð/, etc.), and fricatives for affricates (substitution of /ʃ/ for/tʃ/, etc.).

It is suggested that although faulty techniques in learning English could have been responsible for some of the mistakes of these speakers, it is quite likely that the subjects whose records showed a considerable number of inappropriately placed pauses were either less able linguistically or less experienced in their speaking of English—despite their acquaintance with the language as teachers. The results of this investigation would therefore suggest that literary study of a language (in this case, of English) is inadequate as a means of preparing the non-native teacher to deal with the several systems of the phonological component of his subject.

While there is reason to believe that the nature of the foreign subjects' first language contributed to their abnormal rhythm when speaking English, the differences in the EMG pattern of the internal intercostal muscular activity between the native and the non-native speakers could not be attributed to this cause. Similar deviations from the native EMG pattern were found in the records of all the non-native subjects when speaking English. Furthermore, the speakers of a syllable-timed language used a native-type pattern of internal intercostal activity when using their own language. When speaking English, however, the less fluent non-native speakers, whatever their mother tonque, exhibited quite markedly the EMG features outlined above as "non-native", whereas the better non-native speakers—irrespective of their first language—manifested these features to a considerably less extent. In the absence of further evidence, therefore, it would seem that lack of proficiency in English is of greater significance than the nature of the first language in accounting for a foreign speaker's deviations from the native-type expiratory muscular activity pattern.

Of localized bursts of internal intercostal muscular activity synchronous with the utterance of stressed syllables there was no trace—either in the records of the native speakers or in those of any one of the non-native speakers with their syllable-timed first language. The argument that such localized bursts on stressed syllables might be present in the latter part of each phrase but not apparent because of the overall EMG activity occurring at those times cannot be maintained, since, as we have noted, even in the early parts of the initial and second phrases when EMG activity was minimal or absent, such bursts of activity were not found to be associated with individual syllables—either stressed or unstressed.

Having thus established that increased expiratory muscular activity could not be correlated with syllabic stress in connected speech, my next step was to examine the relationship of some acoustic parameters to perceived stress. If certain words of an utterance are perceived as stressed by the listener the question still remained, what does the speaker *do* to create this impression?

CHAPTER SIX

Acoustic Parameters

In view of the negative results of the EMG investigation of the physiological mechanism believed to be involved in the production of stress, it seemed that my search for the correlates of this feature must surely extend to examination of the acoustic parameters generally regarded as cues to its perception.

As we have seen, it has now been fairly well established that the most consistent acoustic correlates of stress are fundamental frequency, amplitude (or, intensity), and duration, and that, as McClean and Tiffany[1] summarize, in relation to unstressed syllables stressed syllables have increased magnitudes of these parameters. However, although it is generally recognized that no one-to-one correspondence exists between stress and any single acoustic parameter,[2] there is still considerable speculation regarding which of them predominates as a cue,[3] and it would seem that the precise nature of the complex trading relationships[4] between fundamental frequency, amplitude, and duration has not been positively determined for native speakers of English much less even considered for non-native speakers of the language. Yet if the objectives of this study presently reported (examination of the phonetic nature of stress in relation to English speech rhythm, and of the problems associated with the foreign learner's acquisition of stress-timed rhythm) were to be realized, it was felt that analysis of these acoustic parameters in the connected utterance of native and non-native speakers must be the *sine qua non* of any further investigation.

The parameters investigated in this phase of the study, then, were fundamental frequency, envelope amplitude, and duration, which are perceived as pitch, loudness, and length respectively. Again, the instruments used were the Frøkjær-Jensen pitchmeter and intensity meter which recorded these parameters, and the Oscillomink E which displayed them together with time of utterance marked in 0.1 sec.

Sixteen subjects were used in this investigation—8 native speakers of English, and 8 non-native speakers whose native languages were Vietnamese, Bengali, Indonesian, and Cambodian. The test material consisted of the English items set out above in the report on the auditory perception test.

It has been stated that *amplitude*—rather than *intensity*—was measured in this investigation. In view of the fact that these terms are frequently used synonymously in the literature, this exactitude may seem somewhat pedantic. However, the phenomena which they signify are not identical and for this reason the distinction has been observed. According to Fant,[5]

> The term amplitude refers to the instantaneous or time average value of sound pressure, volume velocity, or particle velocity at a particular point in the sound field, or to the corresponding voltages or currents as delivered by a microphone. Any particular numerical value of the amplified, filtered and by other means processed version of this electrical copy of the acoustic wave is also referred to by the term amplitude.
>
> Sound intensity is the energy per unit time transmitted through a unit area. In the *cgs* system, which is the most common reference system in the acoustic literature, . . . the unit of intensity is erg per second per square centimeter. Once such unit is 10^{-7} *watts/cm²*. In a plane or spherical free-progressive sound wave the intensity in the direction of the propagation is
>
> $$W = P^2/qc \; erg\text{-}sec\text{—}^1/cm^2,$$ \hfill (A.1-1)
>
> Speech intensity is almost never measured directly. Pressure-sensitive microphones are utilized and the intensity, if of any interest, is calculated by means of *Eq. A 1-1*. Amplitude and intensity have become synonymous in a general sense because of this one-to-one correspondence. Sound pressure or intensity data are generally specified on a logarithmic scale with the unit decibel (dB) relative to a fixed reference.[6]

The fixed reference in this study was the level of non-speech or ambient sound. Thus any rise in the amplitude of the sound wave envelope was measured relative to this level and not from absolute silence or the threshold of hearing.

The syllables judged as stressed by the adjudicators used in the auditory perception experiment were located on the oscillograms, underlined, and marked off, as can be observed in Figs. 21 and 22, by vertical lines.

Measurements were then taken of the fundamental frequency, amplitude, and duration of each stressed syllable. At a later stage, measurements were also taken of these parameters in a random selection of the same syllables which had not been stressed. This procedure was necessary in order to avoid the possibility of intrinsic intensity and fundamental frequency obscuring

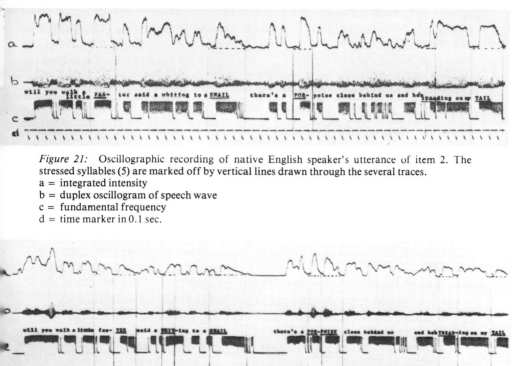

Figure 21: Oscillographic recording of native English speaker's utterance of item 2. The stressed syllables (5) are marked off by vertical lines drawn through the several traces.
a = integrated intensity
b = duplex oscillogram of speech wave
c = fundamental frequency
d = time marker in 0.1 sec.

Figure 22: Oscillographic recording of non-native speaker's utterance of item 2. The stressed syllables (8) are marked off by vertical lines drawn through the several traces. Traces a-c as in Figure 21.

the changes due to stress alone. Obviously, vowel amplitudes are affected by changes in phonetic quality and thus the intensity of a vowel can serve as a cue to stress, as Lehiste points out,[7] only when the vowels of identical spectral structure are being compared. Not only this. As McClean and Tiffany have shown,[8] the position of the syllable within the phrase is a significant conditioner of both fundamental frequency and duration. Thus it was essential that the same syllables in identical contexts should be selected for comparison.

In determining the fundamental frequency, amplitude, and duration, of $home_1$ (item 1, *Home again, home again*), for example, these parameters were measured in both stressed and unstressed versions of the word. It was found, incidentally, that this word was stressed by four native and four non-native speakers, and unstressed in the readings of the remaining subjects. Again, in determining the values of the same parameters in the first syllable (*por-*) of the word *porpoise* (item 2, *There's a porpoise close behind us*), both stressed and unstressed versions of the syllable were measured. The word *porpoise* was given sentence stress by five of the native and seven of the non-native subjects. However, two of the latter stressed both syllables of the word, (Fig. 22) and two placed the stress on the second syllable rather than on the first. Thus the syllable *por-* was analysed as stressed in 10 cases and unstressed in 6 cases.

Generally, the syllable boundaries were determined by reference to a drop in the intensity trace since a period of relative silence usually occurred between the syllables. However, segmentation was sometimes performed by reference to the oscillogram of the speech wave itself or to the fundamental frequency trace.[9] In this investigation, every syllable—stressed and un-stressed—selected for analysis was regarded in the first instance as a linguistic unit, and therefore the acoustic investigation presupposed phonological determination of syllable boundaries.

This accords with the view of von Essen, noted by Kloster Jensen,[10] "Die phonetische Silbe wird also von der mit anderen Methoden bestimmten Silbe abhängig gemacht."[11] As Kloster Jensen himself says,[12] the syllable peak has to be found by quite different criteria from those by which the syllable boundaries are determined. This, because the syllable is a hybrid. As he points out, "Sie hat einen phonetischen Kern und phonemisch und distributionell bestimmte Grenzen."[13]

It seemed to me, therefore, that the whole syllable, rather than the syllable nucleus alone,[14] should be measured. While vowel quality differences may have particular significance in stress judgments, there are nevertheless some features of consonant quality; for example, strength of friction, aspiration, sharpness of onset, increased duration, etc., which are likewise capable of influencing the listener's perception of stress. For this reason, all syllables selected for analysis were measured from onset of the first sound to termination of the last, the precise points having been located by rolling the tape backwards and forwards over the playback head.[15]

Having thus segmented the 192 separate oscillographic recordings used in this phase of the study, I proceeded to measure the fundamental frequency, amplitude, and duration of each of the stressed syllables and a randomly selected sample of the same syllables which had not been stressed.

Five patterns of fundamental frequency variation consistently occurred in the utterance of both native and non-native subjects. While it would have been possible to have classified these systematic variations more precisely,[16] it was felt that the direction of the perceived pitch movement rather than the relative level of the tone was of greater importance in this investigation, and thus all rising fundamental frequency (F_0) glides were subsumed under *Type I*, all falling glides under *Type II*, rising-falling glides under *Type III*, and falling-rising glides under *Type IV*. In addition, a level tone occurred often enough to be classified as *Type V*.

For *Type I* three measurements were taken:
(i) the initial level of the fundamental frequency
(ii) the end level
(iii) the amount of rise
For *Type II* three measurements were likewise taken:
(i) initial level
(ii) end level
(iii) amount of fall
For *Types III and IV* five measurements were taken:
(i) initial level
(ii) peak (Type III)/ trough (Type IV) level
(iii) end level
(iv) amount of rise (Type III)/ fall (Type (IV)
(v) amount of fall (Type III)/ rise (Type IV)
For *Type V* a single measurement was taken of the level of the fundamental frequency on the syllable.

These patterns are represented diagrammatically in Fig. 23.

The means and standard deviations of these several types of fundamental frequency variation are shown in Tables 8a and 8b. The relatively high incidence of *Type I* and *Type II* in both native and non-native speakers should be noted. It may also be observed that the *Type IV* pattern is rare in both native and non-native speakers, but particularly so in both groups' utterance of unstressed syllables. The *Type II* pattern is seen to occur more frequently on stressed than on unstressed syllables in the utterance of native speakers, although this does not apply to the non-native speakers. *Type III* did not occur very frequently in the utterance of either group, although reference to Table 8b will show that 16% of the stressed syllables spoken by the non-native subjects were of this pattern.

In the vast majority (96%) of the syllables analysed, amplitude followed a simple rise-fall pattern. Other types of amplitude recordings were so infrequent that they were disregarded for the purpose of this analysis.

NATIVE SPEAKERS
Fundamental frequency
The mean measurements taken of the initial level and the end level in *Type I* and *Type II* were higher in the former and lower in the latter for stressed than for unstressed syllables. Furthermore, the amount of rise in *Type I* and fall in *Type II* was found to be greater in stressed than in unstressed syllables. The significance levels of these differences are indicated in Table 8a. In *Type III* all five measurements were significantly greater in stressed than in unstressed syllables. Comparison could not be made in the case of *Type IV* since the incidence of this pattern, particularly

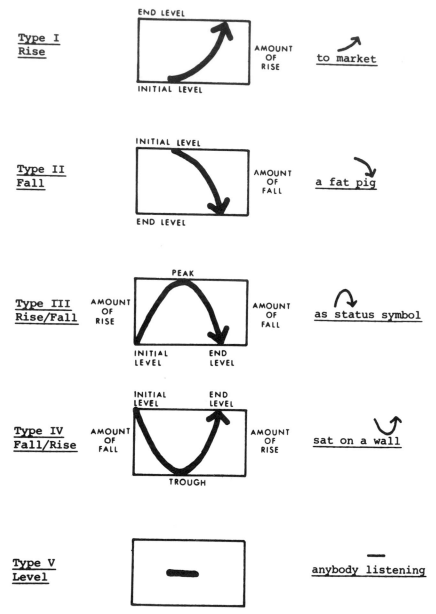

Figure 23. Diagrammatic representation of the five patterns of fundamental frequency variation found in the utterance of 8 native and 8 non-native speakers of English. System of notation adapted from Corinne Adams, (1969), *loc. cit.*, pp. 109, 112.

TABLE 8

Means ($\overline{X}$) and standard deviations (SD) of the fundamental frequency (in Hz) of stressed and unstressed syllables in native and non-native speakers of English, and t-tests showing the significance of the difference between stressed and unstressed syllables

(a) *NATIVE SPEAKERS*

	Unstressed Syllables			Stressed Syllables			
	N	$\overline{X}$	SD	N	$\overline{X}$	SD	t
Type I							
initial level	51 (44%)	137.3	19.8	106 (25%)	142.2	18.5	+ 1.50
end level	51	170.1	21.3	106	177.6	20.6	+ 2.09*
amount of rise	51	32.8	22.7	106	35.4	17.9	+ 0.77
Type II							
initial level	38 (32%)	163.0	18.7	201 (48%)	152.7	20.0	−2.92**
end level	38	128.3	36.6	201	108.1	20.8	−4.73***
amount of fall	38	34.7	18.9	201	44.6	20.7	+ 2.72**
Type III							
initial level	16 (14%)	124.4	8.0	53 (13%)	147.5	18.1	+ 4.88***
peak	16	144.7	11.6	53	181.0	24.8	+ 5.58***
end level	16	123.7	13.3	53	148.6	29.8	+ 3.19**
amount of rise	16	20.3	6.0	53	33.6	20.7	+ 2.50*
amount of fall	16	20.9	7.5	53	32.5	18.7	+ 2.38*
Type IV							
initial level	1 (1%)	150	0	26 (6%)	171.2	17.7	+ 1.15
trough	1	110	0	26	133.5	19.5	+ 1.15
end level	1	170	0	26	167.9	22.6	−0.08
amount of fall	1	40	0	26	37.7	18.3	−0.12
amount of rise	1	60	0	26	34.6	13.7	−1.78
Type V							
level	11 (9%)	122.3	11.3	30 (7%)	129.5	17.9	+ 1.21

N = number of syllables

+ = relevant parameter of stressed syllable > that of unstressed syllable

− = relevant parameter of stressed syllable < that of unstressed syllable

*, **, *** = significance at 5 per cent, 1 per cent, and 0.1 per cent levels respectively.

TABLE 8

Means ($\overline{X}$) and standard deviations (SD) of the fundamental frequency (in Hz) of stressed and unstressed syllables in native and non-native speakers of English, and t-tests showing the significance of the difference between stressed and unstressed syllables

(b)   *NON-NATIVE SPEAKERS*

	Unstressed Syllables			Stressed Syllables			
	N	X̄	SD	N	X̄	SD	t
Type I							
initial level	63 (27%)	147.9	24.1	208 (32%)	154.9	18.2	+ 2.45*
end level	63	173.5	23.1	208	186.5	22.1	+ 4.03***
amount of rise	63	25.6	18.5	208	31.6	19.7	+ 2.13*
Type II							
initial level	91 (39%)	156.2	24.2	205 (31%)	163.8	18.2	+ 2.97**
end level	91	128.6	23.4	205	126.8	26.3	−0.55
amount of fall	91	27.6	18.8	205	37.0	20.3	+ 3.74***
Type III							
initial level	23 (10%)	143.0	17.0	106 (16%)	155.0	18.6	+ 2.82**
peak	23	164.3	17.3	106	184.6	22.1	+ 4.10***
end level	23	146.5	20.4	106	155.2	25.2	+ 1.53
amount of rise	23	21.3	11.5	106	29.5	17.2	+ 2.16*
amount of fall	23	17.8	16.5	106	29.4	16.3	+ 3.06**
Type IV							
initial level	3 (1%)	146.7	5.8	69 (11%)	166.0	15.6	+ 2.10*
trough	3	133.3	5.8	69	143.1	14.8	+ 1.12
end level	3	146.7	5.8	69	170.1	16.8	+ 2.37*
amount of fall	3	13.3	5.8	69	22.9	13.6	+ 1.20
amount of rise	3	13.3	5.8	69	27.0	18.0	+ 1.29
Type V							
level	54 (23%)	158.9	22.9	68 (10%)	170.2	17.5	+ 3.06**

N = number of syllables
+ = relevant parameter of stressed syllable > that of unstressed syllable
− = relevant parameter of stressed syllable < that of unstressed syllable
*, **, *** = significance at 5 per cent, 1 per cent, and 0.1 per cent levels respectively.

in unstressed syllables, was too low. In *Type V*, the fundamental frequency level was higher in stressed than in unstressed syllables, but not significantly so.

Amplitude

The similarity of the mean peak levels in stressed and unstressed syllables and the relatively low standard deviation of these means suggest that under the conditions of this experiment all subjects reached a fairly constant peak level of amplitude for all syllables, stressed and unstressed. However, the fall from this peak was significantly greater in stressed than in unstressed syllables (Table 9).

Duration

Overall, duration was found to be greater in stressed than in unstressed syllables. With all fundamental frequency patterns it was found to be greater, but only significantly so with *Types II, IV* and *V* (Table 10).

TABLE 9

Means ($\overline{X}$) and standard deviations (SD of the amplitude In dB) of stressed and unstressed syllables in native and non-native speakers of English, and t-tests showing the significance of the difference between stressed and unstressed syllables

| | NATIVE SPEAKERS | | | | | | |
| | Unstressed Syllables | | | Stressed Syllables | | | |
	N	$\overline{X}$	SD	N	$\overline{X}$	SD	t
initial level	112	11.5	12.6	399	10.4	11.4	−0.87
peak	112	32.8	3.1	399	32.6	2.9	−0.63
end level	112	16.2	11.2	399	10.6	11.4	−4.60***
amount of rise	112	21.3	12.6	399	22.1	11.1	+0.65
amount of fall	112	16.6	10.4	399	21.9	10.6	+4.68***
	NON-NATIVE SPEAKERS						
initial level	234	12.9	10.1	654	14.0	12.2	+1.23
peak	234	31.7	3.9	654	33.2	2.9	+6.15***
end level	234	15.1	10.6	654	13.3	10.5	−2.24*
amount of rise	234	18.7	10.3	654	19.2	10.4	+0.63
amount of fall	234	16.6.	9.0	654	19.8	9.7	+4.40***

N = number of syllables

+ = relevant parameter of stressed syllable > that of unstressed syllable

− = relevant parameter of stressed syllable < that of unstressed syllable

*, **, *** = significance at 5 per cent, 1 per cent, and 0.1 per cent levels respectively.

TABLE 10

The duration (in msec) of stressed and unstressed syllables in native and non-native speakers of English, and t-tests showing the significance of the difference between stressed and unstressed syllables

| | NATIVE SPEAKERS | | | | | | |
| | Unstressed Syllables | | | Stressed Syllables | | | |
	N	$\overline{X}$	SD	N	$\overline{X}$	SD	t
Type of Fundamental Frequency Curve							
Type I	51	245	57	106	262	84	+1.29
Type II	37	236	74	201	331	95	+5.74***
Type III	16	260	30	53	272	78	+0.59

Table 10 contd.

	Unstressed Syllables			Stressed Syllables			
	N	X̄	SD	N	X̄	SD	t
Type IV	1	190	0	26	329	55	+ 2.43*
Type V	11	192	76	30	264	93	+ 2.24*
Amplitude							
Type III	111	232	74	399	302	99	+ 6.91***

NON-NATIVE SPEAKERS

Type of Fundamental Frequency Curve							
Type I	63	234	78	208	285	89	+ 4.08***
Type II	91	279	89	205	327	99	+ 3.95***
Type III	23	247	63	106	306	89	+ 2.99**
Type IV	3	409	152	69	369	95	−0.68
Type V	54	238	78	68	251	91	+ 0.82
Amplitude							
Type III	234	257	86	654	306	101	+ 6.60***

N = number of syllables

+ = relevant parameter of stressed syllable > that of unstressed syllable

− = relevant parameter of stressed syllable < that of unstressed syllable

*, **, *** = significance at 5 per cent, 1 per cent, and 0.1 per cent levels respectively.

X̄ = mean

SD = standard deviation

NON-NATIVE SPEAKERS

Fundamental frequency

Features similar to those shown for the native speakers were found in the records of the non-native subjects. The one difference which should be noted is that their initial level in *Type II* was significantly higher than that of the native speakers in their utterance of stressed syllables. (cf. Tables 8a and 8b.)

Amplitude

As with the native speakers, the fall from the peak amplitude was significantly greater in stressed than in unstressed syllables. The relative constancy of the peak level should again be noted (Table 9).

Duration

The duration of stressed syllables was greater than that of unstressed syllables. The difference was found to be significant with *Types I*, *II* and *III* fundamental frequency patterns.

In summary, it would appear from these results that stress in connected utterance is associated with:

1. a greater degree of fundamental frequency change (either rising or falling);
2. a greater fall of amplitude from a fairly constant peak level;
3. greater duration.

It was considered that the importance of each of these factors might vary from syllable to syllable and from one individual to another; therefore, the relationships of fundamental frequency, amplitude, and duration, to stress in the individual subject, were explored using Spearman's coefficient of rank order correlation. The aim of the test was to determine which parameter as used by the individual speakers had caused the listeners to perceive certain of the syllables as stressed.

Accordingly, the amount of F_0 change, the peak amplitude, and the duration of all stressed syllables uttered by each of the 16 subjects were ranked. Also ranked were the number of stress judgments awarded by the adjudicators to each syllable. The rank correlation coefficients determined for each subject are shown in Table 11. The significance levels of each of the acoustic parameters were determined from standard correlation coefficient (r) tables.

The analysis presented in Table 11 supports the basic conclusions drawn from the mean figures analysed above. Of the 16 subjects (native and non-native) tested, stress was positively correlated with fundamental frequency in 7 individuals, with amplitude in 4 individuals and with duration in 13 individuals. In one (native) subject there was a significant negative correlation between amplitude and stress, although it may be observed that in his utterance the two other parameters investigated—F_0 and duration—showed a significant positive correlation with it (Table 11).

It is also interesting to observe that in the utterance of another subject (non-native) none of these parameters correlated significantly with stress, while all three showed a positive correlation with it in the utterance of two of the other non-native subjects. It is clear from Table 11 that duration was the parameter most frequently associated with stress, although sometimes in conjunction with one or both of the other parameters.

Although little difference was shown on the whole between the mechanisms used by the native and the non-native subjects to signal stress, it should be noted that fundamental frequency was more often correlated with stress in the utterance of the non-native subjects than in that of the native subjects. This tendency could well be associated with the fairly general belief that F_0 changes are the most usual markers of stress in English—a view certainly based on the findings of experimental phoneticians but not always applicable to stress at the *sentence* level, for despite the fact that they have stated quite explicitly in their reports that

TABLE 11

Acoustic correlates of stress in 8 native and 8 non-native speakers of English by Spearman's coefficient of rank-order correlation
(For explanation *vide supra* p. 145)

NATIVE SPEAKERS

Subjects	Fundamental Frequency N	r	Amplitude N	r	Duration N	r
A	66	0.18	66	0.04	65	0.25*
B	64	0.07	67	-0.03	67	0.41***
C	63	0.12	64	0.18	64	0.35**
D	72	0.07	72	0.29*	72	0.13
E	69	0.36**	69	-0.29*	69	0.47***
F	70	0.08	70	0.09	70	0.32**
G	62	0.08	62	-0.12	60	0.28*
H	61	0.28*	61	-0.02	56	0.34**

NON-NATIVE SPEAKERS

Subjects	N	r	N	r	N	r
A	110	0.18	111	0.08	112	0.25**
B	104	0.17	101	-0.09	103	0.28**
C	109	0.38***	109	0.07	111	0.26**
D	116	0.40***	114	-0.01	114	0.33***
E	116	0.10	116	0.17	112	0.14
F	106	0.26**	108	0.29**	108	0.32***
G	105	0.56***	105	0.30**	105	0.11
H	120	0.27**	120	0.20*	120	0.20*

N = number of observations (stressed syllables)
r = coefficient of rank correlation
*, **, *** = significance at 5 per cent, 1 per cent, and 0.1 per cent levels respectively.

they investigated the acoustic correlates of *word* stress, these investigators, more often than not, have been interpreted as suggesting that stress at all levels in English is produced by pitch variation. From discussions with the non-native speakers who participated in this study and with numbers of my TEFL students in other years, I have ascertained that stress is most often taught on the basis of its contrastive function—the stressed syllable of the noun-verb pair, for example, being uttered with a rising pitch—and that usually this is the only guide the student has been given to the stress system of English. Hence the non-native speaker tends to apply this principle to the marking of stress at the sentence level also. This explanation gains some support from the mean F_0 patterns shown in Tables 8a and 8b.

It will be noted that in the utterance of the non-native subjects 27% of the unstressed syllables analysed were spoken with the *Type I* (rising) F_0 glide, whereas 32% of their stressed syllables were spoken with this pattern. On the other hand, the native subjects used *Type I* for only 25% of their stressed syllables, but for 44% of the unstressed syllables analysed for them. With the other parameters little difference was found between the native and the non-native speakers.

It has been noted that both the mean initial and final levels of *Type I* F_0 glides (rising pitch) were higher in stressed than in unstressed syllables. In the case of the native speakers, although *the amount of rise* from initial to end level was greater in stressed than in unstressed syllables—for example, the unstressed syllables had a mean rise of 32.8 Hz whereas the mean rise of the stressed syllables was 35.4 Hz—only the level on which the glide ended was shown to be significantly higher (Table 8a). However, in the utterance of the non-native speakers all three factors—initial level, end level, and amount of rise—were shown to be significantly different in stressed and unstressed syllables. The unstressed syllables had a mean rise of 25.6 Hz, and the stressed syllables a rise of 31.6 Hz. Thus, it will be observed that the mean *range* of the glides used by these subjects was more restricted than that of the native subjects. It is possible that as speakers in the main of tone languages (and therefore accustomed to using relatively short phonemic glides in their first language) they transferred this characteristic of pitch variation to their speaking of English, whereas the native speakers, when they did use fundamental frequency for syllable prominence, employed what I have elsewhere described as *extended* and *compound* intonemes,[17] these being the more usual pitch sequences used to mark word prominence.[18]

In connection with the native speaker's use of fundamental frequency to signal stress, it is interesting to observe that 48% of the stressed syllables analysed for this group were *Type II* (falling pitch) glides. This supports Bolinger's conclusion that although the "upward obtrusion is basic, pitch prominence need not be merely upward, as commonly supposed, but may take other directions."[19]

In the utterance of both native and non-native speakers, the *amount of fall* from initial to end level was very significantly greater in stressed than in unstressed syllables. For the native speakers, the mean amount of fall on unstressed syllables was 34.7 Hz, and on stressed syllables 44.6 Hz. In view of the fact that the mean vocal range of these subjects was only 120 Hz, this amount of F_0 change was quite considerable. On the other hand, the non-native speakers whose mean vocal range was also 120 Hz but whose pitch generally was higher (91-211 Hz) than that of the native speakers—possibly because of their slighter physique—again used relatively restricted glides. As can be seen from Table 8b, their mean amount of fall on unstressed syllables was 27.6 Hz, and on stressed syllables was 37.0 Hz.

There were also slight differences between the native and non-native subjects in their use of the two compound patterns of fundamental frequency. Both patterns—*Type III* (rise-fall) and *Type IV* (fall-rise)—were used to some extent by the two categories of speakers to signal stress but the non-native speakers used them more frequently. With the exception of the end level in the case of the foreign speakers, statistically significant differences between stressed and unstressed syllables for both groups in their use of Type III can be seen by reference to Tables 8a and 8b. Likewise, the amounts of rise and fall are shown to be significantly different for stressed and unstressed syllables in the utterance of both groups.

The interesting feature of the native speakers' use of *Type III* was that the levels at commencement, peak, and termination were so much higher when it occurred on stressed syllables than when it appeared on the same syllables in unstressed positions; for example,

mean initial level for unstressed syllables	124.4 Hz
" peak " " "	144.7 Hz
" end " " "	123.7 Hz
mean initial level for stressed syllables	147.5 Hz
" peak " " " "	181.0 Hz
" end " " " "	148.6 Hz

The differences between the levels for stressed and unstressed syllables were much less marked in the utterance of the non-native speakers. Although much less frequent than *Type II*, this glide would seem to be important as a cue to stress, especially in the medial position,[20] whereas *Type II* is more likely to be found at or near the end of the sense group, particularly when the word taking the primary stress occurs at the end of the sentence.[21] Since the non-native subjects in this study also failed to manage intonation patterns satisfactorily, frequently using rising intonemes in positions were the native speaker would use falling pitch sequences, (note F_0 trace. Figs. 24 and 25)[22] it is quite possible that the lower incidence of *Type II* glides in their pronunciation could be associated with this factor.

Although the *Type IV* glide was even less used than the *Type III* glide, differences were observed between its production in stressed and unstressed syllables. In the case of the non-native speakers, the differences between the initial and end levels for stressed and unstressed syllables were statistically significant.

Type V glides (level tones) were infrequent in the speech of the native subjects. When they were used, they occurred more often on unstressed than on stressed syllables, although as Kingdon[23] points out, such tones are regularly used in English to give prominence to words which are of less

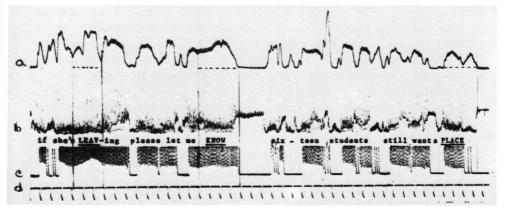

Figure 24. Oscillographic recording of native speaker's utterance of item 10. Traces a-d as in Figure 21. (see text for discussion of fundamental frequency.)

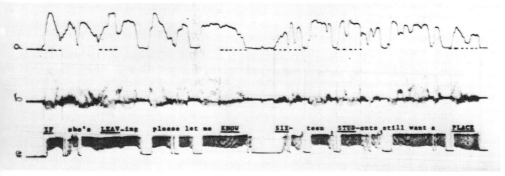

Figure 25. Oscillographic recording of non-native speaker's utterance of item 10. Traces a-c as in Figure 21. (See text for discussion of fundamental frequency.)

importance than the ones ordinarily made prominent by means of kinetic tones. It might well be, then, that they were used by the subjects in this experiment to signal either secondary or tertiary stress. When they occurred on stressed syllables, however, they were found to be several cycles higher than when they were used on the same syllable in an unstressed position. In the speech of the non-native subjects, also, the level tone was significantly higher when it occurred on stressed than when it was associated with unstressed syllables (170.2 Hz compared with 158.9 Hz).

Although several types of amplitude pattern were used, only one type—a rise/fall—occurred consistently. In Figs. 24 and 25 we have excellent examples of the point made by Brosnahan and Malmberg[24] that a syllable containing high frequency sounds such as /s/ may have more than one peak of prominence on the intensity trace. In the syllable *six* (stressed by the speaker in Fig. 25 but not by the speaker in Fig. 24) three peaks are shown. However, the highest of each of these (the syllabic centre /ɪ/) was the level measured for the peak envelope amplitude of the syllable.

The non-native speakers appeared to use amplitude more than did the native speakers as a cue to stress. In the utterance of the foreign subjects there was a significant difference between the peak level recorded for stressed and unstressed syllables (Table 9). No such difference occurred in the case of the native speakers whose mean peak level of amplitude was almost identical for both stressed and unstressed syllables (32.6 dB and 32.8 dB).

There was very little difference between stressed and unstressed syllables with regard to the initial level of the amplitude and the amount of the rise. However, the difference between the end level of the amplitude of stressed and unstressed syllables was shown by t-test to be significant in the utterance of both native and non-native speakers—as was the amount of fall occurring at syllable boundaries. This decrease in the amplitude at the end of stressed syllables could be related to the disjuncture which occurs after stressed syllables but not after unstressed syllables which tend to be harder to distinguish in the stream of speech, by dint of their reduced length (see Table 10 for comparison of the duration of stressed and unstressed syllables) and the narrower intervals of relative silence between them.

The staccato utterance of the non-native speakers was probably accentuated by these falls in amplitude at the boundaries of the stressed syllables. As has already been observed,[25] by comparison with the native speakers these subjects stressed an inordinately large number of syllables, which, being separated by these reductions in the sound pressure produced an auditory impression of discreteness which contributed to the syllable-timed rhythm effect characteristic of their utterance. In Fig. 26 can be seen an oscillographic recording of a Bengali speaker's utterance of item 9. It will be noted that seven of the 16 syllables of the rhyme are stressed and that the amount of fall at the boundaries of these syllables is greater than that following the unstressed syllables, which are nonetheless quite clearly defined. Interesting to note also are the high amplitude levels of the stressed syllables as spoken by this subject.

In the recording of a native speaker's utterance of item 3 shown in Fig. 27 the fall from peak amplitude at the boundaries of stressed syllables is likewise clearly visible. However, the discreteness of the syllables, so noticeable even in the short item shown in Fig. 26 is not evident. A record of a Vietnamese speaker's utterance of the same item is shown by way of contrast in Fig. 28.

Another interesting acoustic feature which recurred consistently in the records of the native speakers was that the amplitude of the whole item tended to decrease as the utterance continued (Fig. 27). It will be noted that

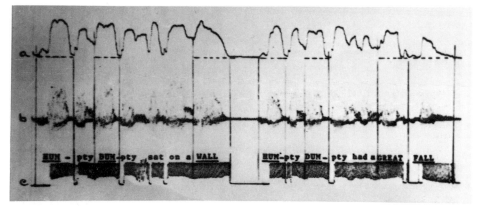

Figure 26. Oscillographic recording of non-native speaker's utterance of item 9. Traces a-c in Figure 21. Time was marked in 0.1 sec. This subject stressed almost half the total number of syllables in the item. The high amplitude levels of the stressed syllables should be noted (trace a, integrated intensity).

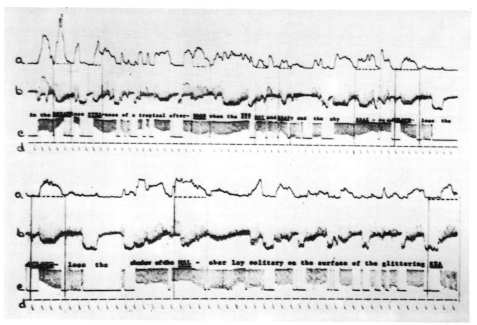

Figure 27. Oscillographic recording of native speaker's utterance of item 3. Traces a-d as in Figure 21. The amplitude level can be observed to decrease progressively to the end of the sentence (trace a, integrated intensity).

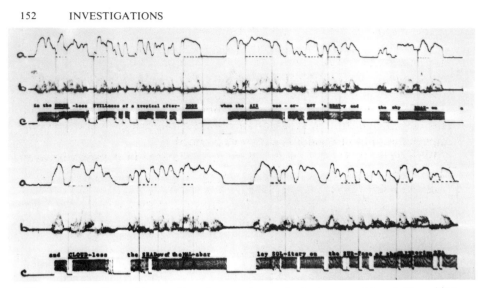

Figure 28. Oscillographic recording of non-native speaker's utterance of item 3. The subject programmed his utterance in a number of short sub-sections. (cf. recording of same item by native speaker, Figure 27.) Traces a-c as in Figure 21. Time was marked in 0.1 sec.

the peaks are higher for both stressed and unstressed syllables at the beginning of the utterance and that the amplitude of the stressed syllables towards the end of the item is lower than that shown on many of the unstressed ones at the beginning of the sentence. On the other hand, the records of the non-native speakers did not always show this overall decrease.

The postulate suggested above[26] that the non-native speakers tended to programme their utterances in shorter sections than the native speakers seems to be supported by this evidence from the amplitude display. If the utterances of the non-native speakers were programmed in short sections, it is possible that the overall amplitude was not allowed to decrease progressively over the whole item, and thus it is not by any means suprising to find relatively high peaks of amplitude at or towards the end of the several subsections. Since the non-native speakers used amplitude to a greater extent than the native speakers to signal stress it is quite feasible that these peaks should occur in any position in the utterance. The native speakers, generally, used amplitude less as a cue to stress, yet the adjudicators were still able to perceive as stressed words which occurred at the very end of the sentence. As can be seen in Fig. 27 the speaker was perceived as having stressed the last word of the item, *sea*, yet the amplitude peak of this word is considerably lower than that of several of the unstressed words of the item. Clearly this speaker could not have relied solely on amplitude to signal stress in this instance.

The mean duration of stressed syllables was shown in practically all instances to be greater than that of their unstressed counterparts in the utterance of both native and non-native subjects. The exception was the non-native speakers' utterance of the *Type IV* F_0 glide with which duration was found to be less (although not significantly so), in the stressed syllables. However, since this pattern occurred in only 1% of the unstressed syllables and 11% of the stressed syllables analysed for this group of speakers, the importance of this irregularity can be discounted.

With *Types I, II,* and *III* F_0 glides the difference in duration between stressed and unstressed syllables was found to be highly significant. Likewise, with *Types II, IV* and *V* F_0 glides the duration difference between stressed and unstressed syllables in the utterance of the native speakers was significant by t-test (Table 10). It will be noted that the two speakers whose oscillographic recordings are shown in Figs. 27 and 28 used the *Type II* F_0 glide and durations of 410 msec. and 510 msec. respectively to signal the stressedness of *sea*, the last word in the sentence. Typically of their respective categories, the amplitude peak was higher in the utterance of the non-native subject (34 dB/30 dB), but the native subject used a greater fall in the fundamental frequency level (200-120 Hz/160-90 Hz).

Further comparison of the recordings of these two subjects will show that there was only a slight difference between the actual duration times of their other stressed syllables. However, the length of the native subject's utterance was 9.7 sec. compared with 13.3 sec. for the non-native subject. This supports the conclusion presented above that the increased length of utterance in the case of the non-native speakers could be attributed to the number and duration of pauses.[27]

The results of the acoustic parameters investigation showed quite clearly that there was very little difference in the duration of stressed syllables as uttered by native and non-native subjects. On the whole, the duration of stressed syllables (Table 10) tended to be slightly longer for the foreign speakers, although, as can be observed in Figs. 27 and 28, native speakers sometimes lengthened the stressed syllables more than did the non-native speakers. Comparison of the records of these two subjects shows that the syllables *noon* (after)*noon*, *braz*(en), and *Mal*(abar), were longer as spoken by the native subject.

A noteworthy feature of the duration results (Table 10) was that the non-native subjects' unstressed syllables were generally slightly longer than those of the native subjects. Thus, in the utterance of the foreign speakers, the difference in duration between stressed and unstressed syllables was less marked than that of the native speakers, and could have contributed to the impression they gave of speaking English with a syllable-timed rhythm. Examination of Figs. 25 and 26 (oscillograms of non-native utterance) will show that in these two short items there was little recorded difference in duration between the stressed and the unstressed syllables. The auditory impression of equivalent length was even more pronounced.

It would seem from the results of this investigation that duration and fundamental frequency are more significant than amplitude in signalling stress in connected English utterance, although the fact that increased magnitudes of all three parameters were found to be involved supports the conclusions of several researchers who have investigated stress at the lexical level. There is little reason to believe that, in general, native and non-native speakers use different parameters as cues to stress although, as we have seen, there were minor differences between the two groups studied, fundamental frequency, and—to a less extent—amplitude being correlated with stress more often in the utterance of non-native than native speakers.

Nevertheless, analysis of the acoustic parameters used by the individual speakers of both categories suggests that both native and non-native speakers individually may use different parameters habitually or according to the context in order to achieve word prominence. It is interesting to observe, for instance, that in one (non-native) speaker none of the parameters investigated correlated significantly with stress—yet he was perceived by the listeners to stress 116 words of the 273 words in the 12 items. It is possible that in this subject's utterance a partial correlation between all three parameters and stress could have summated to signal this feature, or, alternatively, that he used some other parameter not so far investigated to this end. Ando and Canter[28] have also speculated on the possibility of some parameter other than fundamental frequency, amplitude, and duration being used as a cue to stress following their investigation of syllable stress in the utterance of deaf and normal hearing subjects. However, these parameters have been shown quite definitely to be associated with stress, and, as the results of the present investigation indicate, some speakers may even employ all three in a single utterance; fundamental frequency, amplitude, and duration having been found to be positively associated with stress in the speech of two other (non-native) subjects (Table 11).

It would certainly seem that for utterance of the more effective (that is, stylistically) sort, a variety of mechanisms would be more appropriate than a single parameter to convey the semantic component—particularly the attitudinal meaning—of the sentence. However, with the possible exception of item 3, the test material used in this investigation did not require any kind of artistic treatment or special nuances of expression, and therefore the relationships of fundamental frequency, amplitude, and duration were considered only for speech of the most commonplace kind.

The results of this phase of the investigation revealed the acoustic parameters used by 16 speakers of English to create the impression of stress perceived by a group of ten listeners. Contrary to expectation, the non-native speakers' production of stress was found to correspond to the native speakers' production of this feature; the acoustic correlates of fundamental frequency, amplitude, and duration being used, as we have seen, to a greater or less extent by the individual speakers of both groups. Yet the rhythm of the two groups of subjects was different. Stress *per se* was evidently not the root of the problem. The real causes of the rhythm anomalies of the non-native speakers appeared to lie not in their manner of producing stress but rather in the timing of their rhythm units (largely resulting from approximate equivalence of stressed and unstressed syllables), in their surfeit of stressed syllables, and in their frequent and indiscriminate use of the pause—all conditions associated with the syllable-timed nature of their first language, their method of learning English, and their lack of experience in speaking the language.

PART III

Evaluation of an Experimental Programme

CHAPTER SEVEN

(a) The Pre-test

Having concluded on the basis of the results of the several investigations described in Part II that the speech rhythm anomalies of my non-native subjects, manifested in their superfluous and indiscriminate placement of stresses and pauses, could be attributed to
1. the syllable-timed nature of their first language;
2. their method of learning English; and
3. their lack of experience in speaking English;

and having established that increased magnitudes of duration and fundamental frequency are the most consistent acoustic correlates of stress in English, my next step was to devise and test learning experiences by means of which, it was hoped, the foreign student could be assisted to acquire the stress-timed rhythm of English.

It seemed to me that if this experimental learning programme resulted in the speech improvement of a sample of non-native speakers whose difficulties were comparable to those of the subjects who had participated in the other experiments, it could be assumed that my findings had pedagogical as well as linguistic and statistical validity.

In this study rhythm was regarded as the explanatory construct of the organizing principle which underlies both the perception and the production of speech, and therefore the rhythm anomalies of the non-native subjects might well have been interpreted as an indication of their lack of competence[1] had not their very considerable background in English studies been known to me. As graduate teachers of English, they had certainly internalized the system of rules which normally allows the speaker to perceive, interpret, form, or otherwise use a language, yet by dint of their extremely faulty utterance, they exemplified the somewhat unusual case of performance only minimally attesting to knowledge of that language.

My problem, then, was to design a programme which would provide for practice in the recognition and production of credible English rhythm units, organized and timed to establish and maintain the rhythmic impulse in connected speech.

Aware of first language interference in their English pronunciation, and anxious to gain some insights into the principles underlying the rhythm of spoken English, 30 of my TEFL students volunteered to act as subjects. Like the non-native subjects of the previous experiments, they were also teachers of English from Asian, South-East Asian, and Pacific Island countries, and they manifested the same types of pronunciation faults; their native languages being Burmese, Cambodian, Fijian, Indonesian, Japanese, Korean, Malay, Thai, and Vietnamese. Regarding the experiment as a means of obtaining guidelines for the development of their own techniques of teaching stress and rhythm, they were highly motivated, and as members of an experimental class engaged in the learning activities with very considerable enthusiasm and purposefulness.

All wanted to be "learners", but as it was necessary for the purpose of the experiment to compare the progress of two contrasting groups, a division was made into an *experimental* group and a *control* group.[2] The students were randomly selected as members of either the experimental or the control group, but once this division had been made they were carefully matched according to mother tongue, sex, and number of years' experience in speaking English. It did not necessarily follow that the more mature subjects had had greater practice than the younger subjects in their use of the language. "Experience" was assessed on the basis of the number of hours daily that they spoke English in their country of origin. The Fijian, Malay, and Burmese students, for example, were found to speak English much more frequently and for longer periods than most of the others, and in fact taught English as a second, rather than as a foreign language, thus their scores on both pre- and post-tests were generally higher than those of the other students.

The composition of the two groups may be seen in Table 12. It will be noted that each of the 30 subjects has two numbers—the first indicates his or her number on the pre-test, and the second, on the post-test. This system was used so that the adjudicators would not know whether the subject being assessed was from the experimental or the control group, or was on the pre- or the post-test. The initial equivalence of the two groups was shown by means of a paired t-test (Table 12).

Test material

Each subject recorded four passages of English text which ranged from elementary prose structures in simple conversational style to the highly complex verse of T. S. Eliot. The selections were read in the following order:

I. *Simple narrative prose*
   "What's for dinner, Mum?" asked Susan.
   "Are you feeling hungry, dear?"

TABLE 12

Comparison of Control and Experimental Groups on Pre-test—N = 15

Control		Score	Experimental		Score	Language	Sex	Difference
A Nos.	1–31	44	A Nos.	18–48	42	Burmese	F	+2
B ,,	2–32	45	B ,,	17–47	44	Fijian	M	+1
C ,,	3–33	44	C ,,	28–58	45	Indonesian	F	−1
D ,,	4–34	37	D ,,	29–59	46	Indonesian	F	−9
E ,,	5–35	34	E ,,	24–54	43	Indonesian	M	−9
F ,,	6–36	28	F ,,	25–55	37	Vietnamese	M	−9
G ,,	7–37	16	G ,,	23–53	22	Korean	M	−6
H ,,	8–38	34	H ,,	26–56	23	Thai	F	+11
I ,,	9–39	24	I ,,	16–46	25	Thai	F	−1
J ,,	10–40	32	J ,,	21–51	39	Korean	M	−7
K ,,	11–41	35	K ,,	22–52	40	Japanese	M	−5
L ,,	12–42	42	L ,,	19–49	23	Malay	M	+19
M ,,	13–43	43	M ,,	27–57	28	Thai	M	+15
N ,,	14–44	24	N ,,	20–50	18	Cambodian	M	+6
O ,,	15–45	15	O ,,	30–60	22	Cambodian	M	−7
								0

t with 14 d.f. at 5% = 1.76

No significant difference is observable between experimental and control groups on pre-test.

> "Yes, I'm starving," replied Susan.
> Her mother smiled as she knew that was not really true. Susan had eaten a banana, an orange and an apple since her last meal. Susan was always hungry and her mother said that she would get very fat if she didn't eat less. Susan said that she was a growing girl and needed plenty of food to make her strong. Her mother said, "Dinner will be ready in about ten minutes. Can you wait that long?"
> "Well, I'll try," answered Susan.
>
> *Anon.*

II. Literary prose

> Night is a dead monotonous period under a roof; but in the open world it passes lightly, with its stars and dews and perfumes, and the hours are marked by changes in the face of Nature. What seems a kind of temporal death to people choked between walls and curtains,

is only a light and living slumber to the man who sleeps afield. All night long he can hear Nature breathing deeply and freely; even as she takes her rest, she turns and smiles; and there is one stirring hour unknown to those who dwell in houses, when a wakeful influence goes abroad over the sleeping hemisphere, and all the outdoor world are on their feet. It is then that the cock first crows, not this time to announce the dawn, but like a cheerful watchman speeding the course of night. Cattle awake on the meadows; sheep break their fast on dewy hillsides, and change to a new lair among the ferns; and houseless men, who have lain down with the fowls, open their dim eyes and behold the beauty of the night.

R. L. Stevenson, "Night Among the Pines"
from *Travels with a Donkey*.

III *Verse with marked metrical rhythm*

First there were two of us, then there were three of us,
Then there was one bird more,
Four of us—wild white sea-birds,
Treading the ocean floor;
And the wind rose, and the sea rose,
To the angry billows' roar—
With one of us—two of us—three of us—four of us
Sea-birds on the shore.

Soon there were five of us, soon there were nine of us,
And lo! in a trice sixteen!
And the yeasty surf curdled over the sands,
The gaunt grey rocks between;
And the tempest raved, and the lightning's fire
Struck blue on the spindrift hoar—
And on four of us—ay, and on four times four of us
Sea-birds on the shore.

And our sixteen waxed to thirty-two,
And they to past three-score—
A wild white welter of winnowing wings,
And ever more and more;
And the winds lulled, and the sea went down,
And the sun streamed out on high,
Gilding the pools and the spume and the spars
'Neath the vast blue deeps of the sky;
And the isles and the bright green headlands shone,
As they'd never shone before,
Mountains and valleys of silver cloud,

Wherein to swing, sweep, soar—
A host of screeching, scolding, scrabbling
Sea-birds on the shore—
A snowy, silent, sun-washed drift
Of sea-birds on the shore.

Walter de la Mare, *The Storm.*

IV *Verse with more subtle rhythm*

Time present and time past
Are both perhaps present in time future,
And time future contained in time past.
If all time is eternally present
All time is unredeemable.
What might have been is an abstraction
Remaining a perpetual possibility
Only in a world of speculation.
What might have been and what has been
Point to one end, which is always present.
Footfalls echo in the memory
Down the passage which we did not take
Towards the door we never opened
Into the rose-garden. My words echo
Thus, in your mind.
But to what purpose
Disturbing the dust on a bowl of rose-leaves
I do not know.
Other echoes
Inhabit the garden. Shall we follow?
Quick, said the bird, find them, find them,
Round the corner. Through the first gate,
Into our first world, shall we follow
The deception of the thrush? Into our first world.
There they were, dignified, invisible,
Moving without pressure, over the dead leaves,
In the autumn heat, through the vibrant air,
And the bird called in response to
The unheard music hidden in the shrubbery,
And the unseen eyebeam crossed, for the roses
Had the look of flowers that are looked at.
There they were as our guests, accepted and accepting.
So we moved, and they, in a formal pattern.
Along the empty alley, into the box circle,
To look down into the drained pool.
Dry the pool, dry concrete, brown edged,

And the pool was filled with water out of sunlight,
And the lotus rose, quietly, quietly,
The surface glittered out of heart of light,
And they were behind us, reflected in the pool.
Then a cloud passed, and the pool was empty.
Go, said the bird, for the leaves were full of children,
Hidden excitedly, containing laughter.
Go, go, go, said the bird: human kind
Cannot bear very much reality.

T. S. Eliot, *Burnt Norton,*
from *Four Quartets.*

The subjects did not hear their recordings replayed until after the post-test when the two sets of readings were compared. Meanwhile, over a period of six weeks the experimental group of 15 subjects was given 20 hours of class work in the management of English speech rhythm. The classes were held three times weekly and were of one hour's duration. During that time the students were instructed in the principles of English speech rhythm; they compared the rhythm of their native language with that of English; and they did considerable practical work under my direction in the classroom and in the University language laboratory.[3] The control group received no systematic training in the area.

(b) The Programme

The guiding principle of the programme was the organization and timing of the rhythm unit. Thus the learning activities were designed expressly to give the participating students practice in the recognition and production of credible rhythm units organized and timed to establish and maintain the rhythmic impulse in the stream of connected speech. Although the language is composed of linear strings of words, we neither think nor speak in separate words but rather in groups of words, or *sense groups.* These sense groups are hierarchical structures organized according to the meaning we wish to convey. Characteristically, a sense group contains a single idea which achieves its salience by means of the prominence accorded the word in the group which is regarded by the speaker as the most important. The several sense groups of a sentence thus parallel the rhythm groups which, as we have seen, also consist of one stressed syllable and a variable number of unstressed syllables. However, the rhythm group usually commences with the stressed syllable and includes all the unstressed syllables up to, but not including, the next stress; whereas in the sense groups which may subsume a number of rhythm units (some sense groups consisting of a single word and others of a number of words) the nuclear syllable is usually to be found at or near the end of the sequence[4] and is associated with the intonation pattern of the utterance.[5]

By contrast with the meaningful phrasing of the native speakers, the non-native speakers in the investigation emphasized, as we have seen, the separable identity of the words; and by their inappropriately placed stresses and pauses[6] (Tables 1, 6, 7) not only failed to observe the principle of the relative isochrony of the stresses—thereby distorting the rhythm—but also failed to recognize the principle of constituent structure—thereby ignoring sense group organization—and, as a result, in many instances failed completely to convey the meaning intended. Thus, as I observed at the beginning of this report,[7] the phonological transgressions of the non-native speakers were found to have quite serious semantic implications.

Generally, the native speaker of English is able to effect a balance between sound and meaning, and, while creating the impression of sequences of proportionate temporal units, is yet able to use a great variety of stress fluctuations in order to convey the meaning of his utterance. Thus even though several different speakers may phrase a text in different ways according to individual interpretation, the patterning and timing of their rhythm units are so controlled that a credible rhythmic impulse is established and maintained, and this pulse actually reinforces the meaning. The native speaker of English intuitively uses a rhythm which some few modern poets[8] have deliberately exploited in their prosody by mounting the natural speech stress profile above an artificial metrical pattern in order to produce "sprung rhythm"—that is, a rhythm in which the natural and the contrived coexist, the more usual patterns of stress/unstress ratios being dispensed with in favour of patterns based upon stress alone.

In ordinary conversation, the rhythmic pulse established by the speaker is very frequently taken up and continued by the listener, but in stage dialogue, where verisimilitude largely depends upon the art of timing and the ability of the actors to take up their cues on the right beat, the maintaining of the rhythmic impulse is an essential feature of the simulated real-life situation being enacted. It is my belief that in more extended programmes than the one described in this report play-readings could be used very successfully as learning activities in rhythm with students at all levels of ability. As it was, practice in expressive interpretation was confined to poetry and prose excerpts. Even so, such material was presented towards the end of the programme, after the students had gained some insights into the principles governing the rhythm of spoken English. In the early sessions considerable time was spent on the recognition and production of the rhythm unit in connected utterance, on the repetition of rhythm patterns, and on study of the mechanism of English speech rhythm compared with that of the native languages of the students who constituted the class.

If the impression of rhythm in spoken English is produced by the serial recurrence of more or less isochronous intervals marked off by stressed syllables, then it follows that stress, which functions both as the marker of the relative prominence of the syllables of the utterance and as the carrier of the rhythmic impulse, must be the vital element to be considered in the planning of learning experiences. As we have seen, the non-native speakers who participated in the acoustic parameters investigation, did not differ markedly from the native speakers in the mechanisms they used to signal stress but rather in their distribution of this feature and in the timing of their utterances. Thus their problem was actually one of ratio—of the time relations between stresses. Since the impression of isochrony in English is largely dependent upon the quantitative adjustment of unstressed syllables in relation to the fully stressed hub, a second essential feature to be considered was the timing of the constituents of rhythm units and the proportioning of unstressed to stressed syllables in the whole utterance.

As we have also observed, one of the most notable differences between the native and the non-native subjects in all the experiments of this study was the latter group's indiscriminate placement of numerous pauses. Now, in normal English utterance, the pause, as Goldman-Eisler[9] has shown, is as much part of speech as is vocal utterance—disjuncture is the speaker's usual means of delimiting groups of words in close grammatical relationship; and juncture, of preserving the internal structure of the unit. However, as she has concluded,[10] and as we have seen in the present investigation, in fluent speech pauses are integrated into the grammatical structure. Thus, in the planning of the experimental learning programme the crucial question of rhythmic disjuncture was also exploited.

Finally, in order to realize the rhythmic impulse, the speaker must know not only which syllables to stress, and how to create the impression of prominence, how to organize and time the several rhythmic units of his utterance, and how to demarcate these temporal intervals, but also how to maintain the pulse once established.

In order to assist the experimental group to achieve these objectives a programme was devised which featured nursery rhymes and other strongly metrical material. These exercises offered a natural approach to the study of basic rhythms by providing patterns for practice in the organization and timing of rhythm units normally used in more complex connected English utterance. It was hypothesized that certain of the strategies employed by the young native learner in response to his need for rhythmic sounds and movements,[11] if systematically exploited by the second language learner, could lead to the development of a fluency and intelligibility akin to that of native utterance. However, in addition to drills and exercises with *mim-mem* (that is, imitation and memorization) overtones, rules were presented, and these were followed by examples drawn from an extensive range of colloquial and literary material.

It is my belief that, from the pedagogical point of view, the learner approaching the intricacies of English speech rhythm in possession of the basic rules of stress-timing is better equipped for his task than either the learner who, unaware of the principles of the phenomenon, has acquired his knowledge of stress and rhythm only incidentally in the course of his study of the grammatical structures and literature of the target language, or the learner expertly drilled in patterns but unable to comprehend fully or to utter intelligibly sentences not previously learned. Thus the approach used was a combination of two established methods, seemingly contradictory, but in this programme each used to complement the other.

The subjects who participated in this experiment, although hardly "learners", were mainly of the first category, but very few had had specific instruction in the management of any of the prosodic features. For this reason it was considered necessary to give them practice in the five essentials of English rhythm:

1. The organization of words into appropriate sense groups separated by pauses;

2. The correct stress placement on the words within each sense group;

3. The weakening of unstressed syllables in relation to the fully stressed syllable of each rhythm unit;

4. The appropriate signalling of transitions between successive sounds and syllables;

5. Some basic intonation patterns.

No text book was used. As practising teachers, they were familiar with a wide range of standard texts, some of which could provide useful practice material,[12] but none of which was considered completely adequate for the purpose of this programme.

The approach used was derived from the two major learning theories currently observed in language teaching: the *audio-lingual habit theory*, and the *cognitive code-learning theory*. The former is based on the assumption that language is a habit structure, a system of skills, which can be acquired by drills and the formation of stimulus/response association. The latter theory rests in the main upon the neuro-psychological theories of thought and language proposed by the cognitive psychologists, and accords well with contemporary views on the nature of language and how it is acquired. It attaches more importance to the learner's understanding of the system and structure of the target language than to his facility in using it, since it is believed that—provided the learner has appropriate cognitive control over linguistic structures—facility will develop automatically with the use of language in meaningful situations.

Audio-lingual procedures, on the other hand, derive from the mechanist approach to language learning postulated in the 'thirties by the great descriptive linguist, Leonard Bloomfield,[13] who held that language operates in practical situations as a substitute for other kinds of non-symbolic behaviour. Translated into language teaching methodology, the audio-lingual theory has given rise to such techniques as the language laboratory, the structural drill, and *mim-mem*, all of which were used in this programme.

This theory has been criticized in recent years on the grounds that pattern practice drills may bring the student to a high degree of mechanical skill in a relatively short period of time—six months' intensive work sometimes—but because his actual knowledge of the language is superficial, he is usually incapable of operating spontaneously in sustained utterance with anything like the efficiency of a young native speaker—in Piagetian terms,[14] just approaching the *concrete operations*[15] stage of linguistic development. I would agree. I have used the audio-lingual method exclusively with elementary students learning English as a foreign language and I know from experience what its advantages and limitations are. Nevertheless, in some areas of language learning, such as the several features of the phonological system, it can be used very effectively—as I shall show—to effect automatic responses.

On the other hand, the cognitive code-learning theory can be used equally successfully by the learner to acquire conscious control of the target language patterns. According to Carroll,[16] explanation of the differences between the learner's L_1 and the target language in no way confuses the learner—as the audio-lingual habit theorist would claim—but rather facilitates learning through emphasis on deductive presentation.

In his discussion of contrastive analysis and interference theory at Georgetown in 1968, Carroll had this to say:

> . . . there is inferential support for the notion that information from contrastive linguistics can be of use in predicting student difficulties, particularly when the contrasts between the native and the target language systems are pointed out and explained to students so that they will have an opportunity to profit from this information to whatever extent they can.[17]

By way of illustration of the hypothesis that

> to the extent that similarities and contrasts between the native and the target language can be identified and explained or otherwise presented to

the student, facilitation of learning can be increased and interference diminished.[18]

he told the meeting that in teaching students to produce Chinese tones, he had found it helpful to point out that some Chinese tone contours are rather similar to certain intonation patterns in English. I have had similar experience in reverse in teaching the intonation of English to native speakers of other tone languages, such as Thai, Vietnamese, and Burmese.

Likewise, I found in this experimental programme comparison of the rhythms of English nursery rhymes and those of the syllable-timed languages of the participating students to be an extremely useful technique in helping them towards an understanding of the principles of the stress-timed rhythm of English speech. Although, as has been noted above, the learning experiences included activities normally engaged in by first language learners, it was constantly remembered that there is a vast difference between what the L_1 learner brings to the acquisition of his mother tongue and what the second language learner brings to his study of a foreign one.

Whereas conceptually the L_1 learner is at a disadvantage, linguistically it is the L_2 learner who is disadvantaged as a result of his first language rules (or habits) inhibiting, or in some way modifying his learning of the new set. It is Carroll's belief that if the subtle response systems of which the student is usually totally unaware were brought to his notice, negative transfer effects could be reduced "because the student could then better direct his own learning to avoid the interference of his first language system."[19] Likewise, he says, "the pointing out of similarities between aspects of the two languages may facilitate learning."[20] I concur with this view, and it was for this reason that the approach was partly "rule-governed".

An explanation of the pattern was followed by a rule illustrated by means of a simple diagrammatic notation. The pattern was then practised first in the rhymes, next in colloquial sentences, and finally in selections from English literature. For example, the simple rhythm heard in the rhyme,

> *To market, to market to buy a fat pig*
> *Home again, home again, jiggety-jig.*

was read aloud a few times to enable the students to grasp the pattern which was represented[21] as follows:

$$\smile \mid \;—\smile\smile\; \mid \;—\smile\smile\; \mid \;—\smile\smile\; \mid \;—\;_{\wedge\wedge}\; \mid$$
$$\mid \;—\smile\smile\; \mid \;—\smile\smile\; \mid \;—\smile\smile\; \mid \;—\;_{\wedge}\; \mid$$

Once the students had established the rhythmic pulse themselves, they were presented with fabricated equivalents of the rhyme which were first spoken with the beat strongly emphasized—as in the rhyme itself—and subsequently with the speech stress profile counterpointed as it were over the rhythmic pulse which, in the early stages was sometimes maintained with the help of physical movement; for example, clapping, tapping, bouncing a ball, playing a yo-yo, or simply beating time. Such sentences as the following were used at this stage of the programme:

I'd like you to see me tomorrow at three
ᵕ |— ᵕᵕ |— ᵕᵕ |— ᵕᵕ |— ˄˄ |

Where do you come from and what is your name?
— ᵕ ᵕ |— ᵕ ᵕ | — ᵕ ᵕ |— ˄˄ |

Thai has a complex arrangement of tones
— ᵕ ᵕ |— ᵕ ᵕ |— ᵕ ᵕ |—˄˄ |

Hey diddle diddle, the cat and the fiddle,
— ᵕ ᵕ |— ᵕ ᵕ |— ᵕ ᵕ |— ᵕ |

The cow jumped over the moon
ᵕ |— ˄ ᵕ |— ᵕ ᵕ |— ˄ |

The little dog laughed to see such sport
ᵕ |— ˄ ᵕ |— ˄ ᵕ |— ˄ ᵕ |— |

And the dish ran away with the spoon.
ᵕ ᵕ |— ᵕ ᵕ |— ᵕ ᵕ |— ˄˄ |

Lift it up gently and take it inside
— ᵕ ᵕ |— ᵕ ᵕ |— ᵕ ᵕ |— ˄˄ |

The bus is waiting outside
ᵕ |— ˄ ᵕ |— ᵕ ᵕ |— ˄˄ |

The weather is cold now winter's here
ᵕ |— ᵕ ᵕ |— ˄ ᵕ |— ˄ ᵕ |— ˄˄ |

Their results will be published in June
ᵕ ᵕ |— ᵕ ᵕ | — ᵕ ᵕ |— ˄ |

The fabricated equivalents of the rhymes were then divided into sense groups, and the fixed metrical scheme and the speech stress profile were counterpointed; for example,

I'd like you to see me tomorrow at three
ᵕ |— ᵕ ᵕ |— ᵕ ᵕ |— ᵕ ᵕ |— ˄˄ |

I'd like you to sée me│ │tomórrow│ │at thrée│

I'd like you to see me tomórrow│ │at thrée│

I'd like you to sée me│ │tomorrow at thrée│

Lift it up gently and take it inside
— ᵕ ᵕ |— ᵕ ᵕ |— ᵕ ᵕ |— ˄˄ |

Lift it up géntly│ │and take it insíde│

Next, verse with a strong metrical beat was introduced. And, again, correspondences were shown between such lines as,

> *The Owl and the Pussy-Cat went to sea*
> ⏑ | — ⏑ ⏑ | — ⏑ ⏑ |— ˌ⏑ |—|
> *In a beautiful pea-green boat.*
> ⏑ ⏑ |— ⏑ ⏑ |— ˌ ⏑ |— ˌ|
> *They took some honey and plenty of money,*
> ⏑ |— ˌ ⏑ |— ⏑ ⏑ |— ⏑ ⏑ |— ⏑
> *Wrapped up in a five-pound note.*
> ⏑ | — ⏑ ⏑ |— ˌ ⏑ |— ˌ|

and,

> *The news in the paper is not so good.*
> ⏑ |— ⏑ ˙ | — ⏑ ⏑ |— ˌ⏑ |— |
> *The new taxes are hardly fair.*
> ⏑ ⏑ |— ⏑ ⏑ |— ˌ⏑ |— |
> *I doubt that many will ever recover*
> ⏑| — ˌ ⏑ |— ⏑ ⏑ |— ⏑⏑ |— ⏑ |
> *Now interest has jumped so high*
> ⏑ |— ⏑ ⏑ |— ˌ ⏑ |— |

between

> *If you wake at midnight, and hear a horse's feet*
> — ⏑ |— ⏑ |— ˌ|— ⏑ |— ⏑|— ⏑ |— ˌ|
> *Don't go drawing back the blind, or looking in the street*
> — — ⏑ | — ⏑ | — ⏑ | — ⏑|— ⏑ |— ⏑|— |

> *Dreary lay the long road, dreary lay the town,*
> — ⏑|— ⏑ |— ⏑ | — ⏑ |— ⏑ |— ˌ|
> *Lights out and never a glint of moon*
> — ˌ|— ⏑ |— ⏑⏑ |— ⏑ |— |

and sentences which might commonly be heard in everyday conversation; for example,

> *When you go to Denmark, I recommend you see Copenhagen's famous*
> — ⏑ |— ⏑| — ˌ|—⏑ |— ⏑|— — ⏑ |— ˌ|—⏑|— ⏑ |— ⏑ |
> *parks and gardens if you can.*
> — ⏑ | — ⏑|— ⏑|— |

| *When you go to Dénmark,*| |*I recomménd you see Copenhágen's famous*|

| *párks and*| | *gárdens if you cán.*|

Never   leave   the   tap   on.   Always   turn   it   off.   Drought   here   is   one

— ◡ | — ◡ | — ◡͜ | — ◡ | — ◡ | —͜ | —   ◡ ◡ | —

of our greatest plagues.

◡ ◡ | — ◡ | — |

| *Never leave the tа́p on.* | | *Always turn it о́ff.* | | *Drо́ught here* | | *is one of*

| *our greatest plа́gues.* |

It seems to me that a fixed metrical scheme is necessary for the foreign
learner as a guide to his management of the great variety of stress
fluctuations which occur in every sentence of reasonable length in spoken
English, and for this reason, the main emphasis in the programme was on
verse. As comparison of the relatively common-place sentences with the
familiar rhymes and verses given above will show, the two-value system of
accented/unaccented used in scansion is not radically different from the
stress-profile of natural spoken English—understandably enough, since the
former is rooted in the latter. Thus practice with these basic strongly
metrical models can reasonably be expected to familiarize the non-native
speaker with the regular patterns of expectation, and programming
observable in spontaneous native utterance. As McAuley[22] points out,

> Contrast, but not contradiction; freedom within order; variety within
> uniformity; tension and flexibility; the unexpected that nevertheless ful-
> fils the pattern it seems to be overriding, the heightened noticeability of
> each syllable because its actual behaviour is upon a basis of regular
> expectation; the reconciling of the natural and the artificial in the dance
> of language; the sensitive response to logical and emotional nuance—
> these are the reasons that have made accentual-syllabic verse one of the
> great inventions of Western culture, and have enabled its usefulness to
> endure over many centuries. [23]

It must be understood that while I am not advocating the use of our finest
poetry—the form of literature in which the English language excels—as
exercise material for students who could have no appreciation of the
subtleties of its structure, mood, and expression, I do suggest that the
speaking of verse can assist the foreign learner toward an understanding of
the principles underlying the rhythm of English. Despite their acquaintance
with the various *genres* of poetry, the students participating in this programme had had no experience in speaking English verse and only minimal
experience in listening to it (for the most part having been taught by non-
English teachers themselves) and, it later emerged, had not even been aware
of a relationship existing between accentual-syllabic verse and native
English speech.

However, one of the most amazing facts revealed by the investigation was that the foreign subjects generally did not know which words in the English sentence are normally stressed and, consequently, had no idea of the basic principle of sentence stress in English; namely, that the incidence of stress is largely dependent upon the semantic component—that stress placement is governed by the relative importance of words from the standpoint of the meaning or implication of the sentence.

The next stage of the programme, then, was analysis of the normal stress patterning of the parts of speech in English. It was explained to the class that although nouns, verbs, adjectives and adverbs are usually stressed in the sentence, there are a number of instances when they are not. For example, *stick* is unstressed in the expression, *He always'carried a'walking stick*; *is* is unstressed in the sentence, *She is a'teacher at my'school*; *good* is unstressed in the greeting, *Good'morning, Miss'Adams*, and normally in such sentences as *It's a'very good'book*. On the other hand, *very* is unstressed in the sentence, *It's not a very'kind thing to'do to them*.

It was also shown that although the structure words are normally unstressed, numerous examples can be found of these parts of speech receiving stress. For example, in the sentence, *What is it'used for?* the preposition *for* is given its strong form, with the result that it has a prominence which would be incorrect in such a sentence as, *It's for'cleaning the'car*, where the weak form is used. Again, conjunctions—normally unstressed—may be stressed if the subordinate clause which is introduced by one occurs at the beginning of the sentence; for example, *'If you'see her, give her my love.* In this sentence the pronouns are unstressed, but in sentences in which a pronoun is used emphatically or reflexively it *does* receive sentence stress; for example, *The onus was on'her. She did it her'self.* The stressing of demonstratives is likewise variable. Usually unstressed when used as adjectives; for example, *Would you'mind opening that'window?* as pronouns, they usually receive some degree of prominence; for example, *'Where did you find'those?* The indefinite pronouns *some* and *any* are generally unstressed: *You'll'find some on my'desk*, but implying a contrast, and in compounds, they are stressed; for example, *'Some people don't drink 'tea, but there's hardly'anybody who doesn't drink'coffee.*

The anomalous finites or auxiliary verbs—unlike full finites are usually unstressed. In the last example above, for instance, *don't* and *doesn't*, as would be expected, are unstressed. However, when used to introduce a negative question the anomalous finite is frequently stressed; for example, *'Didn't you'see him?* Occurring in positive statements, they are generally used emphatically and are therefore stressed; for example, *I'do apologise for being'late.* Although *shall, will, am, is, was, were, have, had*, etc., are unstressed in positive statements, in negative utterances they are frequently given some degree of prominence: *They 'weren't 'there at the 'time*; *I 'haven't 'seen them for 'ages*. However, in sentences in which *not* is emphasized, the auxiliary is usually unstressed; for example,

   I've 'not 'seen them for 'ages.

When a part of the verb "to be" occurs in the final position of a sentence, it is usually stressed: *Can you 'tell me who she 'is?* However, in a sentence such as, *He wanted to 'know where the 'lecture was*, the *was* is unstressed because it follows immediately after its stressed subject.

   However, despite this attention to exceptional stress placement, the class was given adequate practice in normal stress patterning involving nouns, verbs, adjectives, and adverbs in the sentence, numerous examples such as the following being presented:

1. Stress placement on nouns:
   It had the AP'PEARANCE of 'WOOL.
   We've come to the 'END of the 'EXERCISE.
   Did you 'like the 'SOUND of that 'MUSIC?
   'Best 'WISHES on your '21st 'BIRTHDAY.

2. Stress placement on verbs:
   I 'WANTED you to 'KNOW
   They 'WORKED until they were EX'HAUSTED.
   He 'LEARNED, to his relief, that he had 'PASSED.
   To her conster'nation, she 'REALIZED that she would have to RE'TURN.

3. Stress placement on adjectives:
   The 'cost of 'petrol is very 'HIGH.
   The 'meaning of the 'dream wasn't 'CLEAR.
   The 'top of the 'box was painted 'GREEN.
   It's a 'WARM wind, the 'WEST wind.

4. Stress placement on adverbs:
   Will you have your 'lunch 'NOW?
   On a'rriving at the 'door, he 'opened it 'NOISELESSLY.
   'These students are 'harder 'working than any we have had 'PREVIOUSLY.
   They ME'TICULOUSLY labelled all the 'bottles, and 'THEN they packed them 'CAREFULLY into the 'cartons 'provided.

Special attention was drawn to alteration in stress placement on adverbs as a result of word order; for example, in the sentence,

   'WHILE you were 'OUT, your 'friend called.

the initially placed *while* is given considerable prominence, whereas in the following sentence, where it occurs medially, it is unstressed:

   Your 'friend 'called while you were 'OUT.

Likewise, it was shown that *still* may be stressed or unstressed depending upon its position in the sentence:

> 'These shoes are 'dear but 'those ones are dearer ' STILL

but,

> 'These shoes are 'dear but 'those ones are still 'DEARER.

The principles of sense group organization were then explained to the class, and prose passages were provided for practice in the identification and division of sense groups in the stream of speech.

Sample passages for division into sense groups:

If you hear the colour white mentioned what do you think of? I think of snow. It is interesting to find out what other people think when colours are mentioned. When red is mentioned, a lovely rose comes into my mind. When green is mentioned, fresh leaves appear. I suppose this is because I love nature, especially flowers. A friend of mine said that when these three colours were mentioned to him; he thought of paper, blood, and his school uniform jacket. I wonder if that is because he is a boy and I am a girl. I'm sure girls think of beauty more than boys do.

Anon.

The ground was hard, the air was still, my road was lonely; I walked fast till I got warm, and then I walked slowly to enjoy and analyse the species of pleasure brooding for me in the hour and situation. It was three o'clock; the church bell tolled as I passed under the belfry; the charm of the hour lay in its approaching dimness, in the low-gliding and pale-beaming sun. I was a mile from Thornfield, in a lane noted for wild roses in summer, for nuts and blackberries in autumn, and even now possessing a few coral treasures in hips and haws, but whose best winter delight lay in its utter solitude and leafless repose. If a breath of air stirred, it made no sound here; for there was not a holly, not an ever-green to rustle, and the stripped hawthorn and hazel bushes were as still as the white, worn stones which causewayed the middle of the path. Far and wide, on each side, there were only fields, where no cattle now browsed; and the little brown birds, which stirred occasionally in the hedge, looked like single russet leaves that had forgotten to drop.

Charlotte Brontë,
Jane Eyre, Chapter XII.

To this stage, the class had not dealt systematically with the principle of *gradation*. Thus although the students were becoming reasonably proficient in stress patterning, they were still not able to make the necessary qualitative and quantitative adjustments of unimportant words with any degree of confidence. Semantically, their utterances were accurate, but it was obvious that if their rhythm units were to sound anything like those produced by native speakers of the language they would have to learn how to modify and reduce their pronunciation of the linguistically important but phonetically insignificant structure words.

Accordingly, it was shown that prepositions, articles, pronouns, auxiliary verbs, and conjunctions—important units, structurally, in the sentence—are not usually emphatic and therefore should not be made to seem prominent. Examples of stressed structure words were presented for their consideration, but it was pointed out that generally the weak rather than the strong form would be preferable in connected utterance. Such expressions as the following were practised until the students could recognize the difference between strong and weak forms, and had mastered the rules governing distribution of the weak form:

	Strong Form	Weak Form	Examples of weak form in connected speech
Articles			
a	eɪ	ə	One and *a* half.
an	æn	ən	I waited *an* hour.
the	ðiː	ðə	*The* radio's broken.
	But before vowels the strong form is used		*The* end of *the* affair.
Prepositions			
at	æt	ət	One *at* a time.
for	fɔː	fə	It's a call *for* you.
from	frɒm	frəm	I believe he's *from* England.
of	ɒv	əv	I'd like a cup *of* coffee.
to	tuː	tə	They want *to* leave.
	But before vowels the strong form is used		I suppose we ought *to* ask them.
Personal Pronouns			
he	hiː	iː	Has *he* been waiting long?
her	hɜː	hə	I've met *her* brother several times.
him	hɪm	ɪm	They told *him* not to go that way.
them	ðɛm	ðəm	I haven't seen *them* since Christmas.
you	juː	jə	Do *you* think he'll pass his exams?
your	jɔː	jə	You'd better take *your* overcoat.
us	ʌs	əs	Let *us* go to the circus at Easter.

Impersonal Pronoun

| it | ɪt | ət | I don't know whether *it'll* be delivered. |

Indefinite Adjectives

such	sʌtʃ	sətʃ	All *such* cases have to be examined.
some	sʌm	səm	There were *some* copies in the library.
any	ɛni	ŋi	Have you got *any* coffee?

Conjunctions

but	bʌt	bət	I'd like to meet them *but* I'll be away when they arrive.
than	ðæn	ðən	She's much taller *than* her sister.
and	ænd	ənd	He was both quick *and* accurate.

Auxiliary Verbs

am	æm	m	*I'm* writing to the editor.
are	aː	ə	Where *are* you living now?
is	ɪz	s *or* z	*It's* rained so heavily that the *road's* like a stream.
was	wɒz	wəz	There *was* a time when he needed work.
were	wɜː	wə	We *were* waiting for nearly an hour.
have	hæv	həv *or* əv	*Have* they arrived yet or *have* they only phoned?
had	hæd	həd *or* d	If they *had* asked me I would have been able to help.
has	hæz	həz	*Has* he been appointed yet?

Anomalous Finites

do	du	d (before unstressed *you*)	*Do* you like skiing?
		də (before consonants)	*Do* the students often visit the snow fields?
		dʊ (before vowels)	They enjoy themselves, so *do* I.
does	dʌz	dəz	When *does* the postman come?
can	kæn	kən	*Can* you hear clearly from there?
could	kʊd	kəd	I'm sure you *could* do better.
should	ʃʊd	ʃəd *or* d	How *should* I know?

must	mʌst	məst	*Must* you go now?
will	wɪl	əl *or* l	Everything'*ll* be all right. *He'll* soon be well again.
would	wʊd	d	Had I known about the strike I *would* have bought an extra supply.

These exercises were followed by study and repetition of simple stress patterns in which weak forms of the parts of speech listed above were intermingled with the unstressed syllables of disyllabic and longer words.

Pattern: ˄   ˘   ´

    try again
    not enough
    drive the car
    go to sleep
    change your shoes

Pattern: ˘   ´   ˘

    at dinner
    a lot of
    the paper
    as well as
    for ever

Pattern: ˄   ˘   ˘   ´

    what is the time?
    bright as the day
    heavy as lead
    playing a game
    hardly enough

Pattern: ˘   ´   ˘   ˘   ˋ

    we know what it is
    he wanted us to
    to sharpen it with
    they asked if they could
    a tablespoonful

Pattern: ˘   ´   ˘   ˘   ˋ

    I think he's busy
    They don't believe him
    a bunch of flowers
    he leaves tomorrow
    I haven't read it

Pattern: ˘ ˆ ˘ ˋ ˘ ˊ
I hope they understand
Perhaps you'd care to wait
on Sunday afternoons
the bus is very late
the taxi's due at six

Pattern: ˘ ˋ ˘ ˘ ˆ ˘ ˘ ˊ
We didn't expect to be asked
He's taken the dog for a walk
I'll tell them we haven't the time
She never remembers a thing
They won't be in time for the play

Pattern: ˘ ˋ ˘ ˘ ˆ ˘ ˘ ˊ ˘ ˘
I asked them to wait in the corridor
He said that he couldn't believe in her
They told me they'd left it on Saturday
I hear he's applied for a scholarship
The other men wouldn't agree to it.

From this series of exercises, study developed of the several degrees of stress since it became obvious to the class that although there was always one principal stress in the sense group there might also be present two or more words of less importance which nevertheless required some degree of prominence. This was demonstrated in a series of pyramidal exercises in which the principal stress was retained even though additional words sometimes necessitated varying degrees of stress in order to produce a natural-sounding speech stress profile; for example,

. . . champágne
. . . French champágne
. . . a bottle of French champágne
. . . two bottles of French champágne
. . . two fine old bottles of French champágne
. . . They took two fine old bottles of French champágne
. . . They had taken two fine old bottles of French champágne
It seems they had taken two fine old bottles of French champágne

glásses
a pair of glásses
a pair of réading glasses
a pair of horn-rimmed réading glasses
he wore a pair of horn-rimmed réading glasses
he was wearing a pair of horn-rimmed réading glasses
When I saw him he was wearing a pair of horn-rimmed réading glasses

> *a stíck*
> *a wálking stick*
> *an old wálking stick*
> *an old oak wálking stick*
> *my grandfather's old oak wálking stick*
> *It was my grandfather's old oak wálking stick*

Selections of verse, such as the following, were also used to illustrate regular time spacing of the principal stresses and the counterpointing of metrical rhythm and the speech stress profile.

When men were all asleep the snow came flying,
In large white flakes falling on the city brown,
Stealthily and perpetually settling and loosely lying,
    Hushing the latest traffic of the drowsy town;
Deadening, muffling, stifling its murmurs failing;
Lazily and incessantly floating down and down:
    Silently sifting and veiling road, roof and railing:
Hiding difference, making unevenness even,
Into angles and crevices softly drifting and sailing.
    All night it fell, and when full inches seven
It lay in the depth of its uncompacted lightness,
The clouds blew off from a high and frosty heaven,
    And all woke earlier for the unaccustomed brightness
Of the winter dawning, the strange unheavenly glare:
The eye marvelled—marvelled at the dazzling whiteness;
    The ear hearkened to the stillness of the solemn air;
No sound of wheel rumbling nor of foot falling,
And the busy morning cries came thin and spare.
    Then boys I heard, as they went to school, calling.
They gathered up the crystal manna to freeze
Their tongues with tasting, their hands with snow-balling;
    Or rioted in a drift, plunging up to the knees;
Or peering up from under the white-mossed wonder,
"O look at the trees!" they cried, "O look at the trees!"
    With lessened load a few carts creak and blunder,
Following along the white deserted way,
A country company long dispersed asunder:
    When now already the sun, in pale display
Standing by Paul's high dome, spread forth below
His sparkling beams, and awoke the stir of the day.
    For now doors open, and war is waged with the snow;
And trains of sombre men, past tale of number,

Tread long brown paths, as toward their toil they go;
  But even for them awhile no cares encumber
Their minds diverted; the daily word is unspoken,
The daily thoughts of labour and sorrow slumber
At the sight of the beauty that greets them, for the
  Charm they have broken.

Robert Bridges, London Snow.

It was observed that the stressed syllables occurred at perceptually uniform periods, that they were marked by increased duration, and that they provided the steadily moving pulses, between which the unstressed syllables were accommodated.

The discovery that the rhythmic impulse is not necessarily marked by uniform loudness of the stresses came as a surprise to most of the students, yet, as we have seen, since the time of Joshua Steele it has been recognized that rhythmical pulsation does not necessarily imply sound or noise at all, the essential feature of rhythm being periodicity. However, having realized that undue prominence of any of the syllables of an utterance can result in disturbance of the entire rhythm pattern, the students began to exercise greater care in the arrangement and timing of their rhythm units.

Nevertheless, like the subjects who had participated in the several acoustic investigations, the members of the experimental class experienced considerable difficulty in coping with the features of catenation, and thus as well as learning how to produce structurally credible rhythm units, they had also to study the rules governing liaison and juncture. The ability to move smoothly and steadily from stress to stress taking cognizance of these features is essential to the production of normal English speech rhythm, and thus the students were provided with material for the practice of smooth transitions at word and syllable boundaries. In addition to practice and repetition of linking sounds; for example,

    she teaches‿at‿a high school
    they kept‿asking‿us‿over
    to have‿a cup‿of tea
    sooner‿or later‿I'll‿answer
    I'm‿early, but‿I came to look‿around

they were shown how to use phonetic cues to mark word boundaries—that is, how to use duration and neutralization, pitch change, aspiration, devoicing, etc., to differentiate words in the stream of speech, while at the same time maintaining the impression of an unbroken continuum of connected utterance. Examples such as the following were given:

    a grey day | a grade "A"
    an aim | a name

clear ice | clear rice
pea-stalks | peace talks
a steeled eye | a steel die

and samples of literary material were provided for practice:

> When Marner's sensibility returned, he continued the action which had
> been arrested, and closed his door, unaware of the chasm in his con-
> sciousness, unaware of any intermediate change, except that the light had
> grown dim, and that he was chilled and faint. He thought he had been
> too long standing at the door and looking out. Turning towards the
> hearth, where the two logs had fallen part, and sent forth only a red un-
> certain glimmer, he seated himself on his fireside chair, and was stooping
> to push his logs together, when, to his blurred vision, it seemed as if there
> were gold on the floor in front of the hearth. Gold!—his own gold—
> brought back to him as mysteriously as it had been taken away! He felt
> his heart begin to beat violently, and for a few moments he was unable to
> stretch out his hand and grasp the restored treasure. The heap of gold
> seemed to glow and get larger beneath his agitated gaze. He leaned
> forward at last, and stretched forth his hand; but instead of the hard coin
> with the familiar resisting outline, his fingers encountered soft warm
> curls.
>
> George Eliot, *Silas Marner*, Chapter XII.

The students were next shown the relationship between stress, rhythm, and
intonation, and some basic intonation patterns were introduced in order to
illustrate the linking function of intonation in the chain of speech. The five
types of fundamental frequency variation were represented diagrammatically (Fig. 29), and it was shown how these patterns are used in normal
English utterance.

Practice of these patterns in isolation was followed by readings from
literature in which they occur; for example,

> 'Will you walk a little faster?' said a whiting to a snail.
> 'There's a porpoise close behind us, and he's treading on my tail.
> See how eagerly the lobsters and the turtles all advance!
> They are waiting on the shingle—will you come and join the dance?
> Will you, won't you, will you, won't you, will you join the dance?
>
> 'You can really have no notion how delightful it will be,
> When they take us up and throw us, with the lobsters, out to sea!'
> But the snail replied, 'Too far, too far!' and gave a look askance—
> Said he thanked the whiting kindly, but he would not join the dance.

Would not, could not, would not, could not, would not join the dance.
Would not, could not, would not, could not, could not join the dance.

'What matters it how far we go?' his scaly friend replied,
'There is another shore, you know, upon the other side.
The farther off from England the nearer is to France—
Then turn not pale beloved snail, but come and join the dance.
Will you, won't you, will you, won't you, will you join the dance?
Will you, won't you, will you, won't you, won't you join the dance?

Lewis Carroll, *The Lobster Quadrille.*

It is a truth universally acknowledged that a single man in possession of a good fortune must be in want of a wife.

However little known the feelings or views of such a man may be on his first entering a neighbourhood, this truth is so well fixed in the minds of the surrounding families, that he is considered as the rightful property of some one or other of their daughters.

'My dear Mr. Bennet,' said his lady to him one day, 'have you heard that Netherfield Park is let at last?'

Mr. Bennet replied that he had not.

'But it is,' returned she; 'for Mrs. Long has just been here, and she told me all about it.'

Mr. Bennet made no answer.

'Do you not want to know who has taken it?' cried his wife impatiently.

'*You* want to tell me, and I have no objection to hearing it.'

This was invitation enough.

'Why, my dear, you must know, Mrs. Long says that Netherfield is taken by a young man of large fortune from the north of England; that he came down on Monday in a chaise and four to see the place, and was so much delighted with it that he agreed with Mr. Morris immediately; that he is to take possession before Michaelmas, and some of his servants are to be in the house by the end of next week.'

'What is his name?'

'Bingley.'

'Is he married or single?'

'Oh, single, my dear, to be sure! A single man of large fortune; four or five thousand a year. What a fine thing for our girls!'

'How so? how can it affect them?

'My dear Mr. Bennet,' replied his wife, 'how can you be so tiresome? You must know that I am thinking of his marrying one of them.'

'Is that his design in settling here?'

'Design? nonsense, how can you talk so! But it is very likely that he *may*

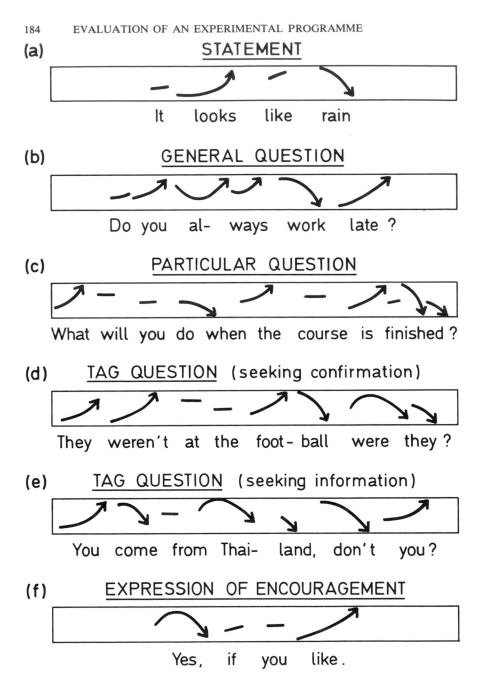

Figure 29.   Diagrammatic representation of intonation patterns used in normal English utterance.
System of notation adapted from Corinne Adams, (1969), *loc. cit.*, pp. 109, 112.

fall in love with one of them, and therefore you must visit him as soon as he comes.'

'I see no occasion for that. You and the girls may go, or you may send them by themselves, which perhaps will be still better; for as you are as handsome as any of them, Mr. Bingley might like you the best of the party.'

Jane Austen, *Pride and Prejudice*,
Chapter I.

Although the experimental programme was of only 20 hours' duration, taped language laboratory programmes were recommended to the students for extra individual work. These programmes which I had prepared at an earlier period for the TEFL students generally were consolidation exercises consisting of 1. description of the sound pattern; 2. presentation of the pattern, first in isolation and subsequently in connected speech; 3. aural discrimination exercises; 4. exercises for repetition; 5. literary material featuring the target sound pattern in combination with other patterns. This last section was given for fluency of expression.

The members of the experimental class varied in the amount of work they did individually in the language laboratory. However, all attended at least four supervised sessions during the course of the programme. The script of the most advanced tape used is shown in Appendix 1.

Outline of Experimental Programme in English Speech Rhythm

Teaching Point	*Learning Activities*
1. Recognition of stress-timed rhythm	1. Listening to readings of English texts
2. Explanation of principles of English speech rhythm and comparison with syllable-timed rhythm	2. Examination of stress placement in strongly metrical material
3. Audio-visual presentation of basic English rhythm patterns	3. Repetition of patterns with fixed metrical scheme contrasted with similar material drawn from the students' native languages
4. Extension of patterns to non-metrical material	4. Practice of fabricated sentences based on simple metrical patterns
5. Analysis of word forms normally stressed in connected utterance	5. Identification of the stressed words in sample texts
6. Organization of the sense group	6. Division of selected texts into sense groups

Outline of Experimental Programme in English Speech Rhythm—Contd.

Teaching Point	Learning Activities
7. Disjuncture and the pause in phrasing	7. Practice in programming the utterance of selected textual material
8. Demonstration of the principle of gradation	8. Practice of strong and weak forms in the rhythm unit, in the sense group, and in the sentence
9. Timing of the rhythm unit	9. Comparison of stressed/ unstressed syllable duration
10. Explanation of the speech stress profile—degrees of stress	10. Repetition of material counterpointing metrical rhythm and the speech stress profile
11. Explication of the rules governing liaison, assimilation, and juncture	11. Examination of samples of liaison, assimilation, and juncture at rhythm group level, at sense group level, and at the level of the whole sentence
12. Relationship between stress, rhythm, and intonation	12. Repetition of some basic intonation patterns

Language Laboratory Consolidation Lessons

Presentation of readings of prose and verse with spaces for repetition	Practice of selected literary material requiring variation in pace, pitch and volume for expressive interpretation

(c) *Post-test*

Two months after the pre-test both experimental and control groups were retested. All subjects showed improved performance in the post-test as comared with the pretest, but it was found that the experimental group had improved twice as much as the control group, the difference in improvement being statistically significant at the 0.1 per cent level.

The three adjudicators who assessed the recorded utterances of the subjects on both tests worked independently evaluating the rhythm of the readings on a rating scale (0-5). All were experienced teachers of English who had a special interest in the spoken language. Nevertheless, they were issued with a few guidelines on the criteria particularly to be observed in their evaluations. In order to obviate the possibility of recognition of students on pre- and post-tests they were presented with tapes of the readings arranged in random order. Thus, order of presentation did not indicate whether the subject being assessed was on his pre-test or his post-test, or whether he was a member of the control or the experimental group. The test material again consisted of items of prose and verse arranged in order of difficulty from simple narrative prose to subtle poetry of considerable structural and conceptual complexity.

The following note was presented to each adjudicator together with a set of the recorded readings:

NOTE TO ADJUDICATORS
The 30 students whom you are asked to assess each recorded the four test items twice—

(i) at the beginning of their course
(ii) two months later, after the experimental group of 15 students had received 20 hours of class instruction in the management of English speech rhythm.

Although all speech rhythm exists in time speakers of different languages divide time differently. In English, the duration of successive portions of a sentence is not strictly proportional to the total number of syllables they contain but rather to the number of stressed syllables in each group. The stressed syllables tend to occur at relatively regular intervals and the unstressed syllables between them are crowded together and their pronunciation modified accordingly. In this way, uniformity of the duration of rhythm groups is preserved even though the actual number of syllables in each group varies. The subjects who participated in this experiment were native speakers of syllable-timed languages and, as you will observe, experienced some difficulty in establishing and maintaining the rhythm of the passages they read. The readings have been arranged in random order, thus order of presentation is not an indication of whether you are listening to the pre-test or the post-test of any student.

You are asked to evaluate the speech rhythm of the readings on a linear scale (0 - 5) marking the place on the continuum representing your estimate of each performance.
0 incomprehensible as English;
1 difficult to follow, extremely jerky—speech a series of isolate word forms without regard to phrasing;
2 comprehensible, but meaning either not understood or insufficiently marked; misplaced stress; staccato rhythm;
3 able to be followed without difficulty but with instances of faulty or inappropriate stress placement; rhythm anomalies;
4 fluent but with occasional errors in stress placement and/or

hesitations; rhythmic pulse realized;

5 basically natural utterance (although that of a foreign speaker); appropriate stress placement at syllable and word level; reasonably expressive phrasing; well sustained rhythm.

Criteria you should observe in your evaluation of the subjects' proficiency in speech rhythm are as follows:

(i) *lexical* (word) and *syntactical* (sentence) *stress* (i.e. appropriately stressed syllables and words);

(ii) *word grouping* (i.e. suitable phrasing, pausing, linking, and rate of utterance);

(iii) *pronunciation*, in so far as it affects the rhythm of the utterance—for example, while substitution of the phoneme /ɔ: / for /əʊ/ in *coat* is likely to occur, from the standpoint of speech rhythm use of the shorter cardinal vowel /o/ in this word would be more serious. Likewise, undue lengthening of short vowels, shortening of long vowels, and use of strong forms would modify the duration of syllables and thus affect the rhythm of the utterance.

Examples of the adjudicators' method of assessment may be seen in Tables 13 and 14 which show the raw scores gained by an experimental subject (No. 22/52) in his pre- and post-tests.

Generally, the consensus of the adjudicators was high. However, it was decided to test the reliability of their ratings by means of statistical analysis. The method selected was that which was described by Ebel in his "Estimation of the Reliability of Ratings" [24] The result of this analysis showed that individual ratings were not sufficiently reliable ($r = 0.7827$) for one adjudicator's scores to be accepted as the final assessment. However, the average index of agreement among the adjudicators was found to be statistically significant at the 1% level (reliability of average ratings = 0.9153).

All subjects (experimental and control) showed improved performance in the post-test as compared with their performance in the pre-test.

This improvement for both groups was shown to be significant by *sign test* at the 1% level [Sign (1%) with 15 d.f. = 2 - 13].

However, out of a possible score of 60, the mean improvement in the control group was 5.3, whereas the mean improvement in the experimental group was 10.6. By *paired t-test* this difference was shown to be significant at the 0.1% level ($t = 4.89$; when $P = 0.001$, $t_{14\,d.f.} = 4.14$).

The difference between the experimental and control groups in the post-test was likewise shown by t-test to be significant at the 5% level ($t = 2.15$; when $P = 0.05$, $t_{14\,d.f.} = 2.1448$).

It would seem that the significance level here—unlike the significance

TABLE 13
Adjudicators' assessment of experimental subject K (No. 22) on pre-test

Test item	Adjudicator 1	Adjudicator 2	Adjudicator 3	Total score
I	0	0	0	10
	1	1	1	
	2	2	2	
	3	3✓	3✓	
	4✓	4	4	
	5	5	5	
II	0	0	0	9
	1	1	1	
	2	2	2	
	3✓	3✓	3✓	
	4	4	4	
	5	5	5	
III	0	0	0	10
	1	1	1	
	2	2	2	
	3✓	3	3✓	
	4	4✓	4	
	5	5	5	
IV	0	0	0	11
	1	1	1	
	2	2	2	
	3	3	3✓	
	4✓	4✓	4	
	5	5	5	
Total	14	14	12	40

Pre-test score = 40

TABLE 14
Adjudicators' assessment of experimental subject K (No. 52) on post-test

Test item	Adjudicator 1	Adjudicator 2	Adjudicator 3	Total score
I	0	0	0	12
	1	1	1	
	2	2	2	
	3	3	3	
	4✓	4✓	4✓	
	5	5	5	

Table 14 contd.

Test item	Adjudicator 1	Adjudicator 2	Adjudicator 3	Total score
II	0	0	0	12
	1	1	1	
	2	2	2	
	3	3	3	
	4✓	4✓	4✓	
	5	5	5	
III	0	0	0	13
	1	1	1	
	2	2	2	
	3	3	3	
	4✓	4✓	4	
	5	5	5✓	
IV	0	0	0	11
	1	1	1	
	2	2	2	
	3	3✓	3	
	4✓	4	4✓	
	5	5	5	
Total	16	15	17	48

Post-test score = 48

level of the improvement—must have been affected by the wide range of ability shown by the individual members of the two groups. Whereas some of the subjects showed a difference of only 2 between their pre- and post-test scores, for some, the difference was as great as 12-17 (Table 15).

A general overall improvement by members of both groups was to be expected, since all subjects—control and experimental alike—lived in an English-speaking environment during the crucial period of two months from pre-test to post-test; they heard lectures in English; many resided in university colleges where they fraternized with native English speakers; and no attempt was made to restrict their use of English for the purpose of this experiment. However, as stated above,[25] the control group received no systematic training during this period. The difference between the two groups as shown in the post-test, then, must be attributed to the experimental group's learning experiences in the course of the programme[26] described in the preceding section.

TABLE 15

Differences between experimental and control subjects' scores on pre- and post-tests

	CONTROL			EXPERIMENTAL		
	Pre-test	*Post-test*	*Difference*	*Pre-test*	*Post-test*	*Difference*
A	44	51	+ 7	42	50	+ 8
B	45	47	+ 2	44	57	+ 13
C	44	53	+ 9	45	57	+ 12
D	37	42	+ 5	46	55	+ 9
E	34	35	+ 1	43	45	+ 2
F	28	30	+ 2	37	44	+ 7
G	16	18	+ 2	22	35	+ 13
H	34	38	+ 4	23	33	+ 10
I	24	30	+ 6	25	37	+ 12
J	32	40	+ 8	39	46	+ 7
K	35	42	+ 7	40	48	+ 8
L	42	53	+ 11	23	37	+ 14
M	43	49	+ 6	28	43	+ 15
N	24	29	+ 5	18	30	+ 12
O	15	19	+ 4	22	39	+ 17

For significance levels of differences, see text.

CHAPTER EIGHT

Conclusion

The starting point of the study of English speech rhythm which has been reported in this book was my concern with the pronunciation of the non-native teachers of English who year by year undertake the course offered by the University of Sydney leading to the Diploma in the Teaching of English as a Foreign Language.

After several years' observation of the spoken English of successive classes of these graduate students, I realized that their foreign accent was due primarily to faulty speech rhythm—an undesirable defect in the utterance of any speaker, but especially serious in their case since it impaired their proficiency as teachers. The cause of the trouble, it seemed to me, was associated with the stressing of the syllables which mark the rhythmic impulse in English and with the disjuncture normally used to separate rhythm units in the stream of connected speech. However, it was first necessary to determine the mechanisms used by native speakers to produce the parameters which actually contribute to the listener's judgment of stress. Thus began the series of investigations through which, I believe, have been elucidated several issues—not only the question of faulty speech rhythm in non-native utterance, but also the riddle of the nature of sentence stress in English, and the problem of selection of appropriate learning experiences in speech rhythm for the foreign learner.

It is my earnest hope that the information which has been brought to light as a result of this study may be of some value in encouraging further research into an elusive and highly complex area of English phonology and, in due course, resolution of associated issues still unanswered.

On the basis of the material analysed in the course of this comparative study of the utterance of native and non-native speakers of English, then, I have drawn the following conclusions:

1. A physiological definition of stress based upon internal intercostal muscular activity is untenable.

2. A pattern of expiratory muscular activity is regularly produced during connected utterance by native speakers, while non-native speakers produce a similar although considerably modified form of this pattern.

3. There appears to be no one-to-one correspondence between stress at the sentence level in English and any single acoustic parameter, individual speakers—native and non-native alike—habitually or in certain contexts signalling this feature by means of one or another and, in some cases, more than one parameter.

4. Duration appears to be the most widely used acoustic correlate of stress in the utterance of both native and non-native speakers.

5. The rhythm anomalies of the non-native speaker of English whose first language is syllable-timed appear to result from superfluous and random placement of stresses and pauses together with failure to neutralize the unstressed syllables of the utterance.

6. In the field of foreign language learning, activities based on the timing and organization of the sense group are crucial for the acquisition of a native-like English speech rhythm.

As I have shown, the object of the whole study was to determine the physiological and/or acoustic correlates of stress by means of a series of investigations of the characteristics of stressed and unstressed syllables in connected speech, and to ascertain whether the rhythm of a group of non-native speakers could be improved as a result of certain learning experiences.

The search for the correlates of sentence stress involved three different areas of investigation; these being, an auditory perception test (Chapter IV); an electromyographic study of respiratory muscles believed to be associated with stress (Chapter V); and examination of the three parameters (fundamental frequency, amplitude, and duration) generally regarded as the most consistent acoustic correlates of this feature (Chapter VI). The learning activities devised on the basis of the findings were then tested on a group of students comparable with those who had participated in these several investigations (Chapter VII).

Despite fairly widespread acceptance of the view that stress is associated with increased respiratory muscular activity, I could find no evidence of increased internal intercostal muscle activity synchronous with the utternace of stressed syllables in connected speech, and must therefore reject a physiological definition of stress based on the expiratory muscular activity of the speaker.

As I have shown,[1] both native English and native Vietnamese speakers produced a typical pattern of internal intercostal muscular activity during connected utterance when the language they spoke was their own mother tongue and, in general, this basic pattern was also produced (although in a considerably modified form) by non-native speakers of English.

It will be remembered that in the "native" pattern a preliminary localized burst of muscular activity before the commencement of speech was followed by an interval in the first part of the utterance during which activity was minimal or absent. After a variable period of time this activity was observed to increase progressively through each successive phrase of the utterance, and, between these phrases, a motor pause in the activity occurred which slightly preceded the linguistic one. The non-native speakers, however, produced patterns of expiratory muscular activity which showed very considerable variability, particularly in that the activity waxed and waned within the several phrases of their utterances rather than increasing progressively to the end, and that repetitions of the pattern of the initial phrase were very common. It was suggested that such "duplications" and "triplications"[2] might have occurred as a result of the tendency of these subjects to programme their utterances in shorter segments. However, neither in their records nor in the records of the native speakers were localized bursts of activity of the internal intercostal muscle found to correlate with the incidence of stressed syllables in connected speech. I can only assume, therefore, that in other studies where increased expiratory muscular activity was found to correlate with stress, the speakers concerned must have uttered each word deliberately after a period of silence so that each stressed syllable became an entity in itself. Thus the stressed syllables would have stood in the same relation to the whole utterance as the first word of each phrase did in my study and, quite typically, would have been preceded by a localized burst of activity.

Although, as we have seen,[3] it is customary to propose a physiological definition of stress when the phenomenon is considered from the speaker's viewpoint and an acoustic explanation when it is considered from the point of view of the listener, I am unable to find support for a physiological definition based upon expiratory muscular activity. However, the acoustic parameters perceived by the listener as the psychological correlates of these physical properties are at the same time fed back to the speaker who, by means of appropriate physiological mechanisms, is able to control their production and adjust their magnitudes at will. Thus an acoustic definition of stress applies equally to speaker and listener. Closely related to auditory perception, the acoustic explanation must nevertheless be regarded—at least in most instances—as physiologically based since the sound of the syllable carrying the stress has to be produced before it can be perceived.

Most of the researchers who have proposed acoustic definitions of stress, however, have used synthesized speech and this, I believe, has perpetuated the dichotomy which originated in the attempts of the early phoneticians to explain the nature of stress either in terms of subjective action on the part of the speaker or by reference to auditory perception on the part of the listener. In this study, however, perceived stress in natural speech was used as the starting-point of the search for the acoustic correlates of stress since one of the main objectives was to determine what the speaker does in order for the listener to receive an impression of stress.

It must be emphasized that no attempt was made to examine the acoustic properties of the several degrees of stress. The 10 adjudicators on whom I relied for judgments regarding stress placement were asked only to indicate on all all-or-none basis which words seemed to them to be stressed—not to state whether they could perceive degrees of stressedness—since it is the periodic alternation of prominence and non-prominence throughout the speech continuum which marks the rhythmic impulse in English, and the purpose of the whole series of investigations was to examine stress in relation to its function as the marker of this pulse.

It may well be that different levels of stress are signalled by different acoustic parameters or that stronger stress requires the use of more than one parameter, for although 81% of the subjects used duration, several of these speakers also used either fundamental frequency or amplitude, while 19% of them used all three parameters. However, this was not examined. In the utterance of 44% of the speakers fundamental frequency was found to correlate with stress but in no case did it occur as a speaker's single cue, being associated with duration in all but one instance when it was found in partnership with amplitude. Amplitude correlated with stress in the utterance of a mere quarter of the subjects and in only one case was used as a speaker's single cue to stress.

The complex trading relationships of these parameters, noted also—as I have pointed out above[4]—by several other researchers, preclude my speculating on the possibility that a one-to-one relationship may exist between any one of them and stress—of any degree whatsoever. Nevertheless, the results show that in this study duration clearly predominated as a cue and there was no evidence to suggest that native and non-native speakers habitually use different cues to signal stress at the sentence level.

However, it is interesting to observe that whereas there was a considerable difference between the duration of stressed and unstressed syllables in the utterance of the native speakers, their non-native counterparts did not mark this distinction with anything like the same degree of consistency. Thus even though 6 out of the 8 non-native speakers used duration to signal stress, the difference between the timing of their stressed and unstressed syllables was frequently minimal. By contrast, the native speakers reduced their unstressed syllables and, by means of this strategy combined with appropriate disjuncture, produced a rhythm consisting of serially recurrent units (each containing one stressed syllable and a variable number of unstressed syllables organized and timed so as to create an auditory impression of relative equivalence) the pulse of which was marked by approximately isochronous stresses.

The anomalous rhythm of the non-native speakers resulted, as I have shown,[5] from their misuse of stress and disjuncture. The numerous pauses made by this group are of interest because they were used not only to delimit sense groups and rhythm units but also to replace the linking mechanisms ordinarily used by native speakers to indicate word and syllable boundaries. The fact that a number of these speakers paused illogically in places where a native speaker would regard a pause as inappropriate seems to indicate that they had not grasped the principle of unitizing sequences of words in conformity with the grammatical rules of the language, and suggests that their comprehension of the test material was insecure. However, the test items were neither structurally nor semantically difficult, and the subjects were, after all, graduate teachers of English with considerable experience in its usage. Moreover, the pauses which they made were often quite short—a fact which suggests that they paused not for the purpose of phrasing but rather because they were experiencing some difficulty at the phonetic level.

Another significant feature of the utterance of the non-native subjects was that it was marked by numerous instances of misplaced stress at the lexical level as well as an overall superfluity of stresses. The discovery that these subjects had stressed 31% of the total 355 syllables in the 12 test items compared with 19% stressed by the native speakers warranted examination of possible reasons for this discrepancy between the two groups. Eventually it emerged that the foreign speakers did not understand the principles of stress placement at the sentence level in English, even though they had studied contrastive stress at the lexical level, and that, in addition, their experience in speaking the language had militated against fluent utterance. I concluded, therefore, that the speech rhythm anomalies of these subjects, manifested in their superfluous and indiscriminate placement of stresses and pauses, were attributable not only to first language interference—particularly in respect of the even-time spacing of their syllables—but also to their limited experience in speaking English and the unsatisfactory methods by which they had learned the language.

As the typical examples of personal data (Appendix 2a and 2b) show, the non-native speakers normally devoted very little time to spoken English outside their teaching work, and in the course of interviews with them, I ascertained that most had learnt English by means of grammar/translation/literary study techniques and that more often than not their work in the spoken language had been limited to the isolate word form. Even those who had studied English by the audio-lingual method appeared not to have had any specific instruction in sentence stress and rhythm.

From the highly successful results of the rhythm-oriented programme I have described above,[6] I am convinced that learning activities based upon organization and timing of stressed and unstressed syllables patterned so as to create an auditory impression of temporal equivalence are essential for the acquisition and development of the stress-timed rhythm of English. As I have shown, one readily available source of material for practice in the organization and timing of the English rhythm unit is the traditional rhyme which, with its strongly metrical beat, provides an excellent foundation for the recognition and production of the basic rhythms which occur in normal connected speech. Such material, regularly practised by the young native learner in response to his need for rhythmic repetitive utterances, emphasizes the cyclic nature of speech rhythm which, as we have seen, is but another manifestation of that periodicity which characterizes all our normal movements.

It seems to me that there are implications for the teacher of English as a foreign language in this study which are nevertheless beyond the scope of this book. It is rare in the process of education for the practitioner to meet with the theorist. The teacher acknowledges the importance of scientific research but all too often regards the researcher as some kind of crank. Theorizing is all very well if one has unlimited time to conduct controlled experiments in laboratories far removed from overcrowded classrooms, but let the theorist join him in the practical situation for a day and he might find cause to review some of his hypotheses. But the researcher, on his part, methodically proceeds with his investigations oblivious, it would seem, of the needs of those in the practical situation. When he speaks, he does so on the basis of evidence painstakingly accumulated and patiently checked. That the teacher might appreciate neither his findings nor the language in which they are expressed seems not to concern him. He will gladly share the results of his investigations with the teacher but he does not regard it as his function to interpret them in the interests of pedagogy.

This lack of liaison is unfortunate, it seems to me, for between the theorist and the practitioner stands the educational technologist—the well-meaning interpreter who frequently mistranslates. More often than not it is through his enthusiastic promotion of technology and software—the products of applied scientific research—that the teacher gains his only tenuous acquaintance with the researcher. But frequently the programmes offered by the technologist are based on the most superficial interpretation of experimental analysis, and the teacher, unaware of the work of the researcher, does not recognize the fact. As Carroll[7] once put it, the teacher has not caught up with the theorist, and this—by and large—is still the case. The result, however, is that misunderstandings are rife. All too often it is naïvely believed that lack of expertise can be offset by the technology package which arrives replete with full instructions for use. Thus teaching materials are frequently procured—and used—uncritically in situations for which they are quite inappropriate. Instructional software is not a guarantee of instant learning, and the possession of a set of attractively presented programmes peddled by the ubiquitous middleman in no way absolves the teacher, as far as I can see, from the responsibility of extrapolating from laboratory theory to classroom practice.

In no area of E.F.L. teaching is this problem more serious than in phonology generally and in speech rhythm in particular, for in this field the teacher's knowledge is usually notoriously insecure and he tends to grasp any proffered technique by means of which he believes he can compensate for his lack of expertise. What he does not realize, however, is that materials and methods of teaching cannot be differentiated solely in terms of their overall results—that what is necessary is a clear understanding of the conditions under which various approaches succeed. Whereas a programme may be successful given certain conditions, it may require considerable adaptation for its objectives to be realized in a different set of circumstances. Furthermore, it is reasonable to suppose that the efficacy of any programme is likely to be influenced by individual student variables.

It is particularly satisfying, therefore, to be in the position not only of having precise knowledge of particular research findings but also of being able to devise a programme of learning activities on the basis of one's own results—further, of being able to test it on students comparable with the subjects who provided the original research data. As I have suggested above,[8] although a researcher's findings may have linguistic and statistical validity it does not follow as a natural corollary that they have pedagogical validity—and the last, I believe, is often the most difficult to establish.

I do not claim that the programme I have outlined would necessarily succeed in all E.F.L. learning situations. Based on the theory that the foreign learner must be taught how to recognize and produce the rhythm units of spoken English in order to establish and maintain the rhythmic impulse in connected utterance, it was devised specifically for native speakers of some Asian languages as a direct result of the research findings I have discussed in Part II of this book. I believe that native speakers of syllable-timed European languages would likewise profit from a rhythm-oriented course although I have no experimental evidence for such an assumption. There seems little doubt, however, that understanding of the principles of word grouping in English and the timing of the constituents of these groups is the *sine qua non* of competence at all levels of usage—both production and perception—in the process of communication. Any approach, therefore, which clarifies the rhythmic patterning that underlies normal English utterance must be of some value to the foreign learner, whatever system of speech rhythm obtains in his native language.

Curiously, it seems to me, the whole area of rhythmicality has been neglected in E.F.L. programmes—largely, I suspect, because its central importance has not been realized. As I pointed out in the *Introduction*, we often become aware of the phenomenon only when a speaker fails either to produce an impression of proportion in his own utterance or to apprehend the intended meaning in the utterance of another. The average teacher, with inadequate knowledge of the nature and function of the prosodic features generally, tends to concentrate his attention on other areas of the spoken language—usually the segmental features of the sound system and the isolate word form—yet the very essence of the communication skills he is presumably trying to develop consists in the external projection of internal processes in the form of chains of events or serial phenomena organized and integrated in time for the primary purpose of linking speaker and listener.

As we have seen, the non-native subjects who participated in the study I have reported here failed to programme their utterances according to the unwritten rules of spoken English and thus produced the anomalies discussed in Part II.

The young native learner, while frequently ignoring structure, is nevertheless unerringly able to produce credible rhythmic units as he progresses through every stage of his language development. This development parallels the development of his cognitive processes and capabilities as his mental activity likewise moves through series of planes from simple to more complex levels of organization. Thus what he wants to say at any stage can be adequately expressed through the medium of his current linguistic usage.

This close relationship between language and cognition is regarded by some observers as evidence of the inevitability of first language acquisition. However, by contrast, subsequent language learning is seen to be far from inevitable. The second language, like any other discipline or subject field, must be consciously learned, for it is impossible even to return the learner to a cognitive state comparable to that, let us say, of an eighteen-month-old child at onset of patterned speech. Nevertheless, as I have shown, at least some of the linguistic material used for amusement by the native learner during the early stages of language acquisition can be adapted successfully for the adult foreign learner. Entertaining as well as educational these learning activities certainly are, but if the native learner can enjoy the process of language acquisition and still achieve mastery, should the pleasure of language learning by painless strategies be denied the non-native speaker? It seems to me that in the area of English speech rhythm there may be found the parallel that Corder[9] sought between the processes of learning the mother tongue and foreign language learning.

THE UNIVERSITY OF SYDNEY

Department of Education

DIPLOMA IN THE TEACHING OF ENGLISH AS A FOREIGN LANGUAGE

RHYTHM

Tape No. 4 in the series Stress and Rhythm Patterns
In this tape you will hear a number of English speech rhythms. All rhythms—the rhythm of dance, the rhythm of the waves of the ocean, the rhythm of the planets, the rhythm of your heart beat—consist of movement in time. Another factor in rhythm is weight. In speech we sometimes refer to this factor as stress. However, the varied and flexible movement of speech rhythm cannot be indicated merely by putting light or heavy stress on certain syllables since rhythm is made up of weight and span and pace in varying proportions and combinations.

It is important to know where the stresses fall in a rhythm group but it is necessary to know, too, the intervals between these points and the time sequences involved in the utterance of them. You are going to hear three poems and three prose passages of increasing difficulty. First listen to the reading, then repeat the selection phrase by phrase. See whether you can find out how the different rhythms are produced.

First we have *Birds of Paradise*.

Golden winged, silver winged,
Winged with flashing flame,
Such a flight of birds I saw,
Birds without a name:
Singing songs in their own tòngue,
Song of songs, they came.

One to another calling
Each answering each,
One to another calling,
In their proper speech:
High above my head they wheeled
Far out of reach.

On wings of flame they went and came
With a cadenced clang
Their silver wings tinkled,
Their golden wings rang:
The wind it whispered through their wings,
Where in heaven they sang.

They flashed and they darted
Awhile before my eyes
Mounting, mounting, mounting still
In haste to scale the skies.
Birds without a nest on earth,
Birds of Paradise.

Where the moon riseth not
Nor the sun seeks the West,
There to sing their glory,
Which they sing at rest,
There to sing their love song
Which they sing their best.

Not in any garden
That mortal foot hath trod,
Not in any flowering tree
That springs from earthly sod,
But in the garden where they dwell,
The Paradise of God.

                                          Christina Rossetti

The West Wind

It's a warm wind, the west wind, full of birds' cries;
I never hear the west wind but tears are in my eyes.
For it comes from the west lands, the old brown hills,
And April's in the west wind, and daffodils.

It's a fine land, the west land, for hearts as tired as mine,
Apple orchards blossom there, and the air's like wine.
There is cool green grass there, where men may lie at rest,
And the thrushes are in song there, fluting from the nest.

"Will ye not come home, brother? ye have been long away,
It's April, and blossom time, and white is the may;

And bright is the sun, brother, and warm is the rain—
Will ye not come home, brother, home to us again?

"The young corn is green, brother, where the rabbits run,
It's a blue sky, and white clouds, and warm rain and sun.
It's song to a man's soul, brother, fire to a man's brain,
To hear the wild bees and see the merry spring again.

"Larks are singing in the west, brother, above the green wheat,
So will ye not come home, brother, and rest your tired feet?
I've a balm for bruised hearts, brother, sleep for aching eyes,"
Says the warm wind, the west wind, full of birds' cries.

It's the white road westward, the road that I must tread,
To the green grass, the cool grass, and rest for heart and head,
To the violets and the warm hearts and the thrushes' song,
In the fine land, the west land, the land where I belong.

John Masefield

The Windhover
To Christ our Lord

I caught this morning morning's minion, king-
  dom of daylight's dauphin, dapple-dawn-drawn Falcon, in
    his riding
  Of the rolling level underneath him steady air, and striding
High there, how he rung upon the rein of a wimpling wing
In his ecstasy! then off, off forth on swing,
  As a skate's heel sweeps smooth on a bow-bend: the hurl and
    gliding
  Rebuffed the big wind. My heart in hiding
Stirred for a bird,—the achieve of, the mastery of the thing!
Brute beauty and valour and act, oh, air, pride, plume here
  Buckle! AND the fire that breaks from thee then, a billion
Times told lovelier, more dangerous, O my chevalier!
No wonder of it: sheer plod makes plough down sillion
Shine, and blue-bleak embers, ah my dear,
Fall, gall themselves, and gash gold-vermilion.

Gerard Manley Hopkins

Now here are some prose passages with pauses for repetition.

Virginibus Puerisque

Pitiful is the case of the blind, who cannot read the face; pitiful that of the deaf, who cannot follow the changes of the voice. And there are others also to be pitied; for there are some of an inert, un-eloquent nature, who have been denied all the symbols of communication, who have neither a lively play of facial expression, nor speaking gestures, nor a responsive voice, nor yet the gift of frank, explanatory speech: people truly made of clay, people tied for life into a bag which no one can undo. They are poorer than the gipsy, for their heart can speak no language under heaven.

R. L. Stevenson

The Four Freedoms

In the future days that we seek to make secure, we look forward to a world founded on four essential freedoms.

The first is freedom of speech and expression—everywhere in the world.

The second is freedom for every person to worship God in his own way—everywhere in the world.

The third is freedom from want which, translated into world terms, means economic understandings which will secure to every nation a healthy peacetime life for its inhabitants—everywhere in the world.

The fourth is freedom from fear which, translated into world terms, means a world-wide reduction of armaments to such a point and in such a thorough fashion that no nation will be in a position to commit an act of physical aggression against any neighbour—anywhere in the world.

This is no vision of a distant millennium. It is a definite basis for a kind of world attainable in our own time and generation. That kind of world is the very antithesis of the so-called new order of tyranny which the dictators seek to create with the crash of a bomb.

Franklin D. Roosevelt,
Message to Congress,
January 6th, 1941.

Love

Though I speak with the tongues of men and of angels, and have not charity, I am become as sounding brass or a tinkling cymbal. And though I have the gift of prophecy, and understand all mysteries, and all knowledge; and though I have all faith, so that I could remove mountains, and have not charity, I am nothing. And though I bestow all my goods to feed the poor, and though I give my body to be burned, and have not charity, it profiteth me nothing.

Charity suffereth long, and is kind; charity envieth not; charity vaunteth not itself, is not puffed up; does not behave itself unseemly, seeketh not her own, is not easily provoked, thinketh no evil; rejoiceth not in iniquity, but rejoiceth in the truth; beareth all things, believeth all things, hopeth all things, endureth all things.

Charity never faileth; but whether there be prophecies, they shall fail; whether there be tongues, they shall cease; whether there be knowledge, it shall vanish away. For we know in part, and we prophesy in part. But when that which is perfect is come, then that which is in part shall be done away.

When I was a child, I spake as a child, I understood as a child, I thought as a child: but when I became a man, I put away childish things. For now we see through a glass, darkly; but then face to face. Now I know in part; but then shall I know even as also I am known.

And now abideth faith, hope, charity—these three. But the greatest of these is charity.

St. Paul, Letter I
to the people of Corinth.
Authorized Version 1611.
Chapter 13.

You have been listening to six passages from literature. Were you able to find out how the different rhythms were produced? They were of course all carefully controlled. See whether you can speak rhythmically using conversational speech.

APPENDIX II(a)

NAME: Subject 4 _____ SEX ___ Male

AGE: _37_____ NATIONALITY ___Vietnamese

PLACE OF BIRTH: Viet Nam _____

NATIVE LANGUAGE: Vietnamese (Northern dialect)_____

OTHER LANGUAGES SPOKEN: English and French _____

_____

NATIONALITY OF PARENTS: Vietnamese _____

IF MARRIED, NATIONALITY OF HUSBAND/WIFE: Vietnamese _____

_____

LANGUAGE SPOKEN AT HOME: Vietnamese _____

LANGUAGE SPOKEN AT WORK: Vietnamese, French and English ___

NUMBER OF HOURS DAILY THAT ENGLISH IS NORMALLY
SPOKEN: 3 hours _____

PERIOD OF RESIDENCE IN ENGLISH SPEAKING COMMUNITY: __
4 months _____

PRESENT COURSE OF STUDY: T.E.F.L. _____

OCCUPATION BEFORE COMMENCING PRESENT COURSE:
Teaching _____

_____

NUMBER OF YEARS ENGAGED IN THIS WORK: 10 years _____

_____

ACADEMIC ACHIEVEMENT
(i)   Certificates: Licence d'Enseignement d'Anglais _____

_____ Institution: Faculty of Pedagogy, Saigon _____
_____ Year: _1961_
(ii)   Diplomas: Diploma of Pedagogy _____

_____ Institution: Higher School of Pedagogy _____
Saigon _____ YEAR: _1956_
(iii) Degrees: B.A. _____

_____ University: _____ YEAR: _1961_

_____

EXTENT OF ENGLISH STUDIES:
(i)   Primary School:
    No   years   English Language
    No   years   English Literature
(ii)   Secondary School:
    4   years   English Language (only in class—grammar translation)
    years   English Literature
(iii)   University:
    4   years   English Language   mainly writing
    years   English Literature
(iv)   Other Institutions:
    years   English Language
    years   English Literature

SPOKEN ENGLISH ACTIVITIES:
(i)   Debating: No
(ii)   Elocution/Speech Training: No

(iii)   Public Speaking: No

(iv)   Drama: No

(v)   Oral reading: No
(vi)   Verse Speaking: No

Singing: No
Other particulars: No
Hearing: Normal, as far as I know
Eyesight: Glasses worn for reading
Teeth: Partial lower denture
Speech defects: None

APPENDIX II(b)

NAME: Subject 7 _____ SEX Male

AGE: 33 _____ NATIONALITY Pakistani

PLACE OF BIRTH: Pakistan _____

NATIVE LANGUAGE: Bengali _____

OTHER LANGUAGES SPOKEN: English, Urdu _____

NATIONALITY OF PARENTS: Pakistani _____

IF MARRIED, NATIONALITY OF HUSBAND/WIFE: Pakistani

LANGUAGE SPOKEN AT HOME: Bengali _____

LANGUAGE SPOKEN AT WORK: Bengali and English (a little bit) ___

NUMBER OF HOURS DAILY THAT ENGLISH IS NORMALLY SPOKEN: _____
Less than one hour—about 6 hours weekly _____

PERIOD OF RESIDENCE IN ENGLISH SPEAKING COMMUNITY: __
previously—3 months _____

PRESENT COURSE OF STUDY: _ Teaching English as a Foreign Language __

OCCUPATION BEFORE COMMENCING PRESENT COURSE:
Teaching _____

NUMBER OF YEARS ENGAGED IN THIS WORK: 6 years _____

ACADEMIC ACHIVEMENT
(i)   Certificates: Matriculation _____

      Institution: High School, Dacca _____
      _____ Year: _____
(ii) Diplomas: _____

      Institution: _____
      _____ Year: _____
(iii) Degrees: B. Ed. _____

      University: Dacca _____
      _____ Year: _____ 1963

EXTENT OF ENGLISH STUDIES:
(i)   Primary School:
          No   years English Language
          --   years English Literature
(ii)   Secondary School:
          4   years English Language
          4   years English Literature
(iii) University:
               years English Language
          4   years English Literature
(iv)   Other Institutions:
          --   years English Language
          --   years English Literature

SPOKEN ENGLISH ACTIVITIES:
(i)   Debating: No
(ii)   Elecoution/Speech Training: No

(iii) Public Speaking: No

(iv)   Drama: No

(v)   Oral reading: Considerable

(vi)   Verse speaking: Considerable

Singing: No
Other particulars: --
Hearing: Normal
Eyesight: Normal/Glasses for reading
Teeth: Normal
Speech defects: None

Notes

Chapter One

1. Thaddeus L. Bolton, "Rhythm", *Amer. J. of Psychology*, Vol. VI, Jan. 1894, No. 2, 145–238.
2. Warner Brown, *Time in English Verse Rhythm*, New York: The Science Press, 1908, p. 4.
3. D. W. Lucas, *Aristotle, Poetics*, Oxford: The Clarendon Press, 1968, p. 58.
4. Plato, *Laws* II, 653, English translation by B. Jowett, *The Dialogues of Plato*, Vol. V, Oxford: The Clarendon Press, 1892, p. 31.
5. Lucas, *op. cit.*, pp. 261–262.
6. *Rhetorica*, 1408^{b}24, cited by D. W. Lucas, *ibid.*, pp. 57–58.
7. W. Thomson, *The Rhythm of Speech*, Glasgow: Maclehose, Jackson & Co., 1923.
8. *ibid.*, p. 28.
9. E. A. Sonnenschein, *What is Rhythm?* Oxford: Blackwell, 1925, p. 18.
10. *Rhythmica Stoicheia* Section 6 (Westphal's edition, Vol. ii, p. 78), quoted Sonnenschein, *ibid.*, p. 18.
11. *ibid.*, Sections 7, 8, quoted Sonnenschein, *ibid.*, p. 8.
12. *ibid.*, p. 16.
13. *ibid.*, p. 28.
14. *ibid.*
15. Elsie Fogerty, "Rhythm", *Proceedings of the Second International Congress of Phonetic Sciences*, Cambridge: The University Press, 1936, p. 92.
16. R. H. Stetson, "Motor Theory of Rhythm and Discrete Succession" I and II, *Psychological Review*, Vol. XII, 1905, 250–269, 293–335.
17. *ibid.*, pp. 258–259.
18. *ibid.*, p. 259.
19. Thomson, *op. cit.*, p. 20.
20. Warner Brown, "Temporal and Accentual Rhythm"—Studies from the Psychological Laboratory of the University of California, *Psychological Review*, XVIII, 1911, 336–346.
21. *ibid.*, p. 344.
22. Bolton, *op. cit.*, p. 174.
23. *ibid.*, p. 168.
24. Brown, *op. cit.*, p. 336.
25. *ibid.*, p. 344.
26. Bolton, *op. cit.*, p. 237.
27. J. E. W. Wallin, "Rhythm and Time", *Psychological Review*, XVIII, 1911, 100–119.
28. I. Miyake, "Researches on Rhythmic Action", *Yale Psychological Studies*, X, 1902, quoted by W. M. Patterson in *The Rhythm of Prose*, New York: Columbia University Press, 1916, p. 23.
29. Wallin, *op. cit.*, p. 110.
30. *ibid.*
31. Stetson, *op. cit.*, p. 256.
32. *ibid.*
33. *ibid.*
34. Christian A. Ruckmich, "The Role of Kinaesthesis in the Perception of Rhythm", *Amer.*

J. of Psychology, Vol. XXIV, July, 1913, 305–359.

35. *ibid.*, p. 311.
36. *ibid.*, p. 359.
37. Bolton, *op. cit.*, p. 163.
38. Norman Triplett and Edmund C. Sandford, "Studies of Rhythm and Metre", *Amer. J. of Psychology*, XII, 1901, 361–387.
39. Bulmer, Darwin, Sweet, Paget, Johannesson, cited by David Abercrombie in *Problems and Principles*, London: Longmans, Green and Co., 1956.
40. *ibid.*, p. 73.
41. John Bulmer, *Chirologia: or the Natural Language of the Hand* (1644) quoted by Abercrombie, p. 73.
42. *vide infra*, Part II—*Investigations*.
43. Triplett and Sanford, *op. cit.*, p. 363.
44. *ibid.*, p. 361.
45. Seymour Chatman, *A Theory of Metre, Janua Linguarum*, The Hague: Mouton and Co., 1965, p. 28.
46. *ibid.*
47. P. F. Swindle, "On the Inheritance of Rhythm", *Amer. J. of Psychology*, Vol. XXIV, 1913, 180–203.
48. *ibid.*, p. 187.
49. *ibid.*, p. 188.
50. Joshua Steele, *Prosodia Rationalis: or, An Essay towards Establishing the Melody and Measure of Speech, to be Expressed and Perpetuated by Peculiar Symbols*, 2nd edition amended and enlarged, London: J. Nichols, 1779.
51. *ibid.*, p. 20.
52. *ibid.*, p. 21.
53. *ibid.*, pp. 21–22.
54. David Crystal, *Prosodic Systems and Intonation in English*, Cambridge: University Press, 1969, p. 26.
55. Sheridan Baker, "English Meter *Is* Quantitative", *College English*, Vol. 21, 1960, 309–315.
56. *ibid.*, p. 311.
57. It should be noted, however, that according to Sonnenschein (*op. cit.*, p. 36) the duration of syllables in Greek and Latin could have varied within limits as wide as those of English.
58. Bolton, *op. cit.*, p. 156.
59. Abercrombie refers to this phenomenon in contemporary English in "Some Functions of Silent Stress", *Edinburgh Studies in English and Scots*, A. J. Aitken, Angus McIntosh and Hermann Pálsson, (Eds.), London: Longman 1971.
60. Bolton, *op. cit.*, p. 168.
61. Frederic G. Cassidy and Richard N. Ringler, (Eds.), *Bright's Old English Grammar and Reader*, Third Edition, New York: Holt, Rinehart and Winston, Inc., 1971, p. 275.
62. John Collins Pope, *The Rhythm of Beowulf*, New Haven: Yale University Press, 1942, Revised edition, 1966.
63. Cassidy and Ringler, *op. cit.*, p. 287.
64. Pope, *op. cit.*, p. 89.
65. *ibid.*, p. 91.
66. James McAuley, "Metrical Accent and Speech Stress", *Balcony/The Sydney Review*, No. 4, Autumn 1966, Sydney: Sydney University Arts Seminar Society.

Chapter Two

1. David Crystal, *op. cit.*, p. 29.
2. Bror Danielsson, *John Hart's Works on English Orthography and Pronunciation*, Part I, *Biographical and Bibliographical Introductions, Texts and Index Verb um*, Stockholm: Almqvist & Wiksell, 1955, Part II, *Phonology*, Uppsala: Almqvist & Wiksell, 1963.

3. *ibid.*, 1955, p. 119.
4. *ibid.*, p. 145.
5. *ibid.*, Chapter 10 (164–165), p. 147.
6. *ibid.*, p. 153.
7. *ibid.*, p. 155.
8. Quoted, Joshua Steele, *An Essay towards establishing the melody and measure of speech*, London: Bowyer and Nichols, 1775, in *English Linguistics*, (1500–1800), Menston, England: The Scolar Press Limited, 1969, p. 3.
9. Joshua Steele, *Prosodia Rationalis, op. cit.*, Preface, p. viii.
10. *ibid.*, p. 18.
11. *ibid.*, p. 67.
12. *ibid.*
13. *ibid.*, p. 68.
14. *ibid.*, p. 11.
15. *ibid.* Second Set of Observations and Queries by the Author of the *Origin and Progress of Language*, Section 10, pp. 105–106.
16. *ibid.*, pp. 87–88.
17. *ibid.*, p. 115.
18. *ibid.*
19. *ibid.*
20. *ibid.*, pp. 115–116.
21. *ibid.*, p. 28.
22. *ibid.*, p. 29.
23. *ibid.*, pp. 18–19.
24. *ibid.*, p. 68.
25. Magdalena Sumera, "The Temporal Tradition in the Study of Verse Structure", *Linguistics*, 61–64, 1970, pp. 44–65.
26. *ibid.*, p. 47.
27. Walter Young, "An Essay on Rhythmical Measures", in *Transactions of the Royal Society of Edinburgh* II, (1790), p. 76. Quoted, Sumera, *ibid.*, p. 47.
28. *ibid.*, pp. 47–48.
29. James Odell, *An Essay on the Elements, Accents, and Prosody of the English Language*, London: 1806, *Anglistica & Americana*, 47, Hildesheim: New York: Georg Olms, 1969, p. 153.
30. *ibid.*, pp. 152–153.
31. *ibid.*, p. 153.
32. *ibid.*, p. 158.
33. *ibid.*, pp. 153–154.
34. *ibid.*, p. 154.
35. *ibid.*, pp. 155–156.
36. *ibid.*, p. 156.
37. *ibid.*
38. James Chapman, *The Music or Melody and Rhythmus of Language*, Edinburgh: 1818, cited Sumera, *op. cit.*, p. 48, and T. S. Omond, *English Metrists*, Oxford: Oxford University Press, 1921, pp. 131–133.
39. Chapman, *op. cit.*, p. 52, quoted in Sumera, *op. cit.*, p. 50.
40. *ibid.*, p. 50.
41. David Abercrombie, "A phonetician's view of verse structure", *Studies in Phonetics and Linguistics*, London: Oxford University Press, 1965, pp. 16–25.
42. Omond, *op. cit.*, p. 131.
43. John Thelwell, *Selections for the Illustration of a Course of Instructions on the Rhythmus and Utterance of the English Language*, London: J. McCreeny, Arch Cornhill, 1812.
44. Coventry Patmore, *Essay on English Metrical Law*, reprinted in *Poems*, Collective Edition: (London, 1886), p. 224, (first published as "English Metrical Critics", *The North British Review*, 27, Edinburgh, 1857).
45. Omond, *op. cit.*, p. 176.
46. Patmore, *op. cit.*, p. 224.

47. *ibid.*
48. Italics, present writer's.
49. *ibid.*, p. 238.
50. Omond, *op. cit.*, p. 172.
51. Patmore, *op. cit.*, p. 237, quoted Omond, p. 176.
52. Omond, *ibid.*, p. 176.
53. *ibid.*
54. *vide infra,* Part II—*Investigations*.
55. E. W. Brücke *Die physiologischen Grundlagen der neuhochdeutschen* Verskunst, Wien, 1871.
56. Patterson, *op. cit.*, p. 17.
57. E. Meumann, Untersuchungen z. Psych. u. Aesth. d. Rhythmus, *Philos. Stud.*, X, 1894.
58. E. Sievers, *Grundzüge der Phonetik*, Leipzig, 5th ed., 1901.
59. Quoted Patterson, *op. cit.*, p. 17.
60. Quoted Patterson, *ibid.*, p. 18.
61. Noted by Patterson, *ibid.*, p. 20.
62. *ibid.*, pp. 21–22.
63. Jakob Schipper, *A History of English Versification*, Oxford: 1910. Reprinted New York, N.Y.: AMS Press Inc., 1971.
64. *ibid.*, p. 24.
65. Quoted Patterson, *op. cit.*, p. 37.
66. *ibid.*, p. 38.
67. J. E. W. Wallin, "Researches on the Rhythm of Speech", *Yale Psy. Stud.*, IX, 1901.
68. Patterson, *op. cit.*, pp. 75–76.
69. *ibid.*, p. 77.
70. *ibid.*
71. E. W. Scripture, *Elements of experimental phonetics*, N.Y.: Scribner, 1902.
72. *ibid.*, p. 554 ff., quoted Patterson, *op. cit.*, p. 25.
73. Scripture, *Researches in experimental phonetics*, Washington: 1906, p. 71, quoted Patterson, *ibid.*, p. 25.
74. P. Verrier, *Essai sur les principes de la métrique anglaise*, Paris: 1909–1910, Vol. III, p. 71, cited by Patterson, *ibid.*, p. 35.
75. *ibid.*, p. 67, quoted by Patterson, *ibid*.
76. *ibid.*, quoted Patterson, *ibid*.
77. *ibid.*, quoted Patterson, *ibid*.
78. Patterson, *ibid.*, p. 36.
79. William Thomson, *The Basis of English Rhythm*, Glasgow: Holmes, 1904.
80. Thomson, *The Rhythm of Speech, op. cit.*
81. *ibid.*, Preface.
82. *ibid.*, p. 27.
83. Italics, present writer's.
84. Cf. Patmore, *vide supra*, p. 37.
85. *ibid.*, pp. 5–6.
86. Thomson, *op. cit.*, pp. 8–9.
87. *ibid.*, pp. 11–12.
88. *ibid.*, p. 11.
89. *ibid.*, p. 28.
90. *ibid.*, p. 21.
91. *ibid.*, Law X, *The Law of Rests*, p. 197.
92. *ibid.*, p. 16.
93. Sumera, *op. cit.*, p. 59.
94. *ibid.*, pp. 39–40.
95. *vide supra*, pp. 31–32.
96. *ibid.*, p. 65.
97. *ibid.*
98. Sonnenschein, *op. cit.*, "To the Reader", p. iv.
99. *ibid.*, p. 123.
100. *ibid.*

101. *vide infra,* Part II—*Investigations.*
102. Sonnenschein, *op. cit.*, p. 124.
103. Henry Sweet, *A Primer of Phonetics*, Oxford: The Clarendon Press, 1906: "There is, however, a natural tendency to pass over the less important unaccented elements of speech, and to dwell on and lengthen the more prominent ones." (p. 72).
104. Sonnenschein, *op. cit.*, p. 121.
105. David Abercrombie, "Syllable quantity and enclitics in English", *Studies in Phonetics and Linguistics, op. cit.*, pp. 26–34.
106. *vide supra*, p. 30.
107. Sonnenschein, *op. cit.*, p. 144.
108. *ibid.*, p. 99.
109. *ibid.*
110. *ibid.*, p. 99 ff.
111. *ibid.*, p. 100.
112. Norton R. Tempest, *The Rhythm of English Prose*, Cambridge: University Press, 1930.
113. Sonnenschein, *op. cit.*, p. 35.
114. Yao Shen and Giles G. Peterson, "Isochronism in English", *Studies in Linguistics*, New York: University of Buffalo, 1962.
115. J. D. O'Connor, "The Perception of Time Intervals", *Progress Report*, Department of Phonetics, University College, London, 1965, pp. 11–15.
116. Elizabeth Uldall, "Isochronous Stresses in R.P.", *Form and Substance*, Phonetic and Linguistic Papers Presented to Eli Fischer-Jørgensen, Akademisk Forlag, Denmark, 1971, p. 209.
117. Thomas Taig, *Rhythm and Metre*, Cardiff: University of Wales Press Board, 1929, p. 24.
118. *ibid.*, p. 25.
119. *ibid.*, p. 29.
120. *ibid.*, p. 26.
121. *ibid.*, p. 30.
122. André Classe, *The Rhythm of English Prose*, Oxford: Basil Blackwell, 1939, p. 132.
123. *ibid.*, p. 100.
124. *ibid.*
125. *ibid.*, p. 50.
126. *ibid.*
127. Verrier, *op. cit.*
128. Patterson, *op. cit.*
129. Classe, *op. cit.*, p. 51.
130. *ibid.*, p. 65.
131. *ibid.*, p. 73.
132. *ibid.*, p. 74.
133. *ibid.*, pp. 86–87. Italics, present writer's.
134. *ibid.*, p. 88.
135. *ibid.*, p. 89.
136. *ibid.*
137. *ibid.*
138. *ibid.*, p. 99.
139. *ibid.*, p. 95.
140. *ibid.*, p. 96.
141. *ibid.*, p. 99.
142. *ibid.*, p. 87.
143. *ibid.*, p. 100.
144. *ibid.*, p. 106.
145. *ibid.*, p. 119.
146. *ibid.*, p. 101.
147. Classe, *op. cit.*, Chapter III.
148. Daniel Jones, *An Outline of English Phonetics*, Leipzig: 1914, and Cambridge: 1932, Section 886 ff.
149. Classe, *op. cit.*, p. 132.
150. *ibid.*, p. 101.

151. Kenneth L. Pike, *The Intonation of American English*, Ann Arbor: University of Michigan Publications, *Linguistics*, Vol. 1, 1945, p. 34.
152. *ibid.*, p. 35.
153. *ibid.*, p. 35.
154. "Practical Phonetics of Rhythm Waves", *Phonetica* 8, 1962, 9–30.
155. *ibid.*, p. 29.
156. Shen and Peterson, *op. cit.*, p. 5.
157. Shen and Peterson, *op. cit.*, p. 34.
158. *ibid.*, p. 6.
159. *ibid.*, p. 34.
160. *ibid.*, p. 13.
161. They say that according to Joos, the average duration of the plus juncture is 1/40 of a second which is half the average time lapse of a phoneme.
162. *ibid.*, p. 14.
163. J. D. O'Connor, *op. cit.*
164. *ibid.*, p. 11.
165. Patterson, *op. cit.*, p. 95.
166. *ibid.*, p. 101.
167. O'Connor, *op. cit.*, p. 12.
168. J. D. O'Connor, "The Duration of the Foot in relation to the number of component sound-segments", *Progress Report*, Phonetics Laboratory, University College, London, June 1968, p. 1.
169. *ibid.*, p. 1.
170. *ibid.*, pp. 2–3.
171. Uldall, *op. cit.*, p. 209.
172. *ibid.*
173. David Abercrombie, *vide supra*, *Studies in Phonetics and Linguistics*, particularly, "A Phonetician's View of Verse Structure", "Syllable Quantity and Enclitics in English", "Steele, Monboddo and Garrick", and *Edinburgh Studies in·English and Scots*, for "Some Functions of Silent Stress".
174. I attended these lectures during November, 1971.
175. *vide infra*, Part II—*Investigations*, for discussion of respiratory muscular activity in speech.
176. During study leave spent at Edinburgh University in 1971.
177. James Duckworth, "The Rhythm of Spoken English", *Selected Conference Papers of The Association of Teachers of English as a Second Language*, (Ed. David C. Wigglesworth), Los Altos, California: Language Research Associates' Press, December, 1967.
178. *ibid.*, p. 12.
179. George D. Allen, "Towards a description of stress-timing in spoken English", *Proceedings of the Conference on Language and Language Behavior*, Ann Arbor: Michigan, 1968(a).
   —"On testing for certain stress-timing effects", *Working Papers in Phonetics, No. 10*, U.C.L.A., 1968(b).
   —"The place of rhythm in a theory of language", *Working Papers in Phonetics, No. 10*, U.C.L.A., 1968(c).
180. *ibid.*, 1968(c), p. 81.
181. *ibid.*
182. Pike, *op. cit.*, 1945, p. 87.
183. Dwight Bolinger, *Forms of English*, (Isamu Abe and Tetsuya Kanekiyo, Eds.), Cambridge, Massachusetts: Harvard University Press, 1965.
184. Allen, *op. cit.*, 1968(c), p. 81.
185. George D. Allen, "The location of rhythmic stress beats in English: An experimental study", *Working Papers in Phonetics*, No. 14, U.C.L.A., 1970.
186. *ibid.*, pp. 81–82.
187. *ibid.*, p. 82.
188. *ibid.*
189. *ibid.*, p. 85.

190. *ibid.*, p. 94.
191. Classe, *op. cit.*
192. W. B. Newcomb, "The perceptual basis of syllable boundary", 1961, unpublished manuscript quoted Allen, (1970), *op. cit.*, p. 125.
193. Allen, *ibid.*
194. *ibid.*
195. *ibid.*, (cf. Noam Chomsky, *Aspects of the Theory of Syntax*, Cambridge, Massachusetts: The M.I.T. Press, 1965).
196. *ibid.*, p. 129.
197. Jones, *op. cit.*, 8th edn., 1956.
198. Bolinger, *op. cit.*, 1965.
199. George D. Allen, "The location of rhythmic stress beats in English: An experimental study I, An experimental study II, *Language and Speech*, 15, 1972, pp. 72–100, pp. 179–195.
200. Crystal, *op. cit.*, pp. 26–29.
201. Sheridan Baker, "English Meter *is* Quantitative", *College English*, Vol. 21, 1960, 309–315.
202. P. Barkas, *A Critique of Modern English Prosody*, (1880–1930) *Studien Zur Englischen Philologie*, Halle (Saale): Max Niemeyer Verlag, 1934.
203. *ibid.*, p. 8.
204. Crystal, *op. cit.*, p. 29.
205. Tempest, *op. cit.*, p. 8.
206. Crystal, *op. cit.*

Chapter Three

1. Ilse Lehiste, *Suprasegmentals*, Cambridge, Massachusetts and London, England: The M.I.T. Press, 1970, p. 106.
2. Jones, *op. cit.*, p. 245, 9th edn., 1969.
3. *ibid.*, section 909.
4. Leonard Bloomfield, *Language*, U.S.A.: 1933. First published in Great Britain, 1935. London and Aylesbury: Compton Printing Ltd., 1967, (8th Reprint).
5. *ibid.*, section 7.3, p. 110.
6. Roger Kingdon, *The Groundwork of English Stress*, London: Longmans, Green and Co. Ltd., 1958, for example, includes a perceptual aspect in his definition, "the force employed in uttering a syllable, giving it a certain degree of prominence," (Glossary, p. ix), yet Jones, *op. cit.*, explicitly states that *stress* and *prominence* should not be confused (section 912).
7. W. S-Y, Wang, "Stress in English", *Language Learning, A Journal of Applied Linguistics*, 1962, 12, 1:67–77.
8. Crystal, *op. cit.*, p. 113.
9. *ibid.*, pp. 114–115.
10. George L. Trager and Henry Lee Smith, Jr., *An Outline of English Structure, Studies in Linguistics, Occasional Papers*, Washington: American Council of Learned Societies, 1957, (7th Printing), p. 35.
11. B. Bloch and G. L. Trager, *Outline of Linguistic Analysis*, Baltimore: Special Publication of the Linguistic Society of America, 1942, p. 35.
12. Crystal, *op. cit.*, p. 115.
13. Lehiste, *op. cit.*, p. 106.
14. Crystal, *op. cit.*, p. 115.
15. A. C. Gimson, "The linguistic relevance of stress", *Zeitschrift für Phonetik*, Berlin: 1956, 9, p. 144.
16. *ibid.*
17. W. Jassem, "Indication of Speech Rhythm in the Transcription of Educated Southern English", *Le Maître Phonétique*, No. 92, Juillet-Décembre, 1949.
18. R. H. Stetson, *Motor Phonetics, A Study of Speech Movements in Action*, 1st edn. 1928,

Archives Néerlandaises de Phonétique Expérimentale, (Vol. III), The Hague. 2nd edn., Amsterdam: North-Holland Publishing Company, 1951.

19. W. F. Twaddell, "Stetson's model and the 'supra-segmental phonemes'", *Language*, 29, 1953, p. 452.
20. *ibid.*
21. Stetson, *op. cit.*, p. 67.
22. *ibid.*, Preface, p. viii.
23. *ibid.*, p. 28.
24. *ibid.*
25. *ibid.*
26. *ibid.*
27. *ibid.*, p. 30.
28. *ibid.*, Preface, p. vii.
29. *ibid.*, p. 1.
30. *ibid.*
31. *ibid.*, p. 2.
32. *ibid.*
33. *ibid.*, p. 7, Note 2.
34. *ibid.*, p. 36.
35. *ibid.*, p. 58.
36. *ibid.*, p. 3.
37. *ibid.*, p. 4.
38. *ibid.*, pp. 97–98.
39. Twaddell, *op. cit.*, pp. 434–435.
40. *ibid.*, p. 443.
41. It is now known that the diaphragm is inactive throughout almost the whole of expiration; thus, diaphragmatic relaxation could not be a significant causal factor in the surge associated with the primary or with the secondary stress.
42. *ibid.* p. 444.
43. It should perhaps be pointed out that the external and internal intercostal muscles run in different directions to each other. It is believed that these muscles are functionally antagonistic in that the external intercostal muscles are associated with inspiration and the internal intercostals are primarily associated with expiration. However, the parasternal part of the internal intercostals is believed to be inspiratory.
44. *ibid.*, pp. 444–445.
45. Stetson, *op. cit.*, p. 67.
46. Twaddell, *op. cit.*, p. 445.
47. *ibid.*, p. 453.
48. Lehiste, *op. cit.*, p. 110.
49. Stetson, *op. cit.*, p. 67.
50. *ibid.*
51. *ibid.*
52. *ibid.*
53. *ibid.*
54. Twaddell, *op. cit.*, p. 453.
55. *ibid.*
56. Stetson used kymographic recordings of the action potentials from the muscles he investigated, and an air-filled balloon in the stomach to record the pressure of air in the lungs.
57. M. H. Draper, P. Ladefoged and D. Whitteridge, "Expiratory muscles involved in speech", *Journal of Physiology*, London: 138, 17P–18P, 1957.
58. I. Fónagy, "Elektrophysiologische Beiträge zur Akzentfrage", *Phonetica*, 2, 1958, 12–58.
59. I. Fónagy, *ibid.* Cited, Elizabeth T. Uldall, "Instrumental investigations of articulatory phonetics: An annotated bibliography", *Work in Progress*, No. 4, Department of Linguistics, Edinburgh University, 1970, p. 12.
60. Peter Ladefoged, "Stress and respiratory activity", *Three Areas of Experimental Phonetics*, London: Oxford University Press, 1967, pp. 46–47.

61. *ibid.*, p. 46.
62. These had been noted by Philip Lieberman, "Some acoustic correlates of word stress in American English", *Journal of the Acoustical Society of America*, 32, 1960, 451–454.
63. *ibid.*
64. *ibid.*
65. Twaddell, *op. cit.*, quoted Ladefoged, *et al.*, "Syllables and Stress", *Miscellanea Phonetica* III, London: International Phonetic Association, 1958, p. 2.
66. *ibid.*
67. *ibid.*
68. According to R. R. Munro,
   "An electromyograph picks up the action currents of contracting voluntary muscle and amplifies them up to 10,000 times. . . . The discharges can be stored on FM magnetic tape for computer analysis; alternatively they can be transferred to a direct recorder or displayed on a cathode ray oscilloscope and photographed. . . .

   Electromyography represents the most sensitive test of muscle function available at the present time. It is the only method which is capable of determining with precision the action of a particular muscle under physiological conditions."
   "Electromyography of the Muscles of Mastication", Chapter 5, *The Temporomandibular Joint Syndrome. The Masticatory Apparatus in Man in Normal and Abnormal Function*, C. J. Griffin and R. Harris (Eds.), Basel, Karger, 1975, p. 87.
69. Ladefoged, *op. cit.*, 1967, p. 6.
70. *ibid.*, p. 9.
71. *ibid.*
72. *ibid.*, p. 1.
73. *ibid.*, p. 2.
74. *ibid.*, p. 20.
75. *ibid.*
76. *ibid.*, p. 21.
77. *ibid.*
78. *ibid.*, p. 25.
79. *ibid.*, p. 22.
80. *ibid.*, pp. 22–24.
81. *ibid.*, p. 25.
82. *ibid.*
83. *ibid.*, p. 46.
84. Lehiste, *op. cit.*, p. 109.
85. G. E. Peterson, "Some curiosities of speech", Paper presented at the 1956 University of Michigan Summer Speech Conference, Ann Arbor, Michigan: 1956.
86. Yvan Lebrun, "Is Stress Essentially a Thoracic or an Abdominal Pulse? A Finding of 'Not Proven'." *Linguistic Research in Belgium*, (Yvan Lebrun, Ed.), Wetteren, 1966.
87. *ibid.*, p. 76.
88. *ibid.*
89. *ibid.*, pp. 71–72.
90. *ibid.*, p. 72.
91. *ibid.*, p. 73.
92. Ladefoged, *op. cit.*, 1967, p. 20.
93. Lebrun, *op. cit.*, p. 74.
94. *ibid.*, p. 75.
95. Iván Fónagy, "Electrophysiological and acoustic correlates of stress and stress perception", *Journal of Speech and Hearing Research*, 9, 1966, 231–244.
96. *ibid.*, p. 236.
97. *ibid.*, p. 238.
98. *ibid.*
99. *ibid.*, p. 239.
100. *ibid.*
101. *ibid.*, p. 239, quoted from Gunnar Fant, *Acoustic Theory of Speech Production*, 'S-Gravenhage: Mouton & Co., 1960, p. 21.
102. *ibid.*

103. Lebrun, *op. cit.*, p. 72.
104. *ibid.*
105. Ilse Lehiste and Gordon E. Peterson, "Vowel amplitude and phonemic stress in American English", *Journal of the Acoustical Society of America*, 31, 1959, 428–435.
106. *ibid.*, p. 429.
107. D. B. Fry, "Duration and intensity as physical correlates of linguistic stress", *Journal of the Acoustical Society of America*, 27, 1955, 765–768.
108. G. Fairbanks, A. S. House and E. L. Stevens, "An experimental study in vowel intensities", *Journal of the Acoustical Society of America*, 22, 1950, 457–459.
109. Lehiste and Peterson, *op. cit.*, p. 429.
110. *ibid.*
111. Lehiste, (1970), *op. cit.*, p. 121.
112. *ibid.*, p. 120.
113. *ibid.*, p. 121.
114. Lehiste and Peterson, *op. cit.*, p. 435.
115. Lehiste, (1970), *op. cit.*, p. 119.
116. *ibid.*, p. 118.
117. *ibid.*, p. 119.
118. Alvin M. Liberman, Franklin S. Cooper, Katherine S. Harris and Peter F. MacNeilage, "A Motor Theory of Speech Perception", *Proceedings of the Stockholm Speech Communication Seminar*, Paper D 3, Vol. II, Stockholm: Speech Transmission Laboratory, Royal Institute of Technology, 1963.
119. *ibid.*, p. 2.
120. Eileen McEntee, "The Perception of English Syllable Stress by Native and Non-Native Speakers of English: An Experiment", Paper presented at the *First International Conference on Foreign Language Testing*, Dublin, 1973.
121. George M. Miller, *Language and Communication*, New York: McGraw-Hill Book Co., Inc., 1951, p. 200.
122. *ibid.*
123. Lehiste and Peterson, *op. cit.*, p. 435.
124. Lehiste, (1970), *op. cit.*, p. 125.
125. *ibid.*
126. Fant described this and other instruments used for speech synthesis in his paper "Acoustic Studies of Speech", *Proceedings of the Eighth International Congress of Linguists*, Oslo: Oslo University Press, 1958.
127. Crystal, *op. cit.*, p. 46.
128. *ibid.*, p. 116.
129. D. B. Fry, "Experiments on the perception of stress", *Language and Speech*, 1, 1958, p. 129.
130. *ibid.*, p. 127.
131. Fry, (1955), *op. cit.*, p. 106.
132. *ibid.*, p. 768.
133. *ibid.*, p. 767.
134. Fry, (1958), *op. cit.*
135. That is, noun-verb pairs, as in his earlier investigation.
136. *ibid.*, p. 151.
137. *ibid.*
138. *ibid.*
139. D. B. Fry, "The dependence of stress judgments on vowel formant structure", *Proceedings of the 5th International Congress of Phonetic Sciences*, Münster, Basel, New York: S. Karger, 1964.
140. *ibid.*, p. 306.
141. *ibid.*, pp. 308, 311.
142. Bolinger, Mol and Uhlenbeck, Lieberman, Morton and Jassem, *vide infra*.
143. Bolinger, *op. cit.*
144. "A Theory of Pitch Accent in English" reprinted from *Word* 14, 1958, (pp. 109–149), in *Forms of English*, p. 17.
145. *ibid.*, p. 55.

146. *ibid.*, p. 20.
147. Italics, present writer's.
148. *ibid.*, p. 55.
149. "Disjuncture as a cue to constructs" reprinted from *Word*, 13, 1957, pp. 246–255, in *Forms of English*.
150. *ibid.*, p. 87.
151. *ibid.*, p. 93.
152. "Pitch accent and sentence rhythm", *Forms of English*, p. 139.
153. Lehiste, (1970), *op. cit.*, p. 128.
154. Philip Lieberman, "Some acoustic correlates of word stress in American English", *Journal of the Acoustical Society of America*, 32, 1960.
155. *ibid.*, p. 453.
156. *ibid.*
157. *ibid.*, p. 454.
158. Philip Lieberman and Sheldon B. Michaels, "Some aspects of fundamental frequency and envelope amplitude as related to the emotional content of speech", *Journal of the Acoustical Society of America*, Vol. 14, No. 7, 1962.
159. H. Mol and E. M. Uhlenbeck, "The linguistic relevance of intensity in speech", *Lingua*, Vol. V, 2, 1965, p. 205.
160. Pike, (1945), *op. cit.*
161. John Morton and Wiktor Jassem, "Acoustic correlates of stress", *Language and Speech*, 8, 1965, 159–181.
162. *ibid.*, p. 163.
163. *ibid.*, p. 178.
164. Lehiste, (1970), *op. cit.*, p. 129.
165. *ibid.*
166. *ibid.*
167. André Rigault, "Rôle de la fréquence, de l'intensité et de la durée vocaliques dans la perception de l'accent en français", *Proceedings of the 4th International Congress of Phonetic Sciences*, Helsinki, 1961, The Hague: Mouton & Co., 1962, pp. 735–748.
168. *ibid.*, p. 741.
169. Ilse Lehiste and Pavle Ivić, "Accent in Serbo-Croation: An Experimental Study", *Michigan Slavic Materials 4*, Ann Arbor: University of Michigan, 1963.
170. Lehiste, (1970), *op. cit.*, p. 138.
171. Classe, *op. cit.*, p. 45.
172. František Daneš, "Sentence intonation in present-day Standard Czech", p. 2, reprinted from *Intonace a věta ve spisovné češtině*, Prague, 1957. Quoted by Bolinger, *Forms of English*, *op. cit.*, p. 167.
173. *vide* also, A. G. H. Strehlow, *Songs of Central Australia*, Sydney: Angus and Robertson Ltd., 1971, who shows that in the verse of the Central Australian languages strong rhythmic measures are found which necessitate the use of both quantity and accent to achieve their effects. It seems that in speaking the verses an accentual pattern of stressed and unstressed syllables is used, but in chanting the strongly stressed syllables lose their accents entirely and the stress falls on relatively unimportant syllables which in normal speech would remain unstressed.
174. David Abercrombie, tutorial, Edinburgh University, 1971.
175. Eric H. Lenneberg, *Biological Foundations of Language*, New York: John Wiley & Sons, Inc., 1967, p. 115 ff.
176. *ibid.*, p. 119.
177. Pike, (1945), *op. cit.*, p. 71.
178. David Abercrombie, "Syllable Quantity and Enclitics in English", *In Honour of Daniel Jones* (Eds. Abercrombie *et al.*), London: Longmans, Green and Co. Ltd., 1964.
179. Examples of the principle of gradation can be observed in the following sentences in which the context determines the pronunciation used:
    What is it used for?   / fɔː /
    It's for cleaning the car.   / fə /

    He often said things like that.   / ðæt /
    He really believed that he was dying.   / ðət /

"But" is a conjunction.   /bʌt/
He's more experienced but she's better qualified.   /bət/

Has anyone seen my pen?   /həz/
It has rolled under the table.   /əz/—/ɪts/
Oh, has it?   /hæz/

180. According to Abercrombie,[181] for example, the sentence *I don't think it matters* can be spoken with three or four feet:

/ ˏ I/ *don't think it* / *matters* / (3 feet)
/ ˏ I* / *don't* / *think it* / *matters* / (4 feet)

181. In the second interpretation *don't* has additional length. The increased duration of the stressed syllable is the most noticeable feature of such an utterance, he says. On this account a syllable constituting a foot must have the *potentiality for salience* (that is, for sentence stress).

182. Abercrombie, "Some functions of silent stress", *op. cit.*, p. 148.
183. *ibid.*, p. 155.
184. Duckworth, *op. cit.*
185. *ibid.*, p. 12.
186. *ibid.*, p. 11.
187. Bolinger, "Pitch Accent and Sentence Rhythm", *Forms of English, op. cit.*, p. 168.

Chapter Four

1. Crystal, *op. cit.*, p. 115.
2. *vide*, A. C. Gimson, *An Introduction to the Pronunciation of English*, London: Edward Arnold Ltd., 1962, p. 24.
3. Fry, (1958), *op. cit.*, p. 130.
4. *vide supra*, p. 79, McEntee, (1973), *op. cit.*, and Miller, (1951), *op. cit.*
5. *vide supra*, p. 14, Ruckmich, (1913), *op. cit.*, and *vide supra*, p. 80, Fry, (1958), *op. cit.*
6. *vide*, A. G. Mitchell and Arthur Delbridge, *The Speech of Australian Adolescents*, Sydney: Angus and Robertson, 1965.
7. *vide infra,* Chapter VII (b), p. 172.
8. *vide supra*, pp. 53–54, Allen (1968 (a), (b), (c), 1970), *op. cit.*
9. Classe, (1939), *op. cit.*
10. P. Verrier, *Essai sur les Principes de la Métrique Anglaise*, Paris: Welter, 1909.
11. I. Miyake, "Researches on rhythmic action", *Studies from the Yale Psychological Laboratory*, 10, 1902, pp. 1–48.
12. *vide infra*, Chapters V and VI.

Chapter Five

1. *vide supra*, Chapter III(a), pp. 69–70, v. also Victoria Fromkin and P. Ladefoged, "Electromyography in Speech Research", *Phonetica*, 15, 1966, 219–242.
2. Ladefoged, (1967), *op. cit.*
3. Stetson, (1928, 1951), *op. cit.*
4. Fónagy, (1958), *op. cit.*
5. Lebrun, (1966), *op. cit.*
6. Ladefoged (1967), *op. cit.*, p. 21.
7. *vide infra, Experimental Programme*, Part III.
8. *vide supra*, Chapter IV, p. 95.
9. This trace is explained in the report on the pause placement experiment, *vide infra*, pp. 121–122.

10. cf. H. Bluhme, "Segmental phonemes versus distinctive features in English", *Linguistics*, 126, 1974, 11–23.

   "Speech as a natural phenomenon is continuous while the discrete units, be they phones or phonemes or distinctive features, are part and parcel of an analytical process carried out by the human brain." p. 11.

11. This phenomenon has been noted in two other studies—those of M. Hoshiko, "Electromyographic investigation of the intercostal muscles during speech", *Arch. Phys. Med.*, 43: 1962, 115–119, and of F. Buchthal and K. Faaborg-Anderson, "Electromyography of laryngeal and respiratory muscles: correlation with phonation and respiration", *Ann. Otol. Rhin. Laryng.*, 73: 1964, 118–124. The later researchers reported that the onset of electrical acvitity in both laryngeal and respiratory muscles occurred between 100 and 200 msec before phonation. The mean interval between the commencement of the localized burst and speech (A), and the mean interval between the termination of the localized burst and speech (B), for each phrase in the utterance of the native speakers in the present study are shown in Table 2.

12. In particular the records of the rhymed items had a greater resemblance to the pattern of activity of the native speakers than did those of the prose passages. On the other hand, the similarity between the records of the rhymed texts and their fabricated equivalents was not as striking as it was in the case of the native speakers.

13. No study was made of native speakers of English reading Vietnamese or any other foreign language text, since the investigation was concerned solely with the pronunciation of English.

14. The numerous pauses made by the non-native speakers increased their overall time of utterance to such an extent that their average for item 4, the longest text (56 syllables), was 13.1 sec. compared with an average of 10.5 sec. by the native speakers for this item.

15. The number of pauses in each item made by the individual subjects is shown in Table 7.

16. *vide*, J. V. Basmajian, *Muscles Alive*, 2nd edn., Baltimore: Williams and Wilkins, 1967.

17. A. Taylor, "The contribution of the intercostal muscles to the effort of respiration in man", *Journal of Physiology*, London, 1960, 151: 390–402.

18. A recent comprehensive account of the function of the respiratory muscles is given in E. J. M. Campbell, E. Agostini, and J. Newsom-Davis, *The Respiratory Muscles: Mechanics and Neural Control*, London: Lloyd-Luke, 1970.

19. *vide supra*, p. 114, ff.

20. *vide supra*, Chapter III (a), Ladefoged, *op. cit.*, Fónagy, *op. cit.*, Chapter V, Hoshiko, *op. cit.*, Faaborg-Anderson, *op. cit.*

21. *Elastic recoil* is the term used to denote the contraction of the elastic tissue in the lungs which has been put under tension by their inflation and does not involve any muscular contraction. More forceful expiration is associated with activity of the expiratory muscles.

22. Ernst Pulgram, *Syllable, Word, Nexus, Cursus, Janua Linguarum* Series, No. 81, The Hague: Mouton, 1970, p. 30.

23. *vide supra*, *rhythmic disjuncture*, Chapter III (b), p. 88, and *silent stress*, *ibid.*, p. 88 ff.

24. *vide supra*, Chapter III (b), p. 87.

Chapter Six

1. M. D. McClean and W. R. Tiffany, "The acoustic parameters of stress in relation to syllable position, speech loudness and rate", *Language and Speech*, 16, July–Sept., 1973, 283–291.

2. Ladefoged, (1967), *op. cit.*, p. 46.

3. W. S. Brown, Jr. and Robert E. McGlone, "Aerodynamic and acoustic study of stress in sentence productions", *J. Acoustical Society of America*, Vol. 56, No. 3, Sept., 1974, 971–974.

4. McClean and Tiffany, *op. cit.*, p. 283.

5. Gunnar Fant, *Acoustic Theory of Speech Production*, 'S-Gravenhage: Mouton & Co., 1960.

6. Fant, *ibid.*, p. 229.
7. Lehiste, *op. cit.*, p. 120.
8. McClean and Tiffany, *op. cit.*, p. 286.
9. *vide supra*, p. 110.
10. M. Kloster Jensen, "Die Silbe in der Phonetik und Phonemik", *Phonetica*, Vol. 9, No. 1, 1963, 17–38.
11. *ibid.*, p. 27.
12. *ibid.*, p. 34.
13. *ibid.*
14. Some researchers have measured only the syllabic peak in their acoustic investigations.
15. cf. Bolinger, "Pitch Accent and Sentence Rhythm", *op. cit.*, p. 166.
16. I recognized 13 intonemes in an earlier study of Australian English intonation patterns.
    vide, Corinne Adams, "A survey of Australian English intonation", *Phonetica*, 20, 1969, 81–130.
17. Corinne Adams, (1969), *ibid.*
18. *ibid.*, p. 124.
19. Bolinger, (1965), *op. cit.*, p. 55.
20. Adams, *op. cit.*, p. 114.
21. Delattre has shown that whereas lexical stress tends to occur on the early syllables of the word in English, "the place of stress in sense groups is as a whole near the end of the group in all four languages."
    P. Delattre, "Comparing the prosodic features of English, German, Spanish and French", *IRAL*, 1, 2: 1963, p. 203.
22. cf. native (Fig. 24) and non-native (Fig. 25) utterance of item 10, *If she's leaving please let me KNOW* . . .
23. Roger Kingdon, *The Groundwork of English Stress*, (1958), *op. cit.*, p. 4.
24. L. F. Brosnahan and Bertil Malmberg, *Introduction to Phonetics*, Cambridge: W. Heffer & Sons Ltd., 1970, p. 143 and Fig. 7.2 facing p. 129.
25. *vide supra*, Chapter IV, p. 97 ff.
26. *vide supra*, Chapter V (c), p. 131.
27. *vide supra*, Chapter V (b).
28. Kyoko Ando and Gerald J. Canter, "A study of syllabic stress in some English words as produced by deaf and normally hearing speakers", *Language and Speech*, Vol. 12, 1969, 247–255.

Chapter Seven

1. *vide* Chomsky (1965), *op. cit.*
2. It should be mentioned that in fairness to all the students who cooperated with me in this phase of the study, the members of the control group were later allowed to follow a similar programme to that which was offered to the experimental group. The results were very satisfying but are not given in this book as the conditions under which these students worked were not as strictly controlled as in the experimental programme.
3. *vide infra*, The Experimental Programme, (*Outline*, pp. 185–186).
4. *vide* Corinne Adams, (1969), *op. cit.*; cf. Delattre, (1963), *op. cit.*
5. *vide* Roger Kingdon, *The Groundwork of English Intonation*, London: Longmans, Green and Co. Ltd., 1958.
6. *vide supra*, Chapter 4, *Auditory Perception Test* and Chapter 5(b), *Pause Interval Investigation*.
7. *vide supra, Introduction*.
8. Notably, Gerard Manley Hopkins and Robert Bridges.
9. F. Goldman-Eisler, *Psycholinguistics: Experiments in Spontaneous Speech*, London and New York: Academic Press, 1968, p. 31.
10. *ibid.*, p. 95.
11. According to Sweet, "if children learnt by eye first they would . . . speak like foreigners

who have begun with the literary language." Henry Sweet, *The Practical Study of Languages*, first published by J. M. Dent & Sons Ltd., 1899, *Language and Language Learning Series*, London: Oxford University Press, 1964, p. 13.

12. W. Stannard Allen, *Living English Speech*, London: Longmans, Green & Co. Ltd., first published 1954, (new edition 1965); and G. A. Pittman, *Activating the use of prepositions*, London: Longmans, Green and Co. Ltd., 1966, are two of the best in this respect.

13. Bloomfield, (1933), *op. cit.*

14. John L. Phillips, Jr., *The Origins of Intellect: Piaget's Theory*, San Francisco: W. H. Freeman and Company, 1969.

15. Piaget regards the *Concrete Operations Period* as the child's development between 7–11 years. It is during this period that the child establishes the foundations of logical thinking.

16. John B. Carroll, "Research on teaching foreign languages", in *Handbook of Research on Teaching*, (Ed. N. L. Gage), Chicago: Rand McNally, 1963.

17. Carroll, (1968), *op. cit.*, p. 121.

18. *ibid.*, pp. 116–117.

19. *ibid.*, p. 121.

20. *ibid.*

21. In this scheme of notation, ˘ = non-stress, — = stress, and ∧ = silence. Where several degrees of stress were to be indicated (as in the stress profile of a sense group) the conventional scheme, ´ = primary, ^ = secondary, ` = tertiary, ˘ = weak, was used.

22. McAuley, "Metrical Accent and Speech Stress", *op. cit.*

23. *ibid.*, p. 24.

24. Robert L. Ebel, "Estimation of the Reliability of Ratings" in *Psychometrika*, Vol. 16, No. 4, 1951, 407–424.

25. *vide supra*, Chapter VII (a), p. 164.

26. The programme was used again with a group of TEFL students in 1975, and once more the results were extremely encouraging. Although no statistical tests were conducted, the fact that a group of sixteen of these students won the open choral verse-speaking championship in the City of Sydney Eisteddfod against native speakers is an indication of the speech proficiency of the individual members of the choir. They were judged by a visiting English adjudicator on their interpretation of two test pieces, *Before Waterloo* (Lord Byron) and *The Storm* (Walter de la Mare).

Chapter Eight

1. *vide supra*, Chapter v (a); pp. 112–115.

2. *vide supra*, p. 116 ff.

3. *vide supra*, Chapter III.

4. *vide supra*, Chapters III (a) and VI.

5. *vide supra*, Chapters IV and V (b).

6. *vide supra*, Chapter VII (b).

7. John B. Carroll, "Contributions of Psychological Theory and Educational Research to the Teaching of Foreign Languages", *Modern Language Journal*, XLIX, May, 1965.

8. *vide supra*, Chapter VII (a).

9. Corder, *op. cit.*

Bibliography

Books

Abercrombie, David
    1956 *Problems and Principles* (London: Longmans, Green and Co.).
    1965a "Syllable Quantity and Enclitics in English", *In Honour of Daniel Jones* (Eds. Abercrombie *et al.*) (London: Longmans, Green and Co. Ltd.).
    1965b *Studies in Phonetics and Linguistics* (London: Oxford University Press).
    1965c "A Phonetician's View of Verse Structure", "Syllable Quantity and Enclitics in English", "Steele, Monboddo and Garrick", all in *Studies in Phonetics and Linguistics* (London: Oxford University Press).
    1971 "Some Functions of Silent Stress', *Edinburgh Studies in English and Scots*, (Eds.) A. J. Aitken, Angus McIntosh and Hermann Pálsson (London: Longman).
Allen, George D.
    1968 "Towards a description of stress-timing in spoken English", *Proceedings of the Conference on Language and Language Behavior* (Ann Arbor: Michigan).
Allen, W. Stannard
    1965 *Living English Speech* (first published 1954) New edition (London: Longmans, Green and Co. Ltd.).
Aristotle
    1968 *Rhetorica*, 1408b24, cited by D. W. Lucas, *Aristotle, Poetics* (Oxford: The Clarendon Press).
Aristoxenus
    1925 *Rhythmica Stoicheia* (Westphal's edition, Vol. ii, p. 78), quoted E. A. Sonnenschein, *What is Rhythm?* (Oxford: Blackwell).
Barkas, Pallister
    1934 *A Critique of Modern English Prosody*, (1880–1930) *Studien Zur Englischen Philologie*, Halle (Saale): Max Niemeyer Verlag.
Basmajian, J. V.
    1967 *Muscles Alive*, 2nd edn. (Baltimore: Williams and Wilkins).
Bloch, B. and Trager, G. L.
    1942 *Outline of Linguistic Analysis* (Baltimore: Special Publication of the Linguistic Society of America).
Bloomfield, Leonard
    1967 *Language*, U.S.A.: 1933. First published in Great Britain, 1935. (London and Aylesbury: Compton Printing Ltd.) (8th Reprint).
Bolinger, Dwight
    1965a *Forms of English*, (Isamu Abe and Tetsuya Kanekiyo, Eds.) (Cambridge, Massachusetts: Harvard University Press).
    1965b "Pitch Accent and Sentence Rhythm", *Forms of English*, (Isamu Abe and Tetsuya Kanekiyo, Eds.) (Cambridge, Massachusetts: Harvard University Press).
Brosnahan, L. F. and Malmberg, Bertil
    1970 *Introduction to Phonetics*, (Cambridge: W. Heffer & Sons Ltd.).
Brown, Warner
    1908 *Time in English Verse Rhythm* (New York: The Science Press).

Brücke, Ernst
  1916 *Die physiologischen Grundlagen der neuhochdeutschen*, Verskunst, Wien, 1871, cited
  by W. M. Patterson, in *The Rhythm of Prose* (New York, Columbia University Press).
Bulmer, John
  1956 *Chirologia: or the Natural Language of the Hand* (1644) quoted by David
  Abercrombie in *Problems and Principles* (London: Longmans, Green and Co.).
Campbell, E. J. M., Agostini, E. and Newsom-Davis, J.
  1970 *The Respiratory Muscles: Mechanics and Neural Control* (London: Lloyd-Luke).
Carroll, John B.
  1963 "Research on Teaching Foreign Languages", in *Handbook of Research on Teaching*,
  (Ed. N. L. Gage) (Chicago: Rand McNally).
  1968 "Contrastive Analysis and Interference Theory", *Report of the Nineteenth Annual
  Round Table Meeting on Linguistics and Language Studies* (Washington D.C.:
  Georgetown University Press).
Cashdan, A. and Grugeon, Elizabeth (Eds.)
  1972 *Language in Education, A Source Book*, Prepared by the Language and Learning
  Course Team at the Open University. (London and Boston: Routledge & Kegan Paul Ltd.).
Cassidy, Frederic G., and Ringler, Richard N. (Eds.)
  1971 *Bright's Old English Grammar and Reader*, Third Edition (New York: Holt, Rinehart
  and Winston, Inc.).
Chapman, James
  1921 *The Music or Melody and Rhythmus of Language*, cited M. Sumera, "The Temporal
  Tradition in the Study of Verse Structure", *Linguistics*, 61-64, 1970, and T. S. Omond,
  English Metrists (Oxford: University Press).
Chatman, Seymour
  1965 *A Theory of Metre, Janua Linguarum* (The Hague: Mouton and Co.).
Chomsky, Noam
  1965 *Aspects of the Theory of Syntax* (Cambridge, Massachusetts: The M.I.T. Press).
Classe, André
  1939 *The Rhythm of English Prose* (Oxford: Basil Blackwell).
Crystal, David
  1969 *Prosodic Systems and Intonation in English* (Cambridge: University Press).
Daneš, František
  1957 "Sentence intonation in present-day Standard Czech", reprinted from *Intonace a věta
  ve spisovné češtině*, (Prague). Quoted by Dwight Bolinger, *Forms of English*. (Eds.
  I. Abe and T. Kanekiyo) (Cambridge, Massachusetts: Harvard University Press).
Danielsson, Bror
  John Hart's Works on English Orthography and Pronunciation.
  1955 Part I, *Biographical and Bibliographical Introductions, Texts and Index Verborum*
  (Stockholm: Almqvist & Wiksell).
  1963 Part II, *Phonology* (Uppsala: Almqvist & Wiksell).
Duckworth, James
  1967 "The Rhythm of Spoken English", *Selected Conference Papers of The Association of
  Teachers of English as a Second Language*, (Ed. David C. Wigglesworth) (Los Altos,
  California: Language Research Associates' Press).
Fant, Gunnar
  1958 "Acoustic Studies of Speech", *Proceedings of the Eighth International Congress of
  Linguists* (Oslo: Oslo University Press).
  1960 *Acoustic Theory of Speech Production*, (The Hague: Mouton & Co.).
Fogerty, Elsie
  1963 "Rhythm", *Proceedings of the Second International Congress of Phonetic Sciences*
  (Cambridge: The University Press).
Fry, D. B.
  1964 "The dependence of stress judgments on vowel formant structure", *Proceedings of
  the 5th International Congress of Phonetic Sciences* (Münster, Basel-New York: S. Karger).
Gage, N. L. (Ed.)
  1963 *Handbook of Research on Teaching* (Chicago: Rand McNally).

Gimson, A. C.
    1962 *An Introduction to the Pronunciation of English* (London: Edward Arnold Ltd.).
Goldman-Eisler, F.
    1968 *Psycholinguistics: Experiments in Spontaneous Speech* (London and New York: Academic Press).
Hart, J., (v. Danielsson, Bror).
Jones, Daniel
    1969 *An Outline of English Phonetics* (Leipzig: 1914, and Cambridge: 1932, W. Heffer & Sons Ltd.) Ninth edition (reprint).
Kingdon, Roger
    1958a *The Groundwork of English Intonation* (London: Longmans, Green and Co. Ltd.)
    1958b *The Groundwork of English Stress* (London: Longmans, Green and Co. Ltd.).
Ladefoged, Peter
    1967 "Stress and respiratory activity", *Three Areas of Experimental Phonetics* (London: Oxford University Press).
Lehiste, Ilse
    1970 *Suprasegmentals* (Cambridge, Massachusetts, and London, England: The M.I.T. Press).
Lehiste, Ilse and Ivič, Pavle
    1963 "Accent in Serbo-Croatian: An Experimental Study", *Michigan Slavic Materials 4* (Ann Arbor: University of Michigan) cited, Ilse Lehiste, *Suprasegmentals* (Cambridge, Massachusetts, and London, England: The M.I.T. Press) 1970.
Lenneberg, Eric H.
    1967 *Biological Foundations of Language* (New York: John Wiley & Sons, Inc.)
Liberman, Alvin M., Cooper, Franklin S., Harris, Katherine S. and MacNeilage, Peter F.
    1963 "A Motor Theory of Speech Perception", *Proceedings of the Stockholm Speech Communication Seminar*, Paper D 3, Vol. II (Stockholm: Speech Transmission Laboratory, Royal Institute of Technology).
Lieberman, Philip
    1967 *Intonation, Perception and Language*, M.I.T. Research Monograph No. 38 (Cambridge, Massachusetts: The M.I.T. Press).
Lucas, D. W.
    1968 *Aristotle, Poetics* (Oxford: The Clarendon Press).
McEntee, Eileen
    1973 "The Perception of English Syllable Stress by Native and Non-Native Speakers of English: An Experiment", paper presented at the *First International Conference of Foreign Language Testing*, Dublin.
Malmberg, Bertil (Ed.)
    1970 *Manual of Phonetics* (Amsterdam-London: North-Holland Publishing Company).
Meumann, E.
    1916 Untersuchungen z. Psych. u. Aesth. d. Rhythmus, *Philos. Stud.* X, 1894, cited W. M. Patterson, *The Rhythm of Prose* (New York).
Miller, George M.
    1951 *Language and Communication* (New York: McGraw-Hill Book Co. Inc.).
Mitchell, A. G. and Delbridge, Arthur
    1965 *The Speech of Australian Adolescents* (Sydney: Angus and Robertson).
Miyake, I.
    1916 "Researches on Rhythmic Action", *Yale Psychological Studies*, X, 1902, quoted by W. M. Patterson in *The Rhythm of Prose*, (New York: Columbia University Press).
Munro, R. R.
    1975 "Electromyography of the Muscles of Mastication", Chapter V. *The Temporomandibular Joint Syndrome. The Masticatory Apparatus in Man in Normal and Abnormal Function* (Eds. C. J. Griffin and R. Harris) (Karger: Basel).
Newcomb, W. B.
    1970 "The perceptual basis of syllable boundary", 1961, unpublished manuscript quoted, George D. Allen, "The Location of Rhythmic Stress Beats in English: An Experimental Study", Working Papers in Phonetics, No. 14 (U.C.L.A.).

Odell, James
    1969 *An Essay on the Elements, Accents, and Prosody of the English Language* (London: 1806) Anglistica & Americana, 47, (Hildesheim, New York: Georg Olms).
Omond, T. S.
    1921 *English Metrists* (Oxford: University Press).
Patmore, Coventry
    1857 *Essay on English Metrical Law*, reprinted in *Poems*, Collective Edition: London, 1886, (first published as "English Metrical Critics", *The North British Review*, 27 (Edinburgh).
Patterson, W. M.
    1916 *The Rhythm of Prose* (New York: Columbia University Press).
Phillips, John L. Jr.
    1969 *The Origins of Intellect: Piaget's Theory* (San Francisco: W. H. Freeman and Company).
Pike, Kenneth L.
    1945 *The Intonation of American English* (Ann Arbor: University of Michigan Publications) *Linguistics*, Vol. 1.
Pittman, G. A.
    1966 *Activating the Use of Prepositions* (London: Longmans, Green and Co. Ltd.).
Plato, *Laws* II, 653
    1892 English translation by B. Jowett, *The Dialogues of Plato*, Vol. V (Oxford: The Clarendon Press).
Pope, John Collins
    The Rhythm of Beowulf (New Haven: Yale University Press).
Pulgram, Ernst
    1970 *Syllable, Word, Nexus, Cursus, Janua Linguarum Series*, No. 81 (The Hague: Mouton).
Rigault, André
    1962 "Rôle de la fréquence, de l'intensité et de la durée vocaliques dans la perception de l'accent en français", *Proceedings of the 4th International Congress of Phonetic Sciences*, Helsinki, 1961 (The Hague: Mouton & Co.).
Ringler, Richard N., v. Cassidy, Frederic G.
Roth, Sister Mary Augustine
    1961 *Coventry Patmore's "Essay on English Metrical Law": A Critical Edition with a Commentary* (Washington D.C.: The Catholic University of America Press).
Schipper, Jakob
    1971 *A History of English Versification*, Oxford: 1910 (Reprinted New York, N.Y.: AMS Press Inc.).
Scripture, E. W.
    1916a *Elements of experimental phonetics*, N.Y.: Scribner, 1902, quoted W. M. Patterson, *The Rhythm of Prose* (New York: Columbia University Press).
    1916b *Researches in experimental phonetics*, Washington: 1906, quoted W. M. Patterson, *The Rhythm of Prose* (New York: Columbia University Press).
Shen, Yao and Peterson, Giles G.
    1962 "Isochronism in English", *Studies in Linguistics* (New York: University of Buffalo).
Sievers, E.
    1916 *Grundzüge der Phonetik*, Leipzig, 5th ed., 1901, cited W. M. Patterson, *The Rhythm of Prose* (New York: Columbia University Press).
Sonnenschein, E. A.
    1925 *What is Rhythm?* (Oxford: Blackwell).
Steele, Joshua
    1775 *An Essay towards establishing the melody and measure of speech* (London: Bowyer and Nichols) in *English Linguistics*, (1500–1800) (Menston: The Scholar Press) 1969.
    1779, *Prosodia Rationalis: or, An Essay towards Establishing the Melody and Measure of Speech, to be Expressed and Perpetuated by Peculiar Symbols*, 2nd edition amended and enlarged, London: J. Nichols, 1779.

Stetson, R. H.,
  1951 *Motor Phonetics, A Study of Speech Movements in Action*, 1st edition, 1928, Archives Néerlandaises de Phonétique Experimentale (Vol. III), The Hague, 2nd edition (Amsterdam: North-Holland Publishing Company).
Strehlow, A. G. H.
  1971 *Songs of Central Australia* (Sydney: Angus and Robertson Ltd.).
Sweet, Henry
  1899 *The Practical Study of Languages*, first published by J. M. Dent & Sons Ltd. *Language and Language Learning Series* (London: Oxford University Press) 1964.
  1906 *A Primer of Phonetics*, Oxford: The Clarendon Press, 1906.
Taig, Thomas
  1929 *Rhythm and Metre* (Cardiff: University of Wales Press Board).
Tempest, Norton R.
  1930 *The Rhythm of English Prose* (Cambridge: University Press).
Thelwell, John
  1812 *Selections for the Illustration of a Course of Instructions on the Rhythmus and Utterance of the English Language* (London: J. McCreeny, Arch Cornhill).
Thomson, William
  1904 *The Basis of English Rhythm* (Glasgow: Holmes).
  1923 *The Rhythm of Speech* (Glasgow: Maclehose, Jackson & Co.).
Trager, George L. and Smith, Henry Lee, Jr.
  1957 *An Outline of English Structure, Studies in Linguistics, Occasional Papers* (Washington: American Council of Learned Societies (Seventh Printing).
Uldall, Elizabeth,
  1971 "Isochronous Stresses in R.P.", *Form and Substance*, Phonetic and Linguistic Papers Presented to Eli Fischer-Jørgensen (Akademisk Forlag, Denmark).
Verrier, P.
  1909-1910 Essai sur les principes de la métrique anglaise (Paris) Vol. III, cited by André Classe, *Rhythm of English Prose* (Oxford: Basil Blackwell) 1939, and W. M. Patterson, *The Rhythm of Prôse* (New York: Columbia University Press) 1916.

Articles

Adams, Corinne
  1969 "A Survey of Australian English Intonation", *Phonetica*, 20, 81-130.
Allen, George D.
  1968a "On testing for certain stress-timing effects", *Working Papers in Phonetics, No. 10*, U.C.L.A.
  1968b "The place of rhythm in a theory of language", *Working Papers in Phonetics, No. 10*, U.C.L.A.
  1970 "The location of rhythmic stress beats in English: An experimental study", *Working Papers in Phonetics, No. 14* (U.C.L.A.)
  1972a "The location of rhythmic stress beats in English: An experimental study I", *Language and Speech*, 15, 72-100.
  1972b "The location of rhythmic stress beats in English: An experimental study II", *Language and Speech*, 15, 179-195.
Ando, Kyoto and Canter, Gerald J.
  1969 "A study of syllabic stress in some English words as produced by deaf and normally hearing speakers". *Language and Speech*, Vol. 12, 247-255.
Baker, Sheridan
  1960 "English Meter *Is* Quantitative", *College English*, Vol. 21, 309-315.
Bluhme, H.
  1974 "Segmental phonemes versus distinctive features in English", *Linguistics* 126, 11-23.
Bolinger, D.
  1957 "Disjuncture as a cue to constructs", *Word* 13, 246-255.
  1958 "A Theory of Pitch Accent in English", *Word* 14, 109-149.
  1961 "Ambiguities in Pitch Accent", *Word* 17, 309-317.
  1972 "Accent is predictable (if you're a mind reader)", *Language* 48, 3, 633-644.

Bolton, Thaddeus L.
  1894 "Rhythm", *American Journal of Psychology*, Vol. VI, No. 2, 145–238.
Brown, Warner
  1911 "Temporal and Accentual Rhythm"—Studies from the Psychological Laboratory of the University of California, *Psychological Review*, XVIII, 336–346.
Brown, W. S., Jr. and McGlone, Robert E.
  1974 "Aerodynamic and acoustic study of stress in sentence productions", *J. Acoustical Society of America*, Vol. 56, No. 3, Sept., 971–974.
Buchthal, F. and Faaborg-Anderson, K.
  1964 "Electromyography of laryngeal and respiratory muscles: correlation with phonation and respiration", *Ann. Otol. Rhin. Laryng.*, 73: 118–124.
Carroll, John B.
  1965 "Contributions of Psychological Theory and Educational Research to the Teaching of Foreign Languages", *Modern Language Journal*, XLIX, May.
Corder, S. Pit
  1967 "Significance of Learners' Errors", *International Review of Applied Linguistics in Language Teaching*, Vol. V, 161–169.
Delattre, P.
  1963 "Comparing the prosodic features of English, German, Spanish and French", *IRAL*, 1, 2: 193–210.
Draper, M. H., Ladefoged, P. and Whitteridge, D.
  1957 "Expiratory muscles involved in speech", *Journal of Physiology* (London) 138, 17P–18P.
Ebel, Robert L.
  1951 "Estimation of the Reliability of Ratings", *Psychometrika*, Vol. 16, No. 4, 407–424.
Fairbanks, G., House, A. S. and Stevens, E. L.
  1950 "An experimental study in vowel intensities", *Journal of the Acoustical Society of America,* 22, 457–459.
Fonagy, I.
  1958 "Elektrophysiologische Beiträge zur Akzentfrage", *Phonetica*, 2, 12–58.
  1966 "Electrophysiological and acoustic correlates of stress and stress perception", *Journal of Speech and Hearing Research*, 9, 231–244.
Fromkin, Victoria and Ladefoged, P.
  1966 "Electromyography in Speech Research", *Phonetica*, 15, 219–242.
Fry, D. B.
  1955 "Duration and intensity as physical correlates of linguistic stress", *Journal of the Acoustical Society of America,* 27, 765–768.
  1958 "Experiments on the perception of stress", *Language and Speech*, 1, 126–152.
Gimson, A. C.
  1956 "The linguistic relevance of stress", *Zeitschrift für Phonetik* (Berlin:) 9, 143–9.
Hoshiko, M.
  1962 "Electromyographic investigation of the intercostal muscles during speech", *Arch. Phys. Med.*, 43: 115–119.
Jassem, W.
  1949 "Indication of Speech Rhythm in the Transcription of Educated Southern English", *Le Maître Phonétique*, No. 92, 22–24.
Jensen, M. Kloster
  1963 "Die Silbe in der Phonetik und Phonemik", *Phonetica*, Vol. 9, No. 1, 17–38.
Ladefoged, P. *et al.*
  1958 "Syllables and Stress", *Miscellanea Phonetica* III, (London: International Phonetic Association) 1–14.
Lebrun, Yvan
  1966 "Is Stress Essentially a Thoracic or an Abdominal Pulse? A Finding of 'Not Proven'." *Linguistic Research in Belgium,* (Yvan Lebrun, Ed.) (Wetteren:) 69–76.
Lehiste, Ilse and Peterson, Gordon E.
  1959 "Vowel amplitude and phonemic stress in American English", *Journal of the Acoustical Society of America*, 31, 428–435.

230   BIBLIOGRAPHY

Lieberman, Philip,
    1960 "Some acoustic correlates of word stress in American English", *Journal of the Acoustical Society of America,* 32, 451–454.
Lieberman, Philip and Michaels, Sheldon B.
    1962 "Some aspects of fundamental frequency and envelope amplitude as related to the emotional content of speech", *Journal of the Acoustical Society of America,* Vol. 14, No. 7, 922–927.
McAuley, James
    1966 "Metrical Accent and Speech Stress", *Balcony/The Sydney Review,* No. 4, 21–31.
McClean, M. D. and Tiffany, W.R.
    1973 "The acoustic parameters of stress in relation to syllable position, speech loudness and rate", *Language and Speech,* 16, July-Sept., 283–291.
Mol, H. and Uhlenbeck, E. M.
    1965 "The linguistic relevance of intensity in speech", *Lingua,* Vol. V, 2, 205–213.
Morton, John and Jassem, Wiktor
    1965 "Acoustic correlates of stress", *Language and Speech,* 8, 159–181.
O'Connor, J. D.
    1965 "The perception of time intervals", *Progress Report,* Department of Phonetics, University College, London, 11–15.
    1968 "The duration of the foot in relation to the number of component sound-segments", *Progress Report,* Department of Phonetics, University College, London, 1–3.
Peterson, G. E.
    1956 "Some curiosities of speech", Paper presented at the 1956 University of Michigan Summer Speech Conference, Ann Arbor, Michigan: cited, Ilse Lehiste, *Suprasegmentals,* (Cambridge, Massachusetts: The M.I.T. Press) 1970.
Pike, K.
    1962 "Practical Phonetics of Rhythm Waves", *Phonetica* 8, 9–30.
Ruckmich, Christian A.
    1913 "The Role of Kinaesthesis in the Perception of Rhythm", *The American Journal of Psychology,* Vol XXIV, 305–359.
Stetson, R. H.
    1905 "Motor Theory of Rhythm and Discrete Succession" I and II, *Psychological Review,* Vol. XII, 250–269, 293–335.
Sumera, Magdalena
    1970 "The Temporal Tradition in the Study of Verse Structure", *Linguistics,* 61–64, 44–65.
Swindle, P. F.
    1913 "On the Inheritance of Rhythm", *The American Journal of Psychology,* Vol. XXIV, 180–203.
Taylor, A.
    1960 "The contribution of the intercostal muscles to the effort of respiration in man", *Journal of Physiology* (London), 151: 390–402.
Triplett, Norman, and Sanford, Edmund C.,
    1901 "Studies of Rhythm and Metre", *American Journal of Psychology,* XII, 361–387.
Twaddell, W. F.
    1953 "Stetson's model and the 'supra-segmental phonemes'," *Language,* 29, 415–453.
Uldall, Elizabeth T.
    1970 "Instrumental investigations of articulatory phonetics: An annotated bibliography", *Work in Progress,* No. 4, Department of Linguistics, Edinburgh University, 2–42.
Wallin, J. E. W.
    1901 "Researches on the Rhythm of Speech", *Yale Psychological Studies,* IX.
    1911 "Rhythm and Time", *Psychological Review,* XVIII, 100–119.
Wang, W. S-Y.
    1962 "Stress in English" *Language Learning, A Journal of Applied Linguistics,* 12, 1:67–77.
Young, Walter
    1970 "An Essay on Rhythmical Measures", in *Transactions of the Royal Society of Edinburgh* II, (1790), quoted Magdalena Sumera, "The Temporal Tradition in the Study of Verse Structure", *Linguistics,* 61–64, 1970, 44–65.

Literary Material Used in Experimental Programme

Austen, Jane
1813 *Pride and Prejudice* (London: Thomas Nelson & Sons Ltd.) (Date of publication of this edition not indicated.)

Bridges, Robert
London Snow, in *Feet on the Ground, An Approach to Modern Verse* (by Margaret J. O'Donnell) (London and Glasgow: Blackie and Son Limited).

Brontë, Charlotte
1847 *Jane Eyre* (London: J. M. Dent & Sons Ltd.) 1950 edition.

Carroll, Lewis
1946 *The Lobster Quadrille*, in *One Thousand Poems for Children*. (Selected and arranged by Elizabeth Hough Sechrist) (Philadelphia: Macrae-Smith-Company).

De La Mare, Walter
1949 *The Storm*, in *Many Voices*, Book III (Compiled by Mona Swann) (London: Macmillan and Co.).

Eliot, George
1861 *Silas Marner* (Chapter XII) (London: J. M. Dent & Sons Ltd.).

Eliot, T. S.
1958 "Burnt Norton", *Collected Poems 1909-1935* (London: Faber & Faber Limited).

Hopkins, Gerard Manley
The Windhover, in *Feet on the Ground, An Approach to Modern Verse* (by Margaret J. O'Donnell) (London and Glasgow: Blackie & Son Limited).

Masefield, John
The West Wind, in *British and Australian Poems*, Series I (Edited by G. T. Spaull) (Sydney: William Brooks & Co. Limited) (Date of publication not indicated.)

Roosevelt, Franklin D.
1950 *The Four Freedoms, Message to Congress, January 6th, 1941*, in *By Word of Mouth* (Compiled by Clive Sansom) (London: Methuen & Co. Ltd.).

Rossetti, Christina
1929 *Birds of Paradise*, in *Certain Poets of Importance; Victorian Verse* (Compiled by Hattie Hecht Sloss) (London and New York: E. P. Dutton and Company).

Stevenson, Robert Louis
1950 "Night Among the Pines", from *Travels with a Donkey* in *By Word of Mouth* (Compiled by Clive Sansom) (London: Methuen & Co. Ltd.).
1946 "The Truth of Intercourse", from *Virginibus Puerisque*, in *The Reciter's Treasure of Scenes and Poems* (Edited by Ernest Guy Pertwee), 4th Impression (London: George Routledge & Sons, Limited).

St. Paul
1611 *I Corinthians xiii, The Holy Bible*, Authorized King James Version (London and New York: Collins Clear-Type Press) 1938.